Rebecca Lemos Igreja, Richard Santos, Carlos Agudelo
Race and Racism in Latin America and the Caribbean

Latin America in Perspective

Society, Culture and Politics

Edited by
Rebecca Lemos Igreja and Camilo Negri

Volume 1

Rebecca Lemos Igreja, Richard Santos, Carlos Agudelo

Race and Racism in Latin America and the Caribbean

—

A Crossview from Brazil

Translated from Brazilian Portuguese by Luiz Costa

DE GRUYTER

Colégio Latino-Americano de Estudos Mundiais

FLACSO BRASIL

ISBN 978-3-11-152302-6
e-ISBN (PDF) 978-3-11-072764-7
e-ISBN (EPUB) 978-3-11-072774-6
ISSN 2749-9367

Library of Congress Control Number: 2022943744

Bibliographic information published by the Deutsche Nationalbibliothek
The Deutsche Nationalbibliothek lists this publication in the Deutsche Nationalbibliografie; detailed bibliographic data are available on the internet at http://dnb.dnb.de.

© 2024 Walter de Gruyter GmbH, Berlin/Boston
This volume is text- and page-identical with the hardback published in 2023.
Cover image: Yalorixás (priestesses) of the Our Lady of Good Death Sisterhood – Salvador, Bahia – preparing the ritual for Obaluaê (deity). © Zezzynho Andraddy

www.degruyter.com

Contents

List of acronyms —— VII

List of figures and tables —— XI

José de Souza Andrade – Photojournalist —— XIII

Introduction —— 1

I   Race, colour and racism in Latin American history and social sciences —— 12
    Race and slavery in the colony —— 12
    Race in the new states/nations of Latin America —— 20
    Racial democracy: ideology and the invisibility of racism —— 33

II Historical predecessors of Black protagonism —— 50
    Black protagonism in the Americas since the end of the 19th century —— 50
    Winds of Negritude —— 52
    Beyond Negritude: the work of Frantz Fanon —— 54
    Rastafarianism —— 55
    The Afromerica Journal. A bold – but fleeting – effort —— 56
    The Dakar Colloquium —— 58
    "Los negros se toman la palabra". The Congresses of the Black Culture of the Americas —— 60
    The *creolité* (*creolización*) of Eduard Glissant —— 62
    The impact of Paul Gilroy and his "Black Atlantic" —— 63
    What the Black cause of the 1970s bequeathed to the Afro-descendant movement of the "multicultural turn" —— 64

III Multiculturalism and new ethno-racial identities in Latin America —— 66
    The advent of multiculturalism and its interpretations —— 66
    Multiculturalism and the emergence of new identities —— 75
    The development of policies concerning Afro-descendants in Latin American in the international sphere —— 86
    International academic projects on Latin American Afro-descendants —— 90

IV The construction of "race" as a foundational category of rights and public policies —— 96
  The identification of Afro-descendants in the Americas: the debate on racial classification —— 96
  Multiculturalist policies, identity politics, and/or racial equality? —— 107
  The Latin American multicultural turn, new constitution and reclaiming the debate on colour/race in Brazil —— 116
  Affirmative Action in Brazil and the identification of race/colour —— 141
  Affirmative Action and the political far-right in Brazil —— 163
  The Black movement in the contemporary context —— 170

V Multiculturalism and the new landscapes: Final thoughts —— 178

References —— 186

List of acronyms

ADC	Declaratory Action for Constitutionality (Ação Declaratória de Constitucionalidade)
ADCT	Transitory Constitutional Disposition Act (Ato das Disposições Constitucionais Transitórias)
ADPF	Claim of Non-Compliance with a Fundamental Precept (Arguição de Descumprimento de Preceito Fundamental)
AFRODESC	Project on Afro-descendants and Slavery: Domination, Identification and Inheritance in the Americas
AFROXXI	Iberoamerican Meeting of the International Year for People of African descent.
ANC	National Constituent Assembly (Assemblea Nacional Constituyente)
APNs	Black Pastoral Agents (Agentes de Pastoral do Negro)
ARAAC	Regional Afro-Descendant Articulation of Latin America and the Caribbean (Articulación Regional de Afrodescendientes de las Américas y El Caribe)
CAN	National Autonomy Commission (Comissión Nacional de Autonomía)
CARICOM	Community of Caribbean Countries
CEAA	Brazilian Centre of Afro-Asiatic Studies (Centro de Estudos Afro-Asiáticos).
CEAP	Centre for the Articulation of Marginalized Populations (Centro de Articulação de Populações Marginalizadas)
CEERT/SP	Centre for the Study of Relations of Work and Inequality (Centro de Estudos das Relações de Trabalho e Desigualdades)
CENARAB	National Centre for the Articulation of Afro-Brazilian Religions (Centro Nacional de Africanidade e Resistência Afro-Brasileira)
CENEG	National Centre for Black Citizenship (Centro de Cidadania Negra do Estado de Goiás)
CLACSO	Latin American Social Science Council (Consejo Latinoamericano en Ciencias Sociales)
CNCD	National Council for Combating Discrimination (Conselho Nacional de Combate à Discriminação)
CNE	National Education Council (Conselho Nacional de Educação)
CNPIR	National Council for the Participation of Racial Equality (Conselho Nacional de Promoção da Igualdade Racial)
CODAE	Afro-Ecuadorian Development Corporation
CONACULTA	Mexican National Council for Culture and Arts (Consejo Nacional para la Cultura y las Artes)
CONAPIR	National Conference on the Promotion of Racial Equality (Conferência Nacional de Promoção da Igualdade Racial)
CONEN	National Coordination of Black Entities (Coordenação Nacional de Entidades Negras)
CUT	Workers' Central Union (Central Única dos Trabalhadores)
DEM	Democratas Party
DGACPV	Deputy Directorate-General of the Population and Housing Census (Dirección General Adjunta del Censo de Población y Vivienda)

List of acronyms

DGES	Directorate-General for Sociodemographic Statistics (Dirección General de Estadísticas Sociodemográficas)
ECLAC	Economic Commission for Latin American and the Caribbean
EIRA	Statute of Racial Equality (Estatuto da Igualdade Racial)
ELSP	Open School of Sociology and Politics (Escola Livre de Sociologia e Política)
ENEN	National Meeting of Black Entities (Encontro Nacional de Entidades Negras)
ENZP	Zumbi dos Palmares National Office (Escritório Nacional Zumbi dos Palmares)
FCP	Palmares Cultural Foundation (Fundação Cultural Palmares)
FESMAN	First World Festival of Black Arts (Premier Festival Mondial des Arts Négres)
FESTAC	World Festival of Black Arts
FNB	Brazilian Black Front (Frente Negra Brasileira)
GELEDES	Institute for the Black Woman (Instituto da Mulher Negra)
GRUCON	Black Union and Awareness Group (Grupo de União e Consciência Negra)
GTAR	André Rebouças Working Group (Grupo de Trabalho André Rebouças)
GTDEO	Working Group for the Elimination of Discrimination in the Workplace and in Careers (Grupo de Trabalho para a Eliminação da Discriminação no Emprego e na Ocupação)
GTI	Working Group for the Valorisation of the Black Population (Grupo de Trabalho Interministerial para Valorização da População Negra)
IBD	Inter-American Development Bank,
IBGE	Brazilian Institute of Geography and Statistics (Instituto Brasileiro de Geografia e Estatística)
ILO	International Labour Organization
INAH	National Institute of Anthropology and History (nstituto Nacional de Antropología e Historia)
INCRA	National Institute of Colonization and Agrarian Reform (Instituto Nacional de Colonização e Reforma Agrária)
INEGI	National Institute of Statistics and Geography (Instituto Nacional de Estadística y Geografía)
INN	National Black Institute (Instituto Nacional do Negro)
INSPIR	Inter-American Institute for Racial Equality (Instituto Sindical Interamericano pela Igualdade Racial)
IPCN	Black Cultures Research Institute (Instituto De Pesquisas Das Culturas Negras)
IPEA	Institute for Applied Economic Research (Instituto de Pesquisa Econômica Aplicada)
IPHAN	National Historic and Artistic Heritage Institute (Instituto do Patrimônio Histórico e Artístico Nacional)
LAPORA	Latin American Anti-racism in a 'Post-Racial' Age
MNU	Black Unified Movement (Movimento Negro Unificado)
MNUCDR	Unified Black Movement against Racial Discrimination (Movimento Negro Unificado Contra a Discriminação Racial)
MPDG	Ministry of Planning, Development and Management (Ministério do Planejamento, Desenvolvimento e Gestão)
MPR	Movement for Reparations (Movimento pelas Reparações)
MST	Landless Workers Movement (Movimento dos Trabalhadores Rurais Sem Terra)
MTE	Ministry for Work and Employment (Ministério do Trabalho e Emprego)
NGOs	Non-governmental organization

NSF	National Science Foundation
OAS	Organization of American States
ODECO	Community Ethnic Development Organization (Organización de Desarrollo Étnico Comunitario)
OFRANEH	The Black Fraternal Organization of Honduras (Organización Fraternal Negra Hondureña)
OJALA	Observatory of Justice for Afro-descendants in Latin America
ORAPPER	Regional workshops for the Analysis and Promotion of Public Policies of Racial Equity (Talleres Regionales de Análisis y Promoción de Políticas Públicas en Equidad Racial)
PALOPs	Portuguese-speaking African Countries (Países Africanos de Língua Oficial Portuguesa)
PANAF	Algeria's first pan-African cultural festival (Premier festival culturel panafricain d'Algérie)
PCERP	Ethno-Racial Characteristics of the Population Research (Pesquisa das Características Étnico-Raciais da População: um Estudo das Categorias de Classificação de Cor ou Raça)
PERLA	Project on Ethnicity and Race in Latin America
PDT	Democratic Worker's Party (Partido Democrático Trabalhista)
PME	Monthly Employment Research (Pesquisa Mensal de Emprego)
PNAD	National Sample Survey of Households (Pesquisa Nacional por Amostra de Domicílios)
PNDH	National Human Rights Programme (Programa Nacional de Direitos Humanos)
PNPIR	National Policy for the Promotion of Racial Equality (Plano Nacional de Desenvolvimento Sustentável dos Povos e Comunidades Tradicionais de Matriz Africana)
PROCEM	National Program for the Centenary of the Abolition (Programa Nacional do Centenário de Abolição da. Escravatura)
PROUNI	University For All Program (Programa Universidade Para Todos)
PSOL	Socialism and Freedom Party (Partido Socialismo e Liberdade)
PT	Worker's Party (Partido dos Trabalhadores)
RAIAR	Antiracist Action and Research Network (Red de Acción e Investigación Anti-Racista)
REUNI	Restructuring and Expansion of Federal Universities (Programa de Apoio a Planos de Reestruturação e Expansão das Universidades Federais)
RMAAD	Network of Afro-Latin American, Afro-Caribbean and Diaspora women (Red de Mujeres Afrolatinoamericanas, Afrocaribeñas y de la Diáspora)
SECAD	Secretariat for Ongoing Education, Literacy, and Diversity (Secretaria de Educação Continuada, Alfabetização e Diversidade)
SEGIB	Ibero-American Secretary General (Secretaría General Iberoamericana)
SEPPIR	Special Secretariat for the Promotion of Racial Equality (Secretaria de Políticas de Promoção da Igualdade Racial)
SINBA	International Brazil-Africa Society (Sociedade de Intercâmbio Brasil-África)
SNDCA	National Secretariat for the Rights of Children and Adolescents (Secretaria Nacional dos Direitos da Criança e do Adolescente)
SNF	National Secretariat of the Family (Secretaria Nacional da Família)
SNJ	National Secretariat of Youth (Secretaria Nacional da Juventude)

SNPIR	National Secretariat of Policies for the Promotion of Racial Equality (Secretaria Nacional de Políticas de Promoção da Igualdade Racial)
SNPM	National Secretariat of Policies for Women (Secretaria Nacional de Políticas para Mulheres)
TEN	Black Experimental Theatre (Teatro Experimental Negro)
TSE	Superior Electoral Court
UERJ	Rio de Janeiro State University (Universidade do Estado do Rio de Janeiro)
UN	United Nations
UNB	University of Brasília (Universidade de Brasília)
UNDP	United Nations Development Programme
UNEGRO	Union of Blacks for Equality (União de Negras e Negros Pela Igualdade)
UNESCO	United Nations Educational, Scientific and Cultural Organization
UNIA	Universal Negro Improvement Association
UNILAB	University of the International Lusophone Afro-Brazilian Integration (Universidade da Integração Internacional da Lusofonia Afro-brasileira)
USP	University of São Paulo (Universidade de São Paulo)
WB	World Bank

List of figures and tables

Figure 1: Abolition of slavery in Latin America —— 12
Figure 2: Afro-descendants in Latin America —— 97
Figure 3: Racial quota system in federal public universities —— 150
Table 1: Ethnicity and/or colour/race by Brazilian demographic census year —— 106
Table 2: Ethno-racial policies implemented in the region —— 110

José de Souza Andrade – Photojournalist

The cover and photos in this book are by José de Souza Andrade, a journalist, cultural producer, and militant of the Brazilian Black movement, also known as "Zezzynho Andraddy". Born in the suburbs of Rio de Janeiro, in the neighbourhood of Anchieta, he is a respected photographer and journalist, who carried with him a view of ethno-racial diversity and plurality.

Born on the 2nd of October 1955, he graduated in journalism at the Faculty of Communication Hélio Afonso; in Professional Photography by the Fina Arts Course of the Liceu de Artes e Ofícios, held by National Commercial Learning Service (SENAC); and in Event Production, also by SENAC.

At the height of the Black Power movement in Brazil he found his path and his collectivity, acting as Soulman in the sessions of the Black dance parties in the Rio de Janeiro suburbs, and being active in the Institute for Research on Black Cultures (IPCN), a traditional Black organization from Rio de Janeiro, where he consolidated his political-ideological formation.

Through these paths and crossroads, José came to be a part of the Black dance party team of the Soul Grand Prix, acting in production and organizing caravans to various Brazilian cities, alongside big national and international names in Soul Music. It was thus that this producer, photojournalist, and photographer became a pioneer of the musical Movement known as "Charme" (Charm), coordinating the trendiest Black dance party in Rio de Janeiro, with the Casino Disco Clube, held at the Marechal Hermes Disco Voador venue for 16 years. He also created one of the first group of Black models in Brazil, turning his event into the main reference for Black culture in the state, through fashion shows, dance competitions, and photography exhibitions.

With the end of the 20th century and the beginning of the new millennium, José de Souza Andrade expands his partnerships and develops cultural occupation projects in the streets of Madureira, a traditional Black neighbourhood in Rio de Janeiro, home of famous samba schools such as Portela, Império Serrano, Tradição and Bloco Afro Agbara Dudú. In Madureira, he takes part in creating the Charme in the Streets Project, now known as the Rio Charme Cultural Project, which is located below the Negrão de Lima Viaduct, and is renowned as one of the main cultural spots in the Rio suburbs.

Through his work as a journalist, photographer, and producer, he also created a series of magazines targeting Black readers and Black Brazilian music, all the while publishing in the mainstream press, including all of the main newspapers in the city of Rio de Janeiro.

A tireless activist and producer, in 2004 he founded Urban Basketball League (LUB) alongside activist colleagues. The institution promotes street basketball as a form of social inclusion for young people from poor communities.

At present, he is responsible for a notable archive from these years, involving various segments of the Black movement in Rio, and also Candomblé. He is active with photography and video recordings of the Rio Carnival, with a special view toward the activity of Black participants. He has acted as a state councillor in the State Council for the Rights of the Negro (Black) (CEDINE), and at the Municipal level in Municipal Council for the Defense of the Rights of the negro (Black) (COMDEDINE). He has been consecrated as a 'King' in the Universal Zulu Nation, an international entity responsible for preserving and developing the Hip Hop movement as a cultural reference point for the Afro diasporic peoples. He is the director of the Black Photographers Collective-RJ.

Photo Section

Cover: Yalorixás (priestesses) of the Our Lady of Good Death Sisterhood – Salvador, Bahia – preparing the ritual for Obaluaê (deity).

Picture 1: Januário Garcia, icon of black photography in Brazil - "There could even be a history of Blacks without Brazil, but there is no history of Brazil without Blacks"

Picture 2: Yalorixá (priestess) Mother Beata of Iemonjá banner – "people of Axé say they are"

Picture 3: Highlighting seed beads at the fair

XVI — José de Souza Andrade – Photojournalist

Picture 4: Cátia Vieira – activist leader of the Black Women Collective of Rio de Janeiro

Picture 5: Conductor Rogério, of the Flor do Oriente street band, the oldest in Rio de Janeiro (150 years)

Introduction

> Every ground is a ground. But no ground can tell its history by itself, can speak of those who have trodden it, of the hidden conversations, of the feet that have passed over it, hurried, fleeing from some hunter. The ground cannot, by itself, say when it is cold or when it is hot, if the liquid that pours over its thick layer of earth, sand, stone or asphalt is the blood of Black or white. The ground also keeps other histories of hurried feet fleeing, below itself. The ground also tells of the layers of life it hides, or which were hidden, there right below today's canopy, which was once shelter for other histories (Ivanir dos Santos, 2018)

There is no doubt that one of the factors that has had the greatest impact on the social, cultural, and political transformation of the last twenty years of the 20th century, influencing the first decades of the 21st, was the prominence of the theme of cultural and ethno-racial diversity. In Latin America and the Caribbean, Indigenous people have been important actors in this process, put Black people have also gained greater visibility in public debates on the theme. The latter make up a significant portion of the total population of the region. Estimates vary between 80 and 150 million people of a total of 900 million inhabitants in the American continent (Antón et al., 2009; Freire, G. et. al., 2018; Santacruz Palacios et al., 2019).

Throughout the region we find diverse Black populations with their own regional or national historical processes, forms of settlement, and socio-cultural and ethnic dynamics. This diversity is also expressed in how they are referred to and classified. The terms that identify them are multiple, varying from one place to another, sometimes within the same country. This variation results from historical contexts, national imaginaries, representations originating in academic studies and in the vocabularies of social movements, political and ideological debates on race and racism, among other factors. The denominations of Black, Negro, and Brown peoples, groups or communities have been superimposed or substituted in different times and places by Afro-Colombians, Afro-Caribbeans, Afro-Latin Americans, among others. However, in general, the term Afro-descendant has been preferred ever since it gained legitimacy with the 3rd World Conference against Racism, Racial Discrimination, Xenophobia and Related Intolerance promoted by the UN and held in Durban, South Africa, between August 30 and September 7, 2001.

Faced with the diversity of existing terms used to denominate the diasporic population, we decided, in this book, to adopt the different forms used in various countries, hence taking into account their different places of enunciation. We do not go into the extensive debates that have existed and are still ongoing regarding the arbitrariness and ambivalence that different denominations can assume according to specific contexts and situations of social interaction. We will use the term Afro-descendant in a more general way, but we will replace it with "negro" or "black" and the "Black" population, especially when dealing with the Brazilian debate, where they are widely used in the country, following a positive political re-signification of the term negro[1].

We must, at the outset, foreground the challenge of translating the racial terms of identification used in Brazil. What we find is great variety in translations into English, according to the choices of different authors. The task becomes even greater when we have to account for classifications common in other Latin American countries. We have decided to use the work of Stanley R. Bailey (2009, pp. 40–45) as a reference, since we believe it comes closer to the facts we explore in this book. To briefly state what we will explore in the chapter on demographic censuses, there are five categories used in Brazil: *branco* (white); *pardo* (brown), *preto* (black), yellow (people of Asian origin) and Indigenous. We have decided not to translate *pardo*, placing 'brown' in parenthesis to differentiate it from *negro* and black in a general way. Due to a political convention, which we will explain further on, *negro* and black are considered to the sum of the categories *pardos* (browns) + *pretos* (black) used in brazilian census questionnaires. We turn to words of Abdias Nascimento (also quoted by Bailey, 2009, p. 46) to explain this choice:

> Official Brazilian census data use two color categories for African descendants: *preto* (literay, "black) for the dark-skinned and *pardo* (roughly, mulatto and mestizo) for others. It is now accepted convention to identify the black population as the sum of the *preto* and *pardo* categories, referred to as *negro*, *afro-brasileiro*, or *afrodescendente*. In English, "black", "African Brazilian", and "people of African descent" refer to this same sum of the two groups [*preto* and *pardo*] (Nascimento & Nascimento, 2001, p. 108).

In the same way, as we will explain in this book, we explore and question the concept of race and its use in public policies considering the national contexts, especially the Brazilian one, where the debate on Afro-descendants and their demands is defined in racial terms, as a debate concerning race relations, wherein discussions of classifications by colour and race, racial identities and the policies of racial equality are on the agenda.

---

[1] In some countries, the self-identification "negro" has been made legitimate by Black Latin American organizations, although other entities have eschewed this category due to its negative historical weight.

Although we deal with different dynamics related to the specificities of the presence of these populations in each country (historical implantation, demographic weight, targeted public policies, processes of political and social mobilization, cultural weight in national societies), there is a set of common elements and global similarities concerning the Black populations in Latin America and the Caribbean. In general, when Latin America started talking about rights for ethnic groups, that is, about the claim for recognition of cultural differences, ethnic identities, inclusionary public policies and other issues that, some 30 years ago, were labelled "multicultural", it was talking about Indigenous peoples. However, since the late 1980s, significant changes have become evident in the "political absence" of Afro-descendants in the region and their demands to be heard in the debate on rights that revolve around cultural difference. The cultural, territorial and political rights of these populations have become part of national and global political agendas.

Historically, the presence of Afro-descendants in national societies has been characterised by the predominance of forms of exclusion, racism and segregation. Their collective political expressions in the region have been episodic. During colonial times, the pioneering example of Haitian independence and the forms of resistance that developed in the face of slavery were a transcendental factor. With the advent of republics and the process of nation-building during the 19th century, the most common political practice for Afro-descendants was militant action in national party forces or participation in political processes through the introduction of specific racial claims. In some of these experiences, dissatisfaction led to the organization of autonomous parties. One example was the Independent Coloured Party in Cuba and the Brazilian Black Front in the early 20th century. We find other experiences of political mobilization throughout this century, the fundamental characteristics of which were the claims, made against the state, for effective policies against racial discrimination and for rights to full citizenship.

Our emphasis in this book is on the elements of the context of what has been called the "multicultural turn" that began in the late 1980s. Since then, multiculturalism, with its various facets, meanings and tensions, has become the pertinent reference for understanding the forms that the processes of recognition of the rights of cultural diversity have assumed, with a stress on Indigenous peoples and Afro-descendants. The Brazilian case, however, brings important inflexions to this context. Although the policies targeting Brazilian Afro-descendant populations have initially been linked to this movement of recognizing the cultural plurality of the region, they later presented themselves as proposals for policies of racial equality, focused especially on the antiracist struggle that results from them. Are we thus witnessing a break with the multicultural turn in Latin America?

We do not understand multiculturalism as a static concept or category, or even as a one-off political phenomenon, but as an "arena" in Bourdieu's (1980, 1994) sense, or a "field of struggle" in the sense of the Manchester School[2]. "Fields of struggle" represent both the actors and their available strategies and resources, which change depending on how actors' acts and the norms and structures within which interactions take place. The political fact – in our case multiculturalism – is, in light of this, an unstable process of interactions between individuals and/or groups based on various power goals. Multiculturalism as a proposal for political action and resistance is installed and constitutes a disputed space submitted to the ups and downs of the correlations of forces, in terms of which it conditions its scope and power relations. It has undergone – and is undergoing – important transformations over these 30 years, with accelerations, setbacks, criticisms and the emergence of new variants.

Our book sits among the various works that study race relations and the presence of Afro-descendants in Latin America and the Caribbean, starting from their common origin in the slave trade, through the processes of abolition and forms of inclusion and exclusion in the national post-independence constructs, up to the contemporary moment of struggle for the recognition of new rights. Between Brazil and the other countries in the region, there are confluences and differences in the dynamics within which the historical and contemporary contextualizing processes are taking place. It is in the to-and-fro of Brazil with the other Latin American and Caribbean peoples that we highlight these confluences, point out differences and particularities and engage in a conversation that, particularly in the case of Brazil, had the United States as a privileged reference point.

Although it is not our aim to provide a historical panorama of the phenomenon, we resort to history in some moments, considering it a necessary requisite in this dialogic gaze between Brazil and the rest of the region. Considering that we take the field of state policies and the social science debate as a focus of analysis, history is revisited as a fundamental position for understanding the construction of the idea of race and racism in Latin America. In particular, we pay attention to the work of Black intellectuals who are often silenced in studies of race relations in the region.

---

[2] The "Manchester School" is an important school of thought in political anthropology. It was officially founded in the Victoria University of Manchester in 1948. It was notable for research carried out in Africa, particularly by Gluckman (1955), Bailey (1969), Barrows (1976), Swartz (1968).

Including older and contemporary Black thought in our analysis is not at all simple, much less easy. Anchoring our reflections in Brazil, a country with a strong African and Indigenous influence, it is notorious that black authors who stand out and register their knowledge are part of a small elite. In certain moments, in association with the interests of the dominant white elite, this black elite found support for their writings, sociological interpretations, historiographical analyses and poetic-literary artistic productions, always with the "lord's" seal of approval or in his shadow. In this case, furthermore, editors and publishers fulfil a thankless role for the subalternized; that is, to re-subalternate their intellectual production, whether they have an academic basis or not.

The quote at the start of this book is by the Ifá priest and Babalorísà Ivanir dos Santos, who is an executive secretary of the NGO Centre for the Articulation of Marginalized Peoples (CEAP), based in Rio de Janeiro. He also holds a PhD from the Federal University of Rio de Janeiro (UFRJ). The extract is from the first paragraph of the first chapter of his doctoral thesis, which has been published (Santos, 2018). It is an ode to Black intellectualness, silenced histories, shattered dreams and invisible publications. Ivanir dos Santos can here be seen as a totem of the Black intellectual in Brazil. We find references to his work in the writings of various European and North American researchers who study subalternized peoples in Brazil, though almost always as a source for the intellectual production of others, and rarely or not at all as an intellectual in his own right, notable for his own output. Having gained access to the space of power that is the university, with his PhD in hand, we see him register his research, his theories and analyses, and yet still needing to overcome the hurdles imposed by access to academic research.

It can be said that this process of erasure of the knowledge and writing of the non-being (recalling, here, Frantz Fanon), is an act with roots as deep as the constitution of the Brazilian state, bringing us to terms with "latter-day slavery", a concept developed by Clóvis Moura (1877, 1990), or to another of his concept, that of "sifting barriers", which Muniz Sodré links to those who monopolize speech and authorize the creation of knowledge, information, registration, and interpretations.

Registering Black intellectual production in our analyses, and bringing to light the work of new authors, is to make visible those who have been rendered invisible, and to reveal the existence of what Richard Santos calls the Minoritized Majority (2020). It is through a Quilombist[3] project, as proposed by Abdias Nas-

---

[3] We will return to Abdias Nascimento's Quilombist project later in the book. We here note that

cimento, that we will be able to listen to the present and to recall the past, the voices of the ground on which we tread and which strengthen us with good energies and vibrations to revert colonial history, as adduced by Ivanir dos Santos.

From the foregoing, we can see that giving centrality to the ideas and theories of Black intellectuals, especially in 20th century Brazil and Latin America, whose worldviews and analyses of the racial issue became central to the construction of a new framework of social understanding of the country and the region, is of fundamental importance for comprehending Latin American society in these first decades of the 21st century. We thus believe that these intellectuals have produced essential contributions to break with the epistemological racism that is institutionalized in traditional Latin American academic thought.

It is important to stress that we follow the geographer and journalist Milton Santos, who seeks to generate social discomfort by defining as "intellectual" anyone who investigates and researches towards transformation, rather than to produce social well-being for protégés. In this view, the intellectual generates critical, transformative knowledge. Milton Santos indirectly agrees with the educator Petronilha Beatriz Gonçalves e Dias (2009), in the sense that research as struggle is only possible when we consider the aims and priorities of social groups that are marginalized by society. In brief, insurgent Black intellectuals who, from the sphere in which they act, are driven to consider their own praxis of Black intellectualness, as a whole distinct from the Eurocentrist and positivist idea of a scientist who produces a knowledge uncontaminated by his experience and corporality[4].

First of all, however, we must provide a very brief context for the genocide[5] of non-white peoples, which is the ground upon which Brazilian (indeed, Latin

---

the reference harks back to the resistance and struggle of the Quilombos (the Brazilian term for 'Maroon', which we will retain throughout the book).

4 In this overview of those who came before so that we may now see the rise of new names in Black intellectuality, with proposals for decentralized thought, a number of study centres and graduate programmes in universities were established, focusing specifically on Blacks. Examples from Brazil include the Graduate Programme in Ethno-Racial Relations and Teaching of the Federal University of Southern Bahia, or even the University of the International Lusophone Afro-Brazilian Integration (UNILAB), a university dedicated to research on the relations between Brazil and Africa.

5 Coined to define the effects of the Holocaust on the Jewish people during the Second World War, the word 'genocide' is used for Brazil by Abdias Nascimento (2016) and for the Caribbean by Aimé Cesaire (1978), to draw attention to the unpunished crimes committed against Africans and their descendants throughout the Americas. Both authors engage the construct as a way of condemning the stolen humanity of Africans and their descendants by European colonizers in the Americas.

American) society is erected, and which leads to the epistemicide[6] of plural and decentred knowledge. We need to recall the past and shed light on the present as an act of the recognition of Black intellectuals, those who have throughout the centuries had their work erased, their skins whitened in official images as a part of the response of the Brazilian state and national intelligentsia, while the former aspired to contribute to a non-Eurocentric epistemology.

In this book we therefore focus particularly on the process that took place after the 1990s, with the mobilisation of Black organisations, when the discourse on racial discrimination is articulated with that of the demand for cultural, territorial and political rights. This transformation is in line with the advent of the multiculturalist wave in the region and the start of the debate on affirmative action. This process has been preceded, since the 1970s, by indigenous mobilisations and by the dynamics generated in the international and national arenas by the context that characterised the last 20 years. In general, it is from the 1980s onwards that the responses of states to these demands began to move in the direction of the institutionalized recognition of the diverse character of societies, constituting a break with the universalist and republican model of homogenizing citizenship or mestizo republics (Wade, 1997; Gros, 1997).

The book is therefore dedicated to a panorama of historical and contemporary debates that follow in the wake of the "multiculturalist turn". It stresses, in particular:
– the characteristics of the period in which multiculturalist policies and legislation of racial equality were enacted;
– the anti-racist struggles and interchanges in the continent, highlighting a history of mobilizations and ancient and contemporary contributions to Black Latin American thought;
– the processes of classification and categorization through which these people were comprehended in the long history of the region;
– finally, a state of the contemporary issue, bringing to the foreground new challenges, new debates that emerge, in large part, from the rise of conservative governments in the region, with a specific focus on Brazil.

As the panorama remains vast, we will focus on the debate on Afro-descendants in Latin America from the perspective of Brazil; that is, our perspective on the issue in Latin America takes the Brazilian case as its vantage point. Brazil, in

---

6 According to Boaventura de Souza Santos (2009), 'epistemicide' is the annihilation of knowledge, wisdom, and cultures which are not assimilated by white/western cultures. It is a subproject of colonialism erected upon the imperialist drive of westernized, European and North American peoples toward orientalized, Asian, African, South American and Caribbean peoples.

turn, is also addressed in its connection with the historical and sociocultural Latin American context as a whole. As we will explain later, Brazil has the largest Black population of the continent, in addition to a history of slavery that stamps the history and the construction of the country's national identity. For this reason, race relations have always been a priority in national public and academic debate. It should be noted that, also for this reason, studies on the Black presence and racism in Brazil tend to focus on the national context, without much dialogue with other Latin American countries, except for some comparative research with the United States, a country that, according to some perspective, shows greater similarities to Brazil. In this book we approach the Brazilian debate from a Latin American perspective, seeing the country as part of the socio-historical context of the region, contesting the common perspective in Brazil which focuses on the national question in isolation, or, at most, in dialogue with the United States.

Brazil is also noteworthy for its experience with implementing affirmative action policies. In this year of 2022, the Law of Quotas in Universities (law 12711, 2012), which provides for access to higher education for Black, Brown, and Indigenous students and people with disabilities, as well as those who attended high school in public schools, is being revised. The Law of Quotas was always intended to be revised ten years after its publication. The current moment raises, yet again, discussions on how to deal with the problem of racism and meet the demands of Black populations. As we will discuss in this book, the question that remains to be addressed in the debate is: are affirmative actions, which require racial identification and classification, the best measures to combat racial discrimination and the exclusion of Blacks?

Finally, the rise to power in Brazil of a far-right government has recently changed the regional landscape. President Jair Bolsonaro promised a major cultural and moral reform in the country and the recovery of Christian and family values. In this sense, he has radically positioned himself against socio-cultural, gender and racial-ethnic agendas, identified as an ideological domination strategy of the international left and as a moral and ideological subversion of traditional Brazilian culture. The president's public manifestations are fundamentally anti-democratic, elitist and racist. To consolidate his reformist project, his government reconstructs the institutional agenda focused on the antiracist struggle and on the Black population, projecting a counter-image of the Black man and a re-discussion of what he considers to be national identity and the Brazilian people. We conclude that this posture, and the conservatives who support it, again cast shadows on the national landscape, conforming what we interpret as a "theatre of shadows". Government and conservatives fabricate images of themselves and the nation, retelling and re-signifying histories, validating their values and representations, thus legitimating, in an extensive setting in which they nominate themselves as representatives of the Brazilian people, a rhetoric that presents itself as universal and inclusive, but which responds only to their interests. They thus reaffirm a speech centred on whiteness and on the Eurocentrism of their values.

This book is the result of research that we carried out during our academic careers. It integrates interdisciplinary perspectives, deriving from our different national and disciplinary origins. A Brazilian anthropologist, a Brazilian communicologist and a Colombian sociologist who converge within the framework of Latin American and Caribbean studies, in that which is characteristic of the field: a comparative, regional, interdisciplinary perspective, engaged with the social reality of the region. These careers are marked by our academic paths, as teachers and university researchers, by our links with social intervention projects and public policies, and, finally, by our interlocution with social activism[7][8]. Even though we are adept at criticizing the social inequalities, Eurocentrism and racism that are equally manifested in the academic field, we cannot forget that we are situated in this privileged space of intellectuals and that it is from this vantage point that we cast our view on themes as complex as racism and race relations in Latin America. For this reason, our effort in this book, and even our experience as educators and researchers, are geared toward promoting a

---

[7] Rebecca Lemos Igreja is an anthropologist, professor at the University of Brasília, and a research associated of the Latin American Social Sciences Faculty (FLASCO/Brasil). She has carried out research in various countries, including Mexico, France, Algeria, the United States, and Brazil, on the theme of multiculturalism, policies of racial equality, racism, discrimination, and ethnic and racial categories. She has been at the head of public policy projects aimed at the inclusion of ethnic/racial minorities, as well as critical efforts at thinking through Latin American academia in a global context. Richard Santos is a communicologist, and professor at Federal University of Southern Bahia. His militant credentials come from his pioneering participation in the Brazilian Hip Hop scene, where he is known as Big Richard. He has headed cultural and political productions, including television shows that have dealt with racial relations and racism in Brazil. Carlos Agudelo is a Colombian sociologist, a researcher associated with the Unit of Joint Research (URMIS – Societies and migrations at the University of Paris, University of Nice), National Research Council – CNRS – and Institute of Research and Development – IRD). He has been a professor and researcher in universities and research centres in Colombia, Central America and France. He has focused on the study of multiculturalism and forms of political action among Afro-descendant peoples, and he has also been linked to the political struggle of Colombian social movements.

[8] Rebecca Igreja thanks the Brazilian Coordination for the Improvement of Higher Education Personnel (CAPES), for the support with funding for postdoctoral research at the Centre d'étude des mouvements sociaux (CEMS/EHESS) in Paris, France, in 2021, when the author also took the opportunity to discuss and advance the conclusion of this book with Carlos Agudelo.

permanent conversation between the different perspectives on the subject, advocated by the different actors participating in the Latin American public debate.

Following our aims, we have organized the chapters in a way which sustains an ongoing dialogue between the Brazilian context and other Latin American countries. The first chapter is called "Race, colour and racism in Latin American history and social sciences", providing a historical dimension on race and racism in Latin America. We focus, in particular, on the colonial period and slavery, on national independence movements, and, finally, going into greater detail on the debate on racial democracy in Brazil. In this latter part we specifically emphasise the Black intellectuals and movements that contributed decisively in this sphere.

The second chapter, "Historical predecessors of Black protagonism" we will turn to certain intellectual movements and examples of Black activism in Latin America, discussed in light of their importance and influence on the debate on race within the context of multiculturalism. Theoretical and methodological proposals, concepts and interpretations that are central in contemporary debates find their inspiration in these earlier movements.

The third chapter, "Multiculturalism and the new ethno-racial identities in Latin America", discusses multiculturalism and its theoretical strands; its introduction in the Latin American context and the emergence of new identity claims; the headways of the political agendas of Latin American Afro-descendants in international spheres; and, finally, an approach to the academic role in this debate, particularly the discussions and research promoted by international projects.

The fourth chapter, "The construction of 'race' as a foundational category of rights and public policies", turns to the debate surrounding racial identification and classification in Latin American censuses, before moving to the public policies targeting Afro-descendants, particularly multiculturalist and racial equality policies, exploring their specificities. After this introduction, we present the contemporary Brazilian context, from the 1988 Constitution, highlighting the associations and movements which have participated in the since the Constituent Assembly. We will then analyse the discussion around the implementation of affirmative action policies, presenting the various social actors and institutions involved with it. We discuss, even if briefly, on the contemporary conjuncture of these policies, how they are being evaluated, and how they have transformed through time. We end by raising questions of the rise of a far-right government in Brazil and its relation to the rights of Blacks and the antiracist struggle.

We conclude the book with a succinct overview of what we have discussed and on our analysis of multiculturalism and Afro-descendant Latin American peoples, again underscoring the complexity of the theme, which involves so many different peoples and distinct historical and national contexts. We return to the Brazilian case one last time, to draw attention once again to the impact of the rise of conservatives to power and how they have dealt with racism and the demands of the Black Brazilian population, ever affected by social inequality, violence and discrimination. We situate racism in a wider context of capitalist domination, showing how, historically, the Black body was treated as a body to be explored, before ending with a nod to the moment of renovation in the debate on the nation and the place of Blacks in its construction.

I Race, colour and racism in Latin American history and social sciences

Race and slavery in the colony

The slavery of Black people stamps the American continent. The trans-Atlantic traffic in enslaved peoples is the largest forced intercontinental migration in world history. Between 1501 and 1867 more than 10 million enslaved people were sent to the Americas from the coastal regions of West Africa. Historians estimate that some 250,000 of these arrived in New Spain, most of them in Mexico and Peru between 1580 and 1640 (Velázquez & Iturralde, 2018). Brazil is estimated to have received some 5 million slaves in over three centuries. Slave trafficking during colonization, and the extended period in which slavery was legal (abolition in Brazil came late, in 1888), left their marks on Brazilian social structure, establishing a hierarchy that persists into the present.

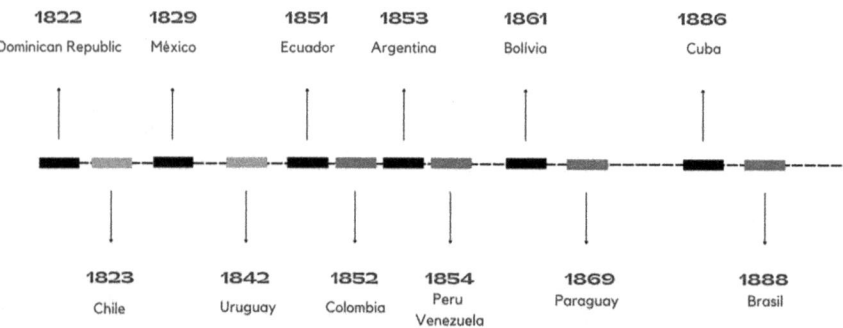

Figure 1: Abolition of slavery in Latin America. Source: Elaborated by the authors

The genesis of the concept of race, like the rhetoric and practice of racism in Latin America and the Caribbean, is therefore not independent from the historical construction of the place of Blacks in the region. The idea of race originates in the European colonial context, but its meanings are transformed within the limits of the political, social and cultural evolution of each society (Banton,

1987; Wade, 1997). It is in this context that we find the variables and specificities for the developmental trajectory of each region and/or country.

While contemporary studies reveal the centrality of racism and ethnic discrimination in accounting for Latin American inequalities, older analyses tended to focus on social class as the structuring basis of the region's societies. The power of the discourse on miscegenation and racial conviviality contrasted with the explicit segregation and racism of the United States. The consolidation of the "multicultural turn", itself preceded by a growing visibility of problems linked to Indigenous and Afro-descendant populations, questions this perspective.

Long before the "discovery" of the Americas[9], Black Africans were already in contact with Europeans through, for example, religious missions and early colonial expeditions in Africa. Before the boom in the Trans-Atlantic trade from the 16th century onwards, there were already African slaves in the Iberian Peninsula, as well as free Blacks. Europeans perceived Africans as being an "heathen people", because of the large number of Muslims in the continent vis-à-vis Christians, although we know that in places such as Ethiopia Christianity existed since ancient times, possibly since the 2nd century (Wade, 1997). Ideas concerning the inferiority and superiority of peoples existed long before the enslavement of Sub-Saharan Africans, although such views were not exclusively linked to a form of racism targeting Black Africans. Aristotelean thought, one of the pillars of the West, legitimated slavery through criteria of power and superiority. Biblical passages were interpreted as showing Black people to be the cursed descendants of Ham, son of Noah (Genesis 9: 20–25, The Curse of Ham or Canaan). In the Middle Ages, Blacks were associated with evil, the demonic, and with sin (Pieterse, 1992). As the Christian faith gained power in Europe, these notions played a legitimizing role in slavery. The progression of the colonization of the Americas consolidates the notion of races of humans in a hierarchy of inferiors and superiors. Thus, slavery in the Americas, initially of Indigenous peoples and later Black Africans, finds a pretext in philosophical and religious precepts, though it can also be justified by the urgent labour needs of colonial expansion as it exploited local resources.

In the "meeting" of worlds, Indigenous Americans first suffered the violence of the conquerors, including slavery. However, this relationship was ambiguous. The colonizers' perceptions of Indigenous people oscillated between attributing to them a savage and fierce character and a gentle and peaceful demeanour.

---

[9] We place "discovery" in quotation marks because the arrival of Europeans is best defined as an invasion, considering the prior existence of diverse civilizations in the continent.

Considered to be subjects of the crown, inhabitants of new imperial territories, native Americans needed to be Evangelized. It should be remembered that the Catholic Church played a key role in colonization, conferring legitimacy to the conquest. Without abandoning their ideas of the superiority of Europeans over native Americans, influential sectors of the Church questioned the extermination of Indigenous peoples and defended an end to their slavery. In the end of the 16th century, colonial empires did just that. We may interpret this period as having developed the "institutionalization" of Indigenous peoples as wards of the crown. In Spanish America, the *encomienda* was instituted, placing Indigenous people under the stewardship of colonial administration, or people designated as *encomenderos* for services rendered to the Spanish crown. Indigenous persons should carry out services and/or pay tribute to the *encomendero* or to the colonial administration; in exchange, they received Christian teaching[10]. This change in the status of Indigenous people did not, evidently, transform the discrimination they suffered, or halt the violence of exploitation, but it did provide a different connotation to the treatment afforded enslaved Africans who were brought to America to, precisely, replace Indigenous labour. Their status as merchandise devoid of rights as persons was only normatively encoded with the Black Codes, long after the start of the slave trade, towards the end of the 18th century.

It is worth reflecting briefly on the role of the Church during colonization and the slave trade. Various colonial legal measures led proprietors to dedicate specific times (Sundays and religious holidays) to promote the Evangelization of slaves. Although this was the general pattern throughout Latin America, in some regions African religiosities fiercely resisted processes of conversion or syncretism, including in Brazil, Cuba, Haiti and other Caribbean regions. (Bastide, 1967; Cotes, 2018).

The Catholic Church remained ambivalent toward the enslavement of Blacks. On the one hand, it provided the ideological ground that made it legitimate, considering it to be aligned with Christian values. While it is true that there were various statements from Church representatives, of all levels, that show reservations, or even condemn the enslavement of Africans (Gutiérrez 1996, pp. 145–160), such positions never congealed into a robust defence of Black populations (Obregón, 2002). On the other hand, the institution of "brotherhoods" as a form of religious, Catholic organization which congregated enslaved and free men of all colours, at times served as springboards for the organization of revolts and escape (Ngou-mve, 2008; Tardieu, 1997; Zuluaga, 1994). It was thus that the institution came to be recognized as a means of support, particularly for

---

10 On this theme, see Pachón (1980) and Minaudier (1992).

runaway slaves who organized *palenques, cimarrons, marrons, cumbes* and/or *quilombos* (denominations for maroons which change according to region), which were communities composed of escaped slaves. We may claim that the Church was, ultimately, reduced to an "assuager" of slavery, itself being the proprietor of enslaved peoples.

Colonial legislation sought to maintain social control of the hierarchy which maintained separated the living spaces of Europeans, Indigenous peoples and slaves. Differences in control over power, material resources, and considerations regarding the inherent dignity of peoples, were based on the stratification of human individuals and groups based on their origins and characteristics of their appearance. However, early hopes of establishing a regime which could accurately separate differentiated human groups was never fully implemented, nor could it be. Reality was more complex, and much racial normativity was subverted in many ways. The notion of 'race' that prevailed in these practices of the colonial system was based on the idea of social differentiations resulting from lineages of purity or impurity of blood, ideas that had been assumed in Europe since the Middle Ages (Hering, 2010).

One of the factors that added complexity to this panorama was the gradual start of miscegenation, which occurred in diverse ways. The most traumatic, but also the earliest, was through the rape of Indigenous or Black women by colonizers. The child of these unions, the mestizo, was a person without a place within this hierarchical schema. Miscegenation also occurred among free Blacks who attained a degree of social mobility after having bought their freedom. Indigenous peoples also moved between their communities and expanding populational conglomerates. Within this context, spaces of social interaction came to be developed, adding further occasion to the dynamic of miscegenation, despite colonial regimentation that sought to curb it.

Colonial authorities never actively promoted miscegenation. Instead, they adapted to the reality of racial mixing. The classification of "castes" in Spanish America, for example, became a common way of defining social stratification, one in which Europeans associated with the idea of whiteness placed themselves at the top of the social pyramid, while Indigenous peoples and Blacks were at the bottom. The use of the word "caste" had the socio-racial connotation of demeaning mulattoes and Brown people, as well as free Blacks, and Indigenous people who did not inhabit native communities (Jaramillo 1994, p. 160). The distinct levels of racial mixing were situated at the intermediary spaces, which, in turn, could generate further classifications of social status premised on other attributes of economic mobility. The caste system could, at times, be highly sophisticated, generating classifications such as *mulato, pardo, moreno, zambo, ladino, cholo*, among many others. These terms, which expressed multiple configurations of racial mixing and miscegenation, were, in some cases, diversified. Castes thereby came to include poor whites, while, in contrast, *mestizos*, *mulatos* and even free Blacks could cease to be considered representative of their respective castes through social advancement and the acquisition of economic capital.

Although it has various meanings, the category of *criollo*[11] was used to classify the descendants of Europeans born in Spanish America. Their European heritage and white colour placed them at the top of the social pyramid, but, in power struggles, the hierarchy always favoured Europeans. Even in the midst of this scenario, the idea of the superiority of Europeans over Indigenous and Black peoples was maintained by the colonial elites. The institutionalization of the 'Indigenous' status enabled certain forms of autonomy and internal hierarchy to survive, placing them in a position of some social recognition within the caste system, above the position of Blacks.

The persistence of racial hierarchy, as well as its tensions, was expressed in the very structure of colonial power, as we can see by, once again, taking Spanish America as an example. This region was constituted by a hierarchical scale that went from the governor, the highest colonial authority of the New Empire, to the "noble" families, the *encomenderos*, Spanish landowners, and, to a lesser degree, their *criollo* descendants who had a near-monopoly of the Cabildo offices. Some of these offices also went to businessmen, owners of mines and plantations. While not part of the nobility, they were arrivistes with economic power. The most difficult barrier to transcend was an "impurity of blood". A mestizo origin remained an almost impossible obstacle to overcome when seeking promotion to positions of prestige in colonial power. *Criollos* and white-skinned mestizos could gain some social notoriety due to economic or cultural factors, but attaining positions of power remained very difficult – a fact that converged in independence struggles during the 19th century (Jaramillo, 1994b). However, in some cases, in the absence of a suitable number of nobles available to occupy positions in councils, certain people of "suspicious origin" might come to compose these governing bodies (Mianaudier, 1988, p. 89). The lower castes, for their part, were excluded, by principle, from all instances of colonial power.

The activity of the cabildos was therefore not exempt from conflicts between families that disputed hierarchically more important roles which conferred not only power but also social prestige. The presence of the not-so-noble *nouveau riche*, often of "suspicious origin", who broke through the formal socio-racial

---

[11] Among its many meanings, *criollo* was also used to distinguish Blacks born in the Americas from Africans, particularly in the Caribbean. It is also used to refer to certain *creole* languages that emerged from the mixture of Indigenous and African languages with English, French, Spanish, Portuguese and/or Dutch.

structure of power, further stoked conflict among elites throughout the 18th century. These conflicts would be carried over, in a modified form, into the Independence period and in the nascent Republics of the 19th century[12]. In this context, new racial components were established, becoming consolidated in the Americas and giving rise to the rhetoric of "racial harmony" which became widespread in Latin America in the first decades of the 20th century (Lasso, 2010).

Studies of Brazil's colonial period tend to take little account of its connection to the experiences of other Latin American countries, despite the fact that colonization was a global process of European expansion the characteristics of which were fundamentally general. Lilia Schwarcz (2019) stresses that Brazil's history has its own particularities when compared with those of its Latin American neighbours, considering that almost one half of all enslaved Africans were brought to the country, and because it had a very popular ruling family for sixty years, thereby securing its borders intact and constituting a large country. Brazil was, furthermore, a Portuguese colony, the population of which speaks a different language from its neighbours. There is no doubt that Schwarcz is right: Brazil displays important historical specificities, which include the constitution of its territory, the proportion of its enslaved peoples, and its demographic formation and socio-political history, including Portuguese colonization. However, the principles that guided and gave justification to the colonization of the Americas do not much differ between Hispanic and Portuguese colonization, as can be discerned from the processes of exploiting slaves in the continent. Perspectives which deny this tend to create an idea of a Brazilian singularity (Dutra & Ribeiro 2021; Tavolaro 2014)[13] which renders invisible wider global and regional processes that have a direct impact on national experiences.

Thus, considering the particularities of the country, the legacy of the colonial period in the formation of contemporary Brazil can be summed up by three dimensions: slavery; patriarchalism; and patrimonialism (Schwarcz, 2019). These

---

12 Debates on what sort of spaces could come to be occupied by these non-noble groups in a new structure of power had already been introduced in the Cadiz Courts, assemblies meant to resist the Napoleonic invasions which met in the eponymous city, in Spain, before the collapse of the Spanish Colonial Empire. What they sought to do at the time was to contain independence.
13 The tendency, within the Brazilian academy, to seek to understand Brazil through its specificities, in isolation from other Latin American countries, is often a reflection of a lack of knowledge of the history of these other countries, as well as of the exchanges of ideas and experiences that have always existed between them (Igreja & Rodrigues Pinto, 2019). This is why we have insisted, since the beginning of this book, on the need to consider the Brazilian perspective on racial relations in conversation with the Latin American context, without thereby ignoring its differences.

three phenomena explain the inequalities, racism and authoritarianism which still prevail in the country. According to Lília Schwarcz (2019), slavery takes centre stage, since it naturalizes racial inequality and the patrimonialism of the landowning class which makes up the oligarchy that still dominates social and economic structure in Brazil.

The enslavement of Blacks in Brazil was a complex system, constituted by a rigid system which submitted slaves to subordination and extreme violence, but which also had its gaps through which they could negotiate their freedom, such as the production of surplus which they could use to buy their manumission and attain a degree of social mobility. It was thus possible to carry out some sort of paid labour or run a commercial activity on nonwork days, although a percentage of the gains thereby obtained were to be passed over to their owners (Reis & Silva, 1999, p. 30). João José Reis and Eduardo Silva (1999) have shown that, while it is important that we recognize the existence of these opportunities, we cannot conclude that relations between slaves and their owners were harmonious or free of conflict – that it was idyllic, as has sometimes been depicted. The authors have observed that, alongside an ever-present violence, there was a social space for bargaining but also conflict. When negotiations broke down, processes of rupture such as escape, rebellion, and the constitution of maroon societies emerged. All of these functioned as a limit to the excesses of the tyranny of slaveowners.

Although the existence of communities of fugitive slaves – the *Mocambos*, as they were first called – is registered in the early days of colonization, it was in 1740 that the Conselho Ultramarino (Overseas Council), a Portuguese colonial administrative agency, defined a *quilombo* as "every settlement of fugitive blacks with over five people, mostly destitute, though without food nor pestles in it". Quilombo is Bantu word which means a "warfare camp in the forest". Palmares was the most well-known Quilombo in the country by far, due to its size and its capacity to resist efforts at destroying it (Gomes, 2015)[14]. Munanga (2001, p. 30) and Moura (2001, p. 104) claim that the Quilombos, communities of refuge, were certainly a means of resistance to the slaveholding structure through the implementation of another political structure, which could harbour all of the oppressed, among them Indigenous peoples. They were also a reaffirmation of African culture and lifestyles. The type of social organization which characterized Quilombos was similar to those that prevailed in African states, which was confirmed by the fact that many heads of Quilombos had only recently arrived from Africa (Carneiro, 2001, p. 11).

---

14 On Quilombos in Brazil, see Reis e Gomes, 1996 and Gomes, 2015.

The rigour of slaveowners and a breakdown in negotiations were not the only cause for escape and the creation of Quilombos. According to Carneiro (2001, p. 12), they were also created out of a situation of local economic anguish which led to a slackening in the disciplinary facets of slavery. Quilombos always appeared at times in which the slave trade became more intense, targeting different parts of Brazil according to fluctuating interests for exploiting one region or another. As Carneiro observes, Quilombos were essentially collective movements, a sort of mass movement that emerged in contexts where economic crises caused slaveowners to neglect their slaves. Nor were Quilombos the only form of collective resistance available to Brazilian slaves. The 19th century was marked by numerous revolts at the height of slavery, particularly during the first half of the century when the country received the highest number of enslaved Africans, despite the ban on the slave trade. Many of these revolts took place in the state of Bahia, the most well-known being the Malê Revolt in 1835 (Reis & Silva, 2018, p. 411).

Nogueira (1998, p. 64) shows that there were different social strata during slavery, forming a hierarchy, with white slaveowners at the top (being a slaveowner was itself a sign of status), followed by whites who worked in commerce, then light-skinned *pardos* (Browns), followed by those with darker skin, moving onto the freed Blacks and, finally, captives, which were themselves distinguished between Believer Blacks (those born in Brazil) and African Blacks. In general, free mulattoes lived in great misery, squeezed between whites and the enslaved, distinguished from the latter only by their legal status. The social structure that became established in the 18th century remained intact until the end of slavery. The correlation between social strata and shades of skin colour is so evident that there is little room for making mistakes. Whitening (*branqueamento*) was a special condition, if not a requisite, for an individual to be accepted on equal terms by the dominant group (even if it was not, of itself, enough). For free mulattoes, social ascent and whitening were two aspects of the same process, just as, for whites, colour justified social status.

Differences in skin colour were evidence of the miscegenation taking place in Brazil, which was later recorded by a number of travellers from Europe. This miscegenation, fuelled by continuous migration to Brazil encouraged by the Portuguese Crown, was often initiated by settlers who arrived in the country without families and who established relations with Indigenous and Black peoples. It should be noted, once more, that this miscegenation did not necessarily imply a rupture in the division between whites and non-whites.

Race in the new states/nations of Latin America

After the processes of independence, which often depended on the participation of the Black population, particularly freemen, the new Latin American states/nations that emerged did not recognize Afro-descendants as full citizens. The liberation movement in different colonial territories resulted from various ongoing historical processes, such as the French Revolution, the Independence of the United States, and the Napoleonic invasion of the Iberian Peninsula, which directly influenced the leadership roles of *criollos* in Spanish America, since their interests were restricted by the power of monarchies over their colonies. These societies' struggle for freedom and rights did not take into account the Black and Indigenous population.

If Independence from European colonies in the Americas is considered to be one of the outstanding events of the start of modernity, a special place must be reserved for the Haitian Revolution[15]. Between 1791 and 1804 we witness a process of struggle and revolt in the French colony of Sainte-Domingue, the richest productive centre in the colonial system of the Americas, with its high concentration of slave labour because of the plantation system. The build-up to the successful revolution and the definitive abolition of slavery, establishing an independent republic, was spearheaded by the leadership of enslaved people and maroons, free Blacks and Mulattoes, it involved a military dimension in articulation with political negotiations, positive developments and setbacks, concessions, tensions, and contradictions within the revolutionary forces, until the definitive attainment of independence from the French Empire in 1804. There were two central aspects to the movement: the unconditionality of the abolition of slavery and autonomy from colonial power.

C.L.R. James (2003) saw the Haitian Revolution as the practical and concrete realization of the universal concept of emancipation by means of slave uprising, a triumph for decolonization and the defeat of the slaveholding system in his country. For Aimé Césaire, the Haitian Revolution was the first material expression of what would later be called 'negritude', understood to be a form of resistance and an affirmation of Blacks as subjects that forge their own liberty. If the independence of the United States in 1775 and the French Revolution in 1789 became major influences in independence processes throughout the Americas, the Haitian Revolution represented the fear of the generalization of slave

---

15 Much of what follows is based on the work of Lao-Montes (2020), particularly on his chapter: "Descolonizar la memoria en aras de forjar futuros de liberación: repensar las independencias a la luz de la revolución haitiana".

revolts with disastrous consequences not only for slaveholding economies and global powers, but also pro-independence lighter-skinned mestizos. Lao-Montes, referring to the work of Haitian thinker Trouillot concludes that:

> ... the Haitian Revolution was an "unthinkable" event in the meaning-horizon of its time, as it constituted the anachronism of a Black republic of freed ex-slaves from Africa in a capitalist Western world where slavery and racist ideologies prevailed, wherein Blacks were qualified less human or nonhuman. It was therefore a revolution silenced by historians through formulas of elimination and formulas of trivialisation, both powerful ways of silencing that constitute "global silences... (Laó-Montes, 2020, p. 176)

The Haitian Revolution was also a veritable coup against the incongruence of the universal values of freedom expressed in the Declaration of the Rights of Man and in the United States declaration of independence, which were elaborated without taking into account the real problem of freedom for millions of human beings subjected to slavery. Yet responses to the movement were swift. Haiti, as an independent nation, was condemned to isolation, boycotts, interventions, resulting in stunted development and conditions of extreme poverty, as well as the image of a country fated to backwardness and chaos.

In practice, the example of Haiti served as a stimulus to ways of resisting slavery which had been in place since the beginning of the slaveholding regime (Dubois, 2005; Geggus, 2002; Geggus & Fiering, 2009). The Haitian Revolution occupies pride of place in the academic output on the history of Afro-descendants in the Americas. Some of the references we cite attest to this. The chapter on Haiti in Lao-Montes's book offers a panorama within which historical elements are articulated with political – and even philosophical – implications in a decolonial perspective of the meanings of this event.

> The legacy of Haiti should not be of regret or a declaration of failure, but of inspiration toward the construction of its incomplete project of social justice and human dignity; the unfinished project of decolonization and the resilience of neocolonial imperialism imply paying attention to the Haitian Revolution and its effects, tracing a genealogy of the classic forms of decolonization and the modalities of coloniality and neocolonialism that we continue to face in the 21st century (Lao-Montes, 2020, p. 186).

In the contemporary context of the mobilization of Afro-descendants for recognition and rights, the Haitian Revolution emerges as an element within a shared historical memory. In what concerns the current plight of Haitian society, one of the demands of some Afro-descendant networks, such as the Regional Afro-Descendant Articulation of Latin America and the Caribbean (ARAAC), is that American states and multilateral organizations implement aid programmes specifically targeting this people.

Without wishing to attenuate the impact of the Haitian Revolution and its representatives, it should be noted that throughout the period of slavery there were events of resistance and Black leaders who rose to prominence. Almost all of the countries in Latin America and the Caribbean that had a contingent of slaves have histories of resistance, some of which remain to be told[16]. Among them, there is much yet to be explored in the history of the Palmares Quilombo, and that of its leader Zumbi, or the San Basílio Palenque, led by Benkos Bioho in Colombia.

A further historical chapter that official narratives tend to conceal is the significant role of contingents of both enslaved and freed Blacks in struggles for independence. We draw attention, for example, to Cuba and leaders such as Antonio Maceo and Quintín Banderas or José Prudencia Padilla in La Nueva Granada (current Andean countries), and also to José María Morelos and Vicente Guerrero in México[17]. Cuba also saw the emergence of the Central Directory of Societies of the Coloured Race and of the Independence Coloured Party, led by Evaristo Estenoz and Gregorio Surín (Lao Montes, 2020, p. 62).

With independence, and later with the definitive abolition of slavery, racial discrimination against Black and Mulatto populations lost much of its normative basis. It should be noted that the possibility of achieving freedom itself, in the period before the abolition of slavery, did not do away with the institutional measures that restrict the rights of these populations. Free Blacks and Mulattoes during the colonial period and in the first years of the new republics continued to be submitted to restrictions that, in some cases, were similar to those that affected the enslaved: they could not dress the same way as whites and Mulattoes, nor carry the same type of weapon; they could not gain access to the same system of education, nor run the same sort of business; they could not ride horses, nor did they have the same freedom of movement as other free peoples. Moreover, their freedom was conditional on the demands of their former owner. The freemen who failed to respect the conditions of their freedom could once again find themselves enslaved.

However, there was also a permanent transgression of the restrictions imposed by legislation. Blacks and Mulattoes took on roles that were prohibited to them by law, whether because of the lack of a suitable workforce that met the standards of racial legislation, the lax surveillance of the authorities, or by their rebellious attitude in relation to instituted power. Consequently, legislation

---

16 A recent book which covers this theme is Aline Helg (2016).
17 For Cuba, see Helg (1998); for Colombia, Chaves (2015); for Mexico, Velázquez (2019).

gradually came to adapt to these social realities (Gutiérrez de Pineda, 1999, pp. 29–133).

The decree that officially abolished slavery legally put Blacks and Mulattoes on an equal footing with the rest of the population, but the conditions which they experienced makes it impossible to speak of "equal conditions" for them and white society. Although individual exceptions always existed, they were still peripheral to the situation of the majority of this population. The rules established during this period (mid-19th century) which intended to "control vagrancy" targeted, in specific, Blacks and Mulattoes who found difficulty in maintaining stable employment (Vieira Júnior, 2006)[18]. Restrictions on occupying public offices, and the prohibition on the participation of illiterate people or those with a minimum economic capital in elections, were also impediments to the majority of the Black population.

The discourse on formal equality, which was now extended to Blacks, did not lead to the end of the stereotypes of racial inferiority that remained in the minds of the dominant society during the colonial period. In the 19th century, these prejudices were adapted to a new ideologically racist rhetoric, the "scientific racism", a line of thought originating in Europe that nurtured a racial social order envisaged by the elites and reproduced as social practice. Latin American national elites were very receptive to this "scientific" rhetoric that came to the Americas along with ideas of progress and liberty.

We can take the Colombian case as an example. In 1850, the year before the abolition of slavery was decreed, the national government created *Comisión Corográfica*. The aim of this agency, composed of a group of academics, was to carry out a complete survey of national geography, its resources and the characteristics of its population. Agustín Codazzi, a geographer of Italian origin and the main member of the commission, wrote of the Black populations, after visiting the North Pacific Coast: "a race that spends its days almost entirely in idleness is not called upon to help the country progress" (Banco da República, 1958, p. 324). Another illustrious member of the commission, Santiago Pérez, commented on the "savage stupidity of the Black race, its ignorant idleness, terrible carelessness, and scandalous cynicism". The intellectual and politician José Maria Samper, one of the figureheads of liberal thought in 19th century Colombia[19], expressed his view of racial differences:

---

[18] For Brazil, see the penal code (Decree n° 847, 1890) and for New Granada, see Escalante, (1964) and Gutiérrez (1980).
[19] J.M. Samper studied in France, and his writings reflect the simultaneous influence of the liberal Romantic theories in vogue at the time in that the mid-19th century, and the conceptions of racial differentiation in "naturalism" as espoused by Gobineau.

> There, primitive man, rugged, brutal, indolent, semi-savage and challenged by the tropical sun, that is, the Colombian fashion, with all his insolence, his stupid fanaticism, cowardly petulance, incredible indolence, and his linguistic cynicism... but here the European, active, intelligent, white and elegant, often blonde... the *boga*[20] descendant of Africa and son of the mixing of degenerate races by tyranny, almost lacks humanity, displaying the external form and necessities of primitive forces... (José María Samper, 1868, p. 16).

The ideological rhetoric which proclaimed racial differentiation and the inferiority of some races in relation to others were accompanied by the acceptance of the mestizo character of Latin American populations, and the conviction that it should, gradually, disappear, reducing the characteristics of the inferior races. Ideal miscegenation should tend, biologically and, above all, culturally, toward the white-European model.

The research of the "scientific racism", promoted in Europe since the mid-19th century, sought to "demonstrate" the relevance of racial hierarchies, the inferiority of non-Europeans, or non-whites, and the negative character of racial mixing. They had a particularly marked impact on the first studies of Black populations in Latin America that analysed the prejudicial influence of these populations in the construction of modern and civilized nations. In parallel with scientific ideas of cataloguing and classifying nature, systems for classifying human beings were developed, such as that developed by Linnaeus in his *Sistema Naturae*, published in 1758. By means of such systems, race emerged as an instrument of classification and a key component for the evolutionary ideas that buttressed the enslavement of Blacks by placing them in a position of inferiority. Efforts at classifying and ideas of the 'purity of blood' had been around since the 15th century and, consequently, inter-racial marriages were re-signified and assumed a scientific content. Such ideas update caste systems and frameworks for social differentiation that sought to order a society already undergoing processes of miscegenation (Velázquez & Iturralde, 2012).

These theories, which preached racial superiority, and which attained a solid legitimacy in Europe and the United States, also had significant repercussions in Brazil, as we will see later. Arthur de Gobineau (1915), a French racist theorist and diplomat, despised the country[21]. He proposed a classification of the three

---

20 This is how men who piloted and rowed boats on the Magdalena River, between the 18th and 19th centuries, were called. The *bogas* were Mulatto, Black and particularly *Zambo* (Indigenous and black mestizos) colonists. The word *boga* comes from *bogar*, which has Latin origin and means 'to row'.

21 Gobineau published "An Essay on the Inequality of the Human Races" (*L'essai sur l'inegalité des races humaines*) where he described his racist ideas, in 1855. He was in Brazil as a representative of France in 1869–1870. The edition quoted here is from 1915.

great races, Black, Yellow, and White, in which the latter were on a superior level. Blacks were here linked to animality, to instinct, to sensuality, while whites were linked to the intellect, rationality, and intelligence.

> The negroid variety is the lowest, and stands at the foot of the ladder. The animal character, that appears in the shape of the pelvis, is stamped on the negro from birth, and foreshadows his destiny. His intellect will always move within a very narrow circle. He is not however a mere brute, for behind his low receding brow, in the middle of his skull, we can see signs of a powerful energy, however crude its objects. If his mental faculties are dull or even non-existent, he often has an intensity of desire, and so of will, which may be called terrible. Many of his senses, especially taste and smell, are developed to an extent unknown to the other two races. ... (1915, p. 205)

> We come now to the white peoples. These are gifted with reflective energy, or rather with an energetic intelligence. They have a feeling for utility, but in a sense far wider and higher, more courageous and ideal... . (1915, p. 207).

Gobineau found Brazilian culture to be stagnated, and he feared for its health, while also despising Brazilians for their miscegenation which, in his view, condemned them to promote racial degeneration. Louis Agassiz, in turn, following a long expedition through Brazil, concluded that although the slaveholding system should be condemned, abolition should come about gradually. Agassiz saw the lack of restrictions on free Blacks in Brazil to be a moral problem, which he linked to a low degree of prejudice based on skin colour, and which he contrasted to the United States, the country in which he resided:

> Those who cast doubt on the pernicious effects of racial mixing, and are drawn, through a false philanthropy, toward bringing down all barriers to it, should come to Brazil. It would be impossible for them to deny the decadence that results from inter-breeding which, in this country, occurs to a greater extent than in others. They would see that this mixture erases the best qualities of whites, Blacks or Indians, and produces an indescribable mestizo type whose physical and mental energy is enfeebled (Agassiz, 2000, p. 282)

A precursor to anti-racist thought was the Haitian anthropologist, politician and diplomat Anténor Firmin, who, in 1855, published a work criticizing the theories of Arthur de Gobineau. Firmin (1855) wrote "The Equality of the Human Races" (De l'égalité des races humaines) in which he refutes Gobineau's theses, affirming the non-inferiority of Black peoples, presenting the Haitian Revolution as an irrefutable demonstration of their capacities. Firmin was the first Black intellectual in Latin America and the Caribbean to author a critical analysis of scientific racism.[22]

Despite contestations, explanations of the economic and social backwardness of Latin American countries still relied on the racial component of their populations. A forum on "Racial Problems in Colombia" was held in 1920, in which the psychiatrist Miguel Jiménez López claimed that Indigenous peoples and Blacks were incapable of producing or assimilating elevated forms of culture (Jiménez, 1920, p. 47). In the same, event, the hygienist Jorge Bejarano expressed the idea that the Black race, "aided by its savage customs and scant intelligence and morality, has reproduced prodigiously" (Jiménez, 1920, p. 192). In the end of the 1920, Laureano Gómez, a well-known conservative politician, claimed that "our race comes from the mixture of Spaniards, Indians, and Blacks. The latter two flows of inheritance are stigmata of complete inferiority". For Gómez, Blacks lived in "a state of perpetual childhood... with a rudimentary and deformed spirit, absorbed in the fog of an eternal illusion...". He proceeded:

> We are a people for whom miscegenation prevails... the primary mestiza is not a useable element for the political and economic unity of America... In the nations of America, wherever Blacks predominate, disorder also reigns... In countries from which Blacks have vanished, such as Argentina, Chile, and Uruguay, it has proved possible to establish economic and political organization, with a solid and stable base (Gómez, 1970, pp. 54–55)

These studies were gradually substituted by another tendency which, while not making the presence of Blacks into a mark of inferiority, tended to deny it by proposing a uniformity of race through racial and cultural miscegenation. In particular during the 1920s and 1930s, these ideas began to question a purported racial degeneration produced by miscegenation, carving, in its place, a positive role for miscegenation and the combined contribution of European, African, and Indigenous components in building Latin American national identities. Major exponents of these ideas include the Mexican intellectual and politician José de Vasconcelos, who claimed that Latin America was the birthplace of the "cosmic race", fruit of the four racial components: European, Indigenous, African, and Asian. Vasconcelos saw this racial melting pot as the ideal future of humanity, thus overcoming older theories of racial superiority which emanated from Europe. While accepting the positive character of these ideas vis-à-vis former racist theories, they helped to cloak ethno-racial differences, as well as the racism and

---

[22] In 1900, Firmin was present in the first Pan-African Conference, held in London (Firmin, 1885).

discrimination that victimized the Black and Indigenous populations in Latin America[23].

In Cuba, Fernando Ortiz developed a new approach in his study of Black peoples in the country. In 1937 he founded the Cuban society of Folklore and Society for Afro-Cuban studies, which carried out important analyses of the culture of Afro-Cubans. Ortiz's concept of 'transculturation' emerged within this context, in a book called "El contrapunteo cubano del tabaco y el azúcar", published in 1940 (Ortiz, 1991). Similar initiatives were developed during the same time in other Latin American countries, such as Venezuela, Colombia, Panama, Uruguay, and Mexico (De la Fuente et al., 2018).

Miscegenation thus became consolidated as a central element of Latin American and Caribbean national identities. Under slogans such as the 'melting point', 'cosmic race' (Vasconcelos, 1948), 'racial harmony', and 'racial democracy', an idea of cultural and racial homogenization (with a tendency towards a white, European paradigm) became consolidated. However, at the same time, miscegenation also established a complex relation with those "others" who remained on the fringes of society, despite being sociocultural components at the forefront of the configuration of national cultures. Claims to difference that become consolidated during the multicultural turn reaffirm this process full of tensions between the ways miscegenation continue to feature, as part of the social and cultural realities of these societies in interaction with various forms of making differences visible.

Turning to Brazil, independence brought no modification to the situation of enslaved Brazilian Blacks, maintaining the slaveholding system intact. However, it did pave the way for liberal ideas that would fuel the abolitionist campaigns that were soon to emerge. It is after the second half of the 19th century, strongly influenced by liberal ideas and practices, that a new positivist-evolutionist ideology grows roots in the country, developing racial models of analysis that sought to demonstrate the biologically inferior status of Blacks.

---

23 "The Cosmic Race", by José Vasconcelos, was published in 1925 after the author travelled to Brazil and Argentina. In an analysis of how Vasconcelos dealt with Blacks in his treaty of the cosmic race, Tardieu shows how many of the theories that came out scientific racism affected the author, particularly in what concerns the structural backwardness of the Blacks of this "cosmic race". "The universal race, upon which the Mexican thinker rests his hopes for the future of humanity, imposes itself by its orderliness, its structure against the disorder of the inferior races... The cosmic race, forged in the crucible of purification, would free itself of all atavistic imperfections. For the Black man, it was seen to be a veritable 'regeneration'" (Tardieu 2015, p. 161).

Da Matta (1987, p. 68) also claims that independence was central insofar as it presented national and local elites with the need to create their own ideologies and mechanisms for rationalizing the country's internal differences. It was impossible to separate from Europe and become independent without seeking out a new identity, one that could justify and legitimate internal differences. According to the author, the solution came through what he calls "the fable of the three races" and "Brazilian racism", an ideology that conciliates a series of contradictory impulses in society without thereby elaborating a plan to transform it in any meaningful way.

Célia Maria Marinho de Azevedo (Azevedo, 2004, pp. 28–30) interprets this moment in Brazilian history as representative of the fear that followed the Haitian Revolution and its declaration of independence, which caused great consternation in slaveowners regarding their family and property. Blacks in Brazil could repeat what happened in Haiti, as attested to by the resilience of the Quilombos, raids on plantations, individual or collective revolts, and the attempted insurrections which occurred throughout the history of slavery in the country.

International pressure on Brazil to bring about the end of slavery was fundamental in strengthening the pressure of the abolitionists. The first step toward abolition was taken in 1871, with the Law of Free Birth which determined that all children born to enslaved mothers would be free. This law, and later the law emancipating those over 60 years of age, began to unravel the slaveholding system.

Before slavery was abolished, the number of freed people was already greater than that of captives. In 1872 there were almost three times as many free men of colour than slaves. They represented 42% of the total population, while the enslaved population was reduced to 16% (Skidmore, 1989, p. 58). It is probable that the lack of a skilled or semi-skilled workforce led white colonizers to allow for the creation of this category of freemen, typically a ruse, who were actually urban workers.

The Lei Áurea (Golden Law) was finally passed on the 13th of May 1888, freeing those people who remained enslaved. Even during the slaveholding period, slaves were able to practice subsistence agriculture, and even to produce some surplus; but with abolition many had to leave the lands that belonged to their former owners, and they were replaced by free workers, many of whom were European immigrants. The enslaved thus saw themselves separated from their small allotments with no means of beginning new lives as freemen.

It must be noted that the historical process which led to the abolition of slavery in Brazil was also marked by Black abolitionist movements and popular unrest. The Malê Revolt in Bahia in 1838, and the uprising of Manuel Congo in Vassouras, in Rio de Janeiro state in the same year, point to pressure mounting against the institution of slavery. In this context, a few prominent Black leaders emerged. Luis Gama, for example, was a freeman who extensively criticized the slaveholding system, and who managed to occupy political and social spaces in which he worked in defence of abolition. There were also a number of Black associations which arranged to purchase manumission and promote the freedom of slaves. The period immediately after abolition was one of conflict and uncertainty. Abolitionists were themselves split between monarchists and republicans, and in many cases the figure of Princess Isabel, who had signed the Golden Law, projected a greater commitment to the freedom of slaves. Within this dispute, the Black Guard was created toward the end of 1888 to defend and ensure the freedom which had been attained. The Republic which began to take shape after abolition took a conservative turn, dominated by former slaveowners and farmers who were dissatisfied with abolition (Gomes, F. S., 2005).

However, with the start of European immigration after abolition, many Blacks saw themselves as being "passed over", in the words of Nogueira (1998), in favour of these new arrivals. Furthermore, there was no official plan to incorporate and account for what was now a massive number of free workers. The end of slavery thus left many Blacks adrift, with neither work nor land. Many turned to subsistence agriculture, often as squatters, while others tried to be reincorporated into rural work, returning to their old farms. Others still headed to the cities, which were ill-equipped to receive such large quantities of unskilled workers, having nothing to offer them but a marginal status.

The arrival of European immigrants to Brazil was a direct consequence of a new form of domination which was based on racist theories that originated in Europe. As of 1890, some three million Europeans settled in Brazil. The state's incentives to European immigration corresponded to the interests of maintaining the dominant status of the elites which were heir to colonization, and to build a whiter national identity, closer to European standards.

It must be kept in mind that what drove segments of the monarchist elite to support the abolition of slavery was not any commitment to the social and human reality, of which Blacks were a part, but an adequation to cultured European thought (Sodré, 1999, p. 79). As Skidmore (1989, p. 43) explains, abolitionist thought, as a reformist doctrine, was born of 19th century European liberalism, which followed in the wake of the Industrial Revolution, accelerated urbanization, and developed the economy. A wager on liberalism was justified by the economic development that was observed in Europe; however, Brazil signed up to this liberal proposal without promoting any deep economic changes. Although a degree of urban growth is detectable after 1850, there was no economic leap in the country.

The adoption of liberalism was decided mostly in an academic environment. As we have mentioned previously for Latin America as a whole, while liberalism preached equality for all before the law, it was handmaiden to the burgeoning racist theories produced by Europeans, such as Louis Agassiz, H.T. Buckle, Arthur de Gobineau, and Louis Couty, many of whom referred to Brazil as a negative example. We here resume an analysis of these theories, which advocated racial superiority, achieving widespread acceptance in Europe, and turn to the discussions they gave rise to in Brazil. Brazilian thinkers found in the racist theories of European thinkers a path for maintaining the powers of the dominant elite[24]. Abolition could unsettle existing social hierarchies, and an ideology that could justify the maintenance of these hierarchies was desirable

Nina Rodrigues, a professor at the Bahia School of Medicine, claimed that the inferiority of Blacks was backed by scientific evidence, based on the work of the Italian criminologist Lombroso, who gained notoriety for measuring cranial capacity in order to determine intelligence. He went as far as to propose that criminal law abide by distinct codes, since Blacks and Indigenous people could not by judged like whites because of their natural tendency to criminality, insanity and paranoia. However, Nina Rodrigues found it difficult to situate Mulattoes in his schema, and he was concerned with the consequences of miscegenation in the formation of the Brazilian people (Rodrigues, 2010).

Brazilian society was already multiracial and miscegenation took place at various social levels. Mulattoes, including Nina Rodrigues himself, looked different from Blacks and pure-blood Indigenous people, but they could not be considered white. It was difficult to determine who was white: as Gobineau said, "not a single Brazilian has pure blood because the pattern of marriages among whites, Indians, and Negroes are so widespread that the nuances of colour are infinite, causing a degeneration of the most depressing type among the lower and upper classes" (quoted in Skidmore, 1989, p. 46).

The literary critic Silvio Romero sought to answer the racist theories proposed by Gobineau, even if in an ambiguous fashion. He saw the problem of de-

---

24 Schwarcz (2001) and Da Matta (1997) argue that the adoption of racist theories in Brazil cannot be seen as a simple interest in copying European thought. While certainly being strongly influenced by Europe, the ideas also responded to specific interests of the white elite. For Schwarcz (2001, p. 19) there was much that was original in Brazilian racial thought, which, adapting exogenous theories, updated what matched with local social reality and discarded what was, in a way, problematic for the construction of a racial argument for the country. As Da Matta reaffirms, in Brazil "racism", much like other imported ideologies, was modified and obeyed the forces that constituted the social totality, that established, within a hierarchical society, a proper "place for each thing".

velopment in Latin America as stemming from the fact that it was colonized by a predatory, parasitic race, originating in the Iberian Peninsula, made up of Portuguese and Spaniards. However, he did not deny a hierarchy among races, considering the possibility that miscegenation might produce a vigorous population growth, and thus benefit the future of all Brazilians (Romero, 1906). Romero believed that the specific character of Brazil came from the mixture of the three races and that each contributed to the formation of mestizo and creole subrace which was distinct from the European race. Observing the lack of a definite ethnic group in Brazil, he elected the mestizo as the "condition for the victory of whites in the country". He thus believed that miscegenation would result from the struggle for the survival of species (Schwarcz, 2001, p. 64).

Abolitionist thought was thus extensive and complex. As Nabuco claimed:

> Slavery, for our contentment, never soured the soul of the slave against the master – collectively speaking – nor did it create between the two races the reciprocal hatred that naturally exists between oppressor and oppressed. For this reason, the contact between them, outside of slavery, always lacked harshness, and the man of colour found all avenues before him open. (Nabuco, 2011, p. 16)

In contrast to the United States, there was, in this view, no prejudice based on colour. Furthermore, most abolitionists predicted an "evolutionist" process in which the white element would gradually triumph as dominant race or social class.

It is this line of thought, and its positive attitude toward miscegenation, which will guide generations of thinkers, with its fundamental principle of promoting the whitening of society. In alignment with the modernizing European project, the new Latin American nations which were being consolidated should be similar to Europe, culturally and racially. It is Brazil, however, which puts into practice a public project anchored in the ideology of whitening the population so as to produce a culturally and genetically superior people.

One year after the abolition of slavery, Brazil's proclamation of the Republic occurred – again, not through the strength of reformist forces, but, rather, as a display of the agrarian elite's power. As well as concern with the mass of free Blacks (or, at least, legally free Blacks), the main issue of the day was peopling the country's vast territories and constituting a contingent of able workers. Encouraging the continuation of European immigration seemed like the best solution, since they could, with one stone, solve the need to people the country and provide workers (Vainer, 1990).

There was a dilemma: there was a state and a national territory before there was a people and a nationality. According to Vainer (1990, p. 105), this meant that it was necessary seek out the bases of nationality. The issue was thus with whom should the territory be occupied, who should make up the workforce, and, finally, who should constitute the basis of the state. The elites and their state would establish goals and means, defining how to construct a Brazilianicity in the name of which, paradoxically, that very same state, despite being inexistent or incomplete, will speak and act. Racism thus served as an instrument for the construction of a country for the future, which would emerge out of a conscious effort expounded in the racial laboratory of the present. The work of Oliveira Viana has focused on this theme, analysing the national melting pots constituted by immigrants, particularly Europeans, and their dialogue with other races, such as Blacks and Indigenous peoples. This is what his study *Raça e Assimilação* (1938) focuses on:

> The fact that ethnicities hailing from all continents have flowed here makes America, on the contrary, the centre *par excellence* of studies of Race, whether from the point of view of physical anthropology or social anthropology (Oliveira Viana, 1938, p. 19).

> We now understand why a nation cannot remain indifferent to the quality or the quantity of the racial elements that participate in its composition. Bringing, to the creation of the racial plasma, their most frequent "types of constitution", these racial elements determine the type of temperament and intelligence that should predominate within the social mass (Oliveira Viana, 1938, p. 52).

The problem lay, precisely, in the impossibility of constructing a nation out of national workers. As Oliveira Viana claims, by defending the re-composition of the national base through migration, considering that, in Brazilian formation, there is a predomination of two inferior bloods (the Black and the Indian), and a people of poorly developed eugenics (Vainer, 1990, p. 105).

Thus, two years after the abolition of slavery, and only seven months after the proclamation of the Republic, Decree n° 528 (1890), aiming to regulate the introduction and distribution of immigrants in the country. Its first article established the free entrance of individuals for work purposes, so long as they did not have a criminal background in their countries of origin, and excepting indigenous Asians and Africans, who could only gain admission with the authorization of Congress. Other laws and projects further organized the admittance of immigrants, including, for example, a law that forbade the admittance of Black people, expanding discriminatory policies to inhibit immigration of Blacks from the North America and the Antilles (Vainer, 1990).

Incentives to immigration practiced as policy the neo-Lamarckian theses of the eugenicists, who believed that genetic deficiencies could be overcome in a single generation. Telles (2003, p. 45) claims that, despite its relatively short popularity, the predominance of this line of thought among Brazilian eugenicists at the turn of the 20th century had enormous implications in interpretations of the idea of race for the succeeding decades. These academics accepted hierarchy among races and, therefore, the inferiority of Blacks and Indigenous peoples; however, they believed that this inferiority could be overcome through miscegenation. It was through their interpretation of eugenics, refuting deterministic ideas which claim that whites were incapable of adapting to tropical climes, that Brazilian academics proposed "whitening" as a solution, by mixing whites and non-whites.

It was in light of this interpretation that the director of the National Museum, João Batista Lacerda, claimed at the 1st National Congress of Races, held in London in 1891, that miscegenation did not result in a degenerate race, but, on the contrary, on a sturdier race that was capable of becoming white, culturally as well as physically. A number of illustrious foreigners welcomed Lacerda's claims, among them Theodore Roosevelt, president of the United States. Guimarães (1999, p. 51) argues that the theory of "whitening" was elaborated out of a wounded national pride, which was ransacked by debts and suspicion regarding its industrial, economic, and civilizational genius. It was, first and foremost, a means of rationalizing the feelings of racial and cultural inferiority instilled by the scientific racism and geographical determinism of the 19th century.

Gilberto Freyre, however, elaborated another interpretation of Brazilian miscegenation, establishing himself as the central reference in discussions of the racial question in the country. The idea of 'racial democracy' is attributed to him, although he never actually used the expression in his work. *The Masters and the Slaves* (Freyre, 2001[1933]), his most debated book, is nonetheless taken to be the most important and sophisticated interpretation of racial democracy in the 20th century.

Racial democracy: ideology and the invisibility of racism

Although, as we have already mentioned, various countries in Latin America have explored the rhetoric on miscegenation and the construction of a racially and culturally homogenous society, we will focus in particular on discussions around racial democracy in Brazil due to the powerful influence it has on the country and the region as a whole.

Gilberto Freyre proposed the end of the myth of the scientific superiority of the white race in contrast to the Black race, rejecting, at the same time, the theory of the degeneration of race through miscegenation. Instead, he stressed the positive contributions of each people toward the construction of the nation through miscegenation. Taking on a culturalist perspective, imported via the anthropology of Franz Boas, Freyre transferred the issue of race to a matter of cultural heritage, in which each – Portuguese, Black, Indigenous, and immigrant – contributed to the construction of the country. In his view, the basic mould of Brazilian society is unique because it stems from a particular type of miscegenation, occurring within an agrarian-patriarchal context (Sodré 1999, p. 99).

Freyre's studies were based on the inter-racial relations of the landowning and slaveholding patriarchal families of the 16th and 17th centuries. His focus is on the institution of the Big House (*casa grande*), which represents a whole economic, social and political system vying with the Church to attain control over the land. "With the Jesuit vanquished, the master of the sugar mill dominated the Colony almost by himself" (Freyre, 2001, p. 50). The history of the Big House is the intimate history of almost every Brazilian, his history of domestic life, conjugality, slaveholding and polygamous patriarchy, his childhood, and his Christianity reduced to a family-based religion and influenced by proximity to the slave quarters (Freyre, 2001, p. 56). It was within the Big House that Blacks and whites lived in intimacy, and where cordial relations were established between them, which conferred a lighter tone on the institution of slavery. Miscegenation is the result of this relation: "miscegenation, which was widely practiced here, corrected the social distance which would otherwise have been firmly retained between the Big house and the tropical forest; between the Big House and the slave quarters" (Freyre, 2001, p. 46). There is little reference in Freyre's work to how whites exploited the labour of Blacks in the plantations. Based on his work, Brazilian thought widely adopted the notion that different races lived in perfect harmony in the country. Thus, the answer to the question of how to incorporate various races was the promotion of the Mestizo as a national product.

Freyre's work does not deal with the actual contradictions of the historical-social process, the classes and their ranks in accordance with their specific dynamics and conflicts and mismatches within the global social system. His views on the interethnic relations between whites, Blacks, and Indigenous people ultimately corroborated the ideology of whitening. According to Skidmore (1989, p. 211), "the practical value of his analysis was not, however, in promoting racial equality. The analysis served first and foremost to strengthen the ideal of whitening, vividly showing how the (primitively white) elite acquired precious cultural traits from intimate contact with the African and, to a lesser degree, the Indian". Guimarães (1999, p. 52), although allowing that the early work of Freyre, later followed by Melville Herskovitz, Donald Pierson, and Charles Wagley, decreed the death of the explicit racism present in the ideas of the time, also stresses that it is a mistake to conclude from this that there was any radical break with these racist presuppositions. In his view, the thesis of whitening was merely adapted to the canons of social anthropology, coming to refer to the social ascension of mestizos within the social hierarchy. Likewise, Marcelo Paixão (2014) shows how racial prejudice, in the form of the differential position of the lighter-skinned mulatto and those closer to Blacks, is evident in Freyre's work.

However, Muniz Sodré (1999, p. 101) stresses that although Freyre ignores armed revolts, the Quilombos, and all forms of explicit resistance of slaves, his work shows that Blacks sought to circumvent the victim ethos strategically, through the use of symbols that obeyed their own logic, committed to the survival and expansion of Afro-descendants. Blacks thus impregnated Brazilian culture, a fact that analyses that focus only on the interests of the white elite and on the ideology of whitening do not take into account. For Sodré, the landed elites were engaged in elaborating particular forms of commitment to the human aspects of territorial diversity. The major issue, them, was their excessive proximity to dark-coloured individuals, in contrast to Indigenous peoples. Freyre's work is evidently attractive for those who believe in racial democracy and its cordiality. These criticisms would not therefore lack foundation, since it is clear that Freyre's work is a fountain of conciliatory formulas and that the cultural synthesis put into effect by mestizaje was unable to eradicate racism from national society because "conciliation and synthesis are means of discrimination that do not assume themselves to be stereotypes of domination" (Sodré, 1999, p. 104).

Authors such as Thomas Skidmore and Roberto da Matta argue that Freyre's thinking and his discourse on miscegenation reflect strategies for the surreptitious maintenance of power. The authors explain that hierarchization in Brazilian society was based on "white superiority" and not on "supremacy" as such. According to this line of thought, miscegenation was a rationalization of the elites who, in the end, sought the whitening of the country's population. Sérgio Costa also sees Freyre's work as a manifesto for the (re)foundation of the Nation, which cannot be understood simply as the construction of a racial ideology, but above all as a deep and definitive inflection in the process of the redefinition of national identity. (Costa, 2002, p. 42).

The debate surrounding Freyre's work is an example of the complexity of interpreting race relations in Brazil. On the one hand, it is evidence that the construction of Brazilian national identity found its core in discussions surrounding race, and it underwent a period in which whitening the population was the goal, itself a refraction of the influence of eugenicist European thought in the country. On the other hand, it demonstrates how the belief in, or the ideology of, a 'racial democracy' penetrated Brazilian society, establishing itself as a foundational myth. Between the real miscegenation that is observed in Brazilian society and the ideological construct that emerges from it, what we find is the resilience of a society that renders invisible the contributions and heritage of African culture in the formation of the nation and the racism that characterizes it. If Freyre's work were a testament to the indisputable contributions of Blacks to the construction of the Brazilian people, it fails to consider the obstacles that prevent the true recognition of these contributions.

Alongside the promotion of Freyre's work to the position of a "genesis of nationality", we witness a process of 'de-Africanization' of various cultural elements which become symbolically whitened. As Schwarcz (2002, p. 277) notes, the examples are many and can be found in the officialization of capoeira and samba, in the end to persecutions of Afro-Brazilian religions, such as Candomblé, and even in the choice of Our Lady Aparecida as the patron saint of Brazil, who was mestiza "like Brazilians". For a while, Freyre's idea of a cultural exchange between groups prevailed.

The presidency of Getúlio Vargas, the historical context in which the debate surrounding racial democracy takes hold, must be considered. Vargas became president in 1930, after the Great Depression of 1929 which had a devastating impact on the export of Brazilian coffee. He was considered to be a populist, supported by the Brazilian working classes (he was known as the "father to the poor"), who came to power amidst revolts that were occurring throughout the country, and the growing conflict between communists and integralists (members of the Brazilian Integralist Action, a fascist organization). Head of a popular government, which many identify as having had fascist tendencies, Vargas was concerned with gathering the entire population within the arch-idea of "the Brazilian people".

In 1930, when the Vargas provisional government begins, the Brazilian Black Front (FNB), a political organization originating in the Southeast of the country, became a political party. It had a markedly integrationist profile, developing ideas such as the importance of moral advancement, work and education as necessary and sufficient elements for bringing an end to prejudice against people of colour and to promote the integration of Black people. FNB rapidly expanded to various parts of the country, promoting demonstrations and even presenting proposals to the 1933 Constituent Assembly. It later declined, due mostly to internal political divisions, until it was finally extinct during the Vargas dictatorship in 1937, when all political parties were outlawed.

In the Vargas government, however, the laws which regulated immigration into Brazil were ambiguous in what pertains to race. For example, the 1934 Constitution restricted the immigration of Africans, although it emphasized equality before the law regardless of race. Through the Council on Immigration and Colonization, Vargas retained his policies, restricting immigration based on origin. Immigration quotas were established according to the capacity of immigrants to adapt and be assimilated. Many of these policies made no efforts to conceal the perpetuation of the drive to 'whiten' the population. Be that as it may, from the 1930s until the 1970s, the 'racial democracy' becomes present in the rhetoric of the Brazilian state, cloaking the existence of racism in the country.

With the consolidation of the ideology of a racial democracy, differences between whites and Blacks in Brazil come to be interpreted by many intellectuals as a simple difference in social class. Blacks were in a worst social condition merely because they were mostly from the lower classes, heirs to their poor socio-economic inclusion in the aftermath of slavery. This new interpretation of the racial issue – which was no longer, strictly, a racial issue – turns out to be a means of inhibiting Black political and anti-racist mobilization.

It is during this period, in 1944, that the Black Experimental Theatre (TEN) is created in Rio de Janeiro, including towering intellectuals such as Abdias Nascimento and Guerreiro Ramos. Abdias Nascimento was one of the most prominent anti-racist activists, as well as an artist, playwright, politician and poet. He took part in the FNB during the 1930s, and also organized historical events such as the First Brazilian Black Congress (1950) and the National Black Convention (1945–1946), which proposed affirmative policies to the National Constituent Assembly of 1945, as well as the definition of racial discrimination as a crime against country. In his own view, TEN sought to reclaim the values of the Black-African person and culture, which had been degraded and denied by a dominant society which, since colonial times, revealed the mindset of its metropolitan European formation, imbued with pseudoscientific concepts regarding the inferiority of the Black race. Ten sought not only to establish a Black theatre, but also to be a "forum for ideas, debates, proposals, and action geared toward the transformation of the structures of racial domination, oppression and exploitation which were implicit in society" (Nascimento, 2004, p. 221).

Alberto Guerreiro Ramos may be considered the brainchild of the condemnation of the ideas of whitening and epistemicide. He was at the centre of intellectual reflections on the nation, being particularly active from 1950 to 1970. This influential Black thinker from the Northeastern state of Bahia was precursor and source of many of the discussions which have since gained ground in peripheral countries, such as decoloniality and non-dependent development.

The applied sociology of Guerreiro Ramos, characteristic of his early work, acquired greater visibility with his role in TEN, with his growing critique of academic social sciences and, more specifically, with the anthropological approach to Brazilian Blacks, conceived mainly as an object of study and not as people whose living conditions needed to be transformed. Guerreiro Ramos stresses the necessity of a Black elite, an intelligentsia who, alongside white intellectuals, would formulate a policy for defeating racism and appreciating Black lives as more than mere objects of research (Ramos, 1950, p. 34).

Defining an agenda for TEN, Guerreiro Ramos took part in the National Black Conference, having been elected to the organizing committee of the 1st Brazilian Black Conference along with Abdias Nascimento and Édison Carneiro. He became the director of the National Black Institute (INN), and was responsible for holding courses on education, culture, and professional development, as well as holding theatrical activities of group dynamics and those of a psychotherapeutic nature. He coordinated a group therapy seminar for students at TEN seeking to develop a workforce able to "act in the favelas, shrines of Afro-Brazilian religions, and associations of people of colour". He believed that group therapy, through theatre, offered opportunities for Blacks to face up to their fears and resentments, purging from their personality the racial stereotypes and self-depreciative views that had been incorporated since childhood (Ramos, 1950, p. 46).

A pioneer in the analysis of the forging of a Brazilian intelligentsia, and of the need for it to express ethno-racial plurality, Guerreiro Ramos developed a theoretical proposal for sociological reduction; or, rather, a method for conceptualizing the reality of the peripheries, the development of their inclusive and aggregating productive forces, which the national elite, in collusion with international capital, had always ignored, and still ignores.

> Sociological reduction is a method destined to allow students to practice the transposition of knowledges and experiences from one perspective to another. What inspires it is the systematic conscience that there exists a Brazilian perspective. Every national culture is a particular perspective. Hence sociological reduction is, merely, a restricted modality of a general attitude, which must be assumed by any culture in its process of foundation (Ramos, 1996, p. 42).

By making headways towards assuming agonistic positions in the academy, condemning the physical and intellectual elimination of the Black Brazilian population, and the subalternization of its intellectuals, Alberto Guerreiro Ramos discovered, in sociological reduction, the means to recover a critical strand of Latin American thought which stressed the production of autonomy and the dignity of producing a social science that is not imported from abroad, and the methods of which were disfigured when applied to Brazil.

Guerreiro Ramos' sociological work not only showcases his mastery of sociology and the scientific method, but reaches beyond the academy, revealing the impact of these investigations in the practice of social sciences in Brazil. He collates analyses and understandings of the psyche of the Black citizen submitted to whitening, and establishes a dialogue with what was being produced, at the time, by the pioneer sociologist and psychoanalyst Virginia Leone Bicudo.

TEN was born in a context critical to the Estado Novo. The Democratic Afro-Brazilian Committee was, in this sense, a social movement which defended a more inclusive democracy. According to Abdias Nascimento (2004), the primary aim of the Committee, composed of Black activists, was to free political prisoners, most of whom were white. However, as soon as they began to discuss problems peculiar to the Black population, the group split. A focus on the black question was seen to be an obstacle for the formation of a unified and homogenous working class.

According to Guimarães (2002, p. 146), during the 1940s and 1950s, Brazilian Blacks continued to be mestizo and hybrid, but would soon gain an increasing Black essence, culturally African. TEN represented this change perfectly, since it shifted between trying to overcome the "African" and "backward" cultural practices of Black people while, at the same time, affirming the Black ethos, also African, linked to emotivity and expressivity, manifest spontaneously in the arts. It did not seek to break with the values of white society, so much as to include Blacks through education, by improving their self-esteem and furthering the adoption of white behaviour typical of the upper classes.

Guimarães (2002, p. 89) also argues that TEN does not break with the belief in the value of racial democracy, since not all of its intellectuals censured Vargas' nationalist and populist policies. The author refers, again, to the work of Guerreiro Ramos, for whom Blacks *were* the Brazilian people, and that therefore there was little sense in speaking of the "Black question", or in cultivating exotic forms of cultural expression (such as Afro-Brazilian religions) which were proper to the condition of misery and ignorance in which most of the poor found themselves. Guimarães also observes that Guerreiro Ramos, exaggerating the *mulato* paradigm of Gilberto Freyre, transformed 'negritude' into an assumption of Brazilian national identity that was free of the inferiority complex bequeathed by Portuguese colonization. As Bastide (1961) claimed, Brazilian Blacks absorbed the Négritude movement in a manner all their own, refusing its cultural aspects and stressing its libertarian and nationalist character.

It is equally important to stress the role of Black women in the Brazilian Black Movement and its associations at this time. Werneck (2009, p. 19) claims that it is already possible to identify female leadership in colonial Quilombos, though indirectly through an analysis of available reports, as attested to by the presence of women such as Aqualtune, Acotirene, Mariana Crioula, and others, and their part in the economic and political articulation of resistance. Equally central was the creation of the first association of domestic workers, which brought together women who worked in the state of São Paulo in the 1930s, the main leader of which was Laudelina Campos Melo, who was also a member of the FNB (Werneck 2009, p. 11). As the author stresses, domestic work is crucial to the economic history of Brazil because it is a professional activity developed primarily by Black women (and remains so today). In May of 1950, the National Council of Black Women was created as a branch of TEN, an initiative of Maria de Lourdes Vale Nascimento. Nascimento would also occupy a prominent role in 1st National Black Congress, held in August of 1950, where she staunchly defended Black women and drew attention to the psychosocial problems of prostitutes, for those engaged in this activity, and to the rights of domestic workers (Silva, J., 2005).

The Brazilian governments that succeeded Vargas continued to feed the ideal of racial democracy, without thereby promoting policies that might realize it. Nonetheless, a few anti-racist laws were elaborated, particularly in response to external demands. In 1951, The Afonso Arinos Law was passed, which threated any act of "prejudice" with a penalty. The term "racism" was judged to be completely inadequate, and the term "prejudice" was used instead. The Law (Law n° 1,390, 1951) stated: "it is a penal infraction (penal contravention), punishable under the terms of this Law, for a commercial or educational establishment, of any nature, to refuse to host, serve, attend to, or receive clients, whether buying clients or not, because of prejudice of race or colour". This law, however, attests to the existence of racism, or "prejudice", in Brazil, even if the idea was denied in practice.

A turn in the debate surrounding racism and racial inequalities in Brazil came through research carried out by UNESCO in the 1950s. Following the horrors of the Second World War, Brazil had acquired an international reputation as the country of racial democracy. UNESCO backed a number of studies seeking to understand how the country had established racial harmony. Various intellectuals took part, among them Charles Wagley, Thales de Azevedo, Marvin Harris, René Ribeiro, Costa Pinto, Roger Batista, Oracy Nogueira and Florestan Fernandes. These studies, particularly those of Florestan Fernandes, sought to reveal obstacles to the integration of Blacks in class-based society, and the particularities of Brazilian racism, probing the image of a racial democracy.

Before appraising the conclusions of the UNESCO project, we find it important to shed light on the silence surrounding the contributions of Virgínia Leone Bicudo. Between 1945 and 1995, the Black sociologist, psychiatric social worker, and psychoanalyst Virgínia Leone Bicudo wrote two pioneering studies of racial relations in Brazil. The first, *A Study of Racial Attitudes of Blacks and Mulattoes in São Paulo (Estudo de atitudes raciais de pretos e mulatos em São Paulo)*, was her MPhil dissertation concluded at the Open School of Sociology and Politics (ELSP) (Bicudo, 1955). In her dissertation, she inaugurates a discussion on the role of Black associations, such as the FNB, in mobilizing against hurdles in the social ascension of the Brazilian Black population. The second study, published in 1955, is *Attitudes of Students in School Groups in Relation to the Colour of their Colleagues* (*Atitudes de Alunos de Grupos Escolares em Relação com a Cor dos seus Colegas*), which resulted from research carried out under the auspices of the UNESCO-Anhembi Project in São Paulo, under the supervision of Roger Bastide and Florestan Fernandes. This study was considered to be a "mere" appendix to the project's final report (Bicudo, 1955; Bicudo & Chor Maio, 2010, p. 46). Researchers who have since recovered Bicudo's seminal work, which remained without reedition for 65 years, and whose contribution to the UNESCO research was effaced, have asked why this should have been so. Gomes (2012, p. 22), whose thesis concerns the sociologist's career, draws attention to the fact that nowhere is there any mention to the fact that a Black woman was a researcher in the UNESCO project. After all, "if a Black woman worked in the UNESCO Project, then this should be duly registered somewhere, even if only as a mere curiosity, since it was itself, in a way, testament to their social ascension in the period, which seems to be far from a trivial fact".

By studying the subjective dimensions of prejudice, Virginia Bicudo inaugurated lines of research that would later be developed by Black intellectuals such as Frantz Fanon and Guerreiro Ramos. Her work does not privilege an analysis of the relations that structure the processes of Brazilian history and its institutions. Rather, she focused on the quotidian register: teaching processes and their complex environments; constraints to personal careers and the social fate of her interviewees; contacts established with subjects on the street, in the city, in private and public interactions; affective and matrimonial strategies, seeking to strengthen the group or annihilate it (marriages intended to *darken* or *whiten the race*); views on feelings of beauty, affection, suffering, inferiority or equality; good and bad manners, public and private; and so forth. She thus starts from the micro-level and moves to the macro-level, without losing sight of the social subject and the construction of an imagery.

Born in São Paulo, in the traditional Luz neighbourhood, in the year of 1910, Virgínia Leone Bicudo was the daughter of a Black father, Theofilo Júlio Bicudo, born free on the 8th of January 1888, named after the Saint of the day of his birth. His daughter's career is indicative of processes such as the professionalization of women in higher education, and the social ascension of Black and mestizo families. Certain historical moments, such as the hygienist drive as a means of social regulation, not only sealed her professional destiny early on, but also her academic reflection, which was often in conflict with new models of social analysis. Her experience as a student during the Vargas era occurring with the rise of sociology as a discipline capable of analysing and understanding Brazil, and its institutionalization through graduate programmes. By studying her career, we also see in the introduction of psychoanalysis in Brazil, and the zone of conflict that took hold of the Brazilian Society of Psychology through a perspective leaning more towards mental hygienist positions.

Through a singular biography for her time, and still exceptional today, she was the only woman to obtain a bachelor's degree in Social and Political Sciences in 1938, at the newly created ELSP. She joined the school in 1936, as she considered it to be less elitist than the University of São Paulo. Years later, she abandoned her career as a sociologist and turned to psychology, believing that sociology was unable to understand her suffering, let alone to resolve it.

We must, however, consider that not all participants in the UNESCO project reached similar conclusions. Studies carried out in Bahia, Recife, and the North, particularly does by Charles Wagley and Marvin Harris, reiterated the conclusions of Gilberto Freyre and Donald Pierson (1945) that racial prejudice was weak, if not inexistent.

> There is little racial prejudice in Bahia (if it exists at all), in the sense that this expression is used in the United States. There are no castes based on race; there are only classes. This is not to say that there is not something that we might properly call "prejudice", but rather that the prejudice that exists is a prejudice of class, not race. It is the type of prejudice that exists among men of colour themselves in the United States, the intensity of which is, truth be told, quite large (Pierson, 1945, p. 402).

In the studies carried out in the Southeast of the country, in São Paulo and Rio de Janeiro, the emergence of racial tensions was widely registered, revealing that while prejudice was strong, it was also denied or underplayed. Florestan Fernandes strongly rejected the conclusions of his colleagues regarding the North and Northeast. In response to Donald Pierson's hypothesis and the proposal of the UNESCO Project, he comments:

> Yet what is a racial democracy? Is the absence of open tensions and permanent conflict, of itself, an index of a "good" organization of racial relations? On the other hand, what is more important for the "negro" and the "mestizo", an ambiguous and disguised consideration or a real condition of economic, social, and cultural humanity equal to that of whites? (Fernandes, 1972, pp. 21–22)

In his analysis of what resulted from the social order linked to slavery, Florestan Fernandes concludes that miscegenation and vertical social mobility were limited by their convenience for the existing social order, which sought continuity with the racial stratification engendered by slavery, and which remained unaltered after abolition. Racial democracy was anchored in this structure and constituted a source for a peaceful solution to the racial question in Brazil. Fernandes sought to show:

> The fact is that, even today, miscegenation is not part of a societal process of integration of the "races" in conditions of social equality. The universalization of free labour did not benefit the "negro" and the "mulatto" submerged in subsistence economy (which, by the way, was also the case for the "whites" who were part of this sector); but, in the conditions in which it took place, the rule was prejudicial the "negro" and the "mulatto" who were part of waged occupations, more or less victimized by the competition of the immigrant (Fernandes, 1972, p. 28)

The author thus affirms that the idea of a "racial democracy", a true myth, ultimately served to accommodate a reality in which black people lived in poorer social conditions of labour, in systematic misery and in permanent social disorganization. In his words, what was generated was the most extreme indifference and lack of solidarity toward a sector that did not have the conditions to face the changes that came with the universalization of free labour and competition. The Brazilian dilemma would hence be this contrast between ideal norms, democratic presuppositions, and effective behaviour, which reflect a process of incomplete decolonization. Great historical changes in the country were always overseen by conservative powers, the supreme power of the white minorities. In this sense, decolonization is an ongoing process, since the colonial world subsists, institutionally and functionally (Fernandes, 1972, p. 260). For Fernandes, the discrimination that still exists is for this reason a product of this persistence of the past in all spheres of human relations.

Telles (2003, p. 60) interprets these differences between "schools" as resulting from distinct foci. Those in the Bahia School who follow Freyre tended to give emphases to horizontal relations of sociability to the detriment of vertical economic relations, presumably because they believed that the indicators of the integration of minorities in society, such as miscegenation and inter-racial marriage, were the best sources for projecting future racial relations. Optimistically interpreting the Brazilian racial system as being more benign that its counterpart in the United States, they identified racial inequality as a consequence of the recent abolition of slavery rather than of existing racial discrimination. The São Paulo School, in contrast, concentrated on the hierarchical relations of racial inequality and the racism they caused. Florestan Fernandes, for example, ignored the mixing of races that was more positively valued in the North of the country. In São Paulo, an ethnic mosaic created by intense immigration, Blacks were only one of the various ethnicities, even if they were the most stigmatized. The relative lack of importance afforded to the mixture of races can also involve the association between Florestan Fernandes and Abdias Nascimento, who associated the elite's support for miscegenation with a strategy for whitening the population.

Lília Schwarcz (2002) claims that the innovation of the São Paulo School was to apply sociological analyses centred on the modernization of the country, in lieu of culturalist analyses. By investigating the shift from the traditional world to the modern, a discussion of the role of social classes in Brazil imposed itself. According to Schwarcz (2002, p. 285), the studies of the São Paulo School were key to unpacking the "myth" of racial democracy; however, by unpacking it, they, in a way, transfigured the theme of race into one of class and abandoned culture, understood as models of "culture of" and "culture for" which enable an understanding of universes of sociability and representations, customs settled in the *longue durée*. It was through modernization and democratization that the racial question, and other questions, were to find a solution in Brazil which did not involve tackling, head on, their specificities. The contrasting conclusions of the researchers of the Project take us back, once again, to the debate surrounding interpretations of Gilberto Freyre, shining a spotlight on the cultural or social aspects of racial relations in Brazil.

During the 1960s and 1970s, discussions of racial inequalities went cold because of the limits imposed by the military dictatorship on intellectual and political freedom. Nonetheless, in 1965 Brazil ratified Convention 111 of the ILO which was concerned with discrimination in the workplace and in the job market, even if this ratification had no internal impact on the racial question. In the end of the 1970s, however, while the country was still under a military dictatorship, a new movement of contestation emerged. The Black Movement was reborn, under a new guise, seeking to denounce the myth of racial democracy, still under the inspiration of the work of Florestan Fernandes but also taking on a new character. According to Hanchard (2001, p. 132), what was unprecedented in the appearance of protest groups and organizations in the 1970s was the confluence of race and class with the Black Movement. Activists and followers abandoned the belief in conformism and social ascension which had prevailed in the 1930s and 1940s.

In the mid-1970s, when the military dictatorship was undergoing a process of "distension" which would, in 1979, result in the political amnesty of exiles, repatriating old activists who had been exposed to new political ideas abroad, in Europe, the United States, and other Latin American countries. By absorbing these ideas, former exiles, along with new and old Brazilian activists, elaborated a new rhetoric in which the influence of the civil rights struggle of Black North Americans was evident, drawing the attention of Brazilians toward political struggle based on racial questions. Equally evident was the influence of the decolonization of Africa and the non-white insurrection movements in Asia, Africa, Latin America and the Caribbean.

These changes also left their mark in the academic field. In the 1970s and 1980s, Carlos Hasenblag and Nelson do Valle Silva (Hasenbalg, 1979; Silva, 1978; 1985; 1999), through quantitative studies of the differential insertion of

Blacks and whites, observed that race, as an ascriptive criterion, had mostly favoured white people in the job market. They also show that Browns presented socioeconomic indexes which were not that different from those of Blacks, and both were very distant from those of whites. This work sought to shake up the myth of racial democracy, putting the notion of 'race' again in evidence, proving the existence of racial discrimination. Their aim was to show that social class, and the legacy of slavery, was not enough to explain the subordinate position of contemporary Blacks in Brazilian society. These were the first in a line of statistical studies that crossed socioeconomic data with "race/colour" in order to reveal the different conditions of Blacks and whites.

In this context, in 1978, the Unified Black Movement against Racial Discrimination (MNUCDR), was founded, its name later changing to the Black Unified Movement (MNU). With the clear bankruptcy of the idea of racial democracy, which had failed to promote the inclusion of Black people, many newly created organizations called for mobilization, raising the awareness of intellectuals and researchers, aiming to condemn the existence of racism in Brazilian society and take a stand against socio-racial inequalities (Cardoso, 2002, p. 38).

The MNU emerged with three aims in its political agenda: a) denounce the racism, racial discrimination and prejudice to which Blacks were victims; b) denounce racial democracy as a myth; c) construct a positive racial identity through Afro-centrism and 'Quilombism', which sought to recuperate African heritage in Brazil (Guimarães, 1999, p. 160).

Abdias Nascimento (2000, p. 220), having returned to Brazil, participated directly in the foundation of the MNU, which was publicly consolidated on the stairs of the Municipal Theatre of São Paulo, was to play a key role by giving expression ta new generation of Black militants. He had always claimed that the racial question was a national question, and that, therefore, it was impossible to think of models of development that excluded from its beneficiaries over half of the population. In this sense, Nascimento's contribution that we will focus on here concerns the elaboration of a socio-political proposal for Brazil, formulated form the vantage point of the Brazilian people, which he terms "Quilombism". Although the word Quilombo originally designated Brazilian maroon settlements, where escaped Blacks would seek shelter during slavery, beginning in 1920s the word took on new meanings as 'political resistance' through the thought of Astrogildo Pereira, Edson Carneiro and Maria Beatriz Nascimento.

Maria Beatriz Nascimento's[25] studies highlighted Black resistance, among them the Quilombo and its political-ideological resignification for the anti-racist struggle.

> And when I went to university, the thing which shocked me the most was the endless studying, in what concerns Blacks, of the slave, as if all through Brazilian history we had only ever existed in the nation as slave labour, as labour for plantations and mines (Nascimento, B., 1977, p. 3).

Criticizing dominant historiography, she sees in the Quilombo not only a refuge for runaway Blacks, but also an effort toward independence of men who sought to establish their own lives, to establish their own form of social organization (Nascimento, 1977, p. 4).

> I want to say the following: the Black man facing the History of Brazil feels eternally a slave, eternally vanquished, incapable of reacting before the situation in which he was placed. But this is a complete deformation of historiography which no longer corresponds to the situation of the lower classes to which Brazilian Blacks usually belong, with their lack of education, economic conditions, yet basically structured within an ideological framework with great implications. [...] So, the Quilombo, for us, for Blacks, has a fundamental importance because, as slavery, Blacks as slaves, historically cease to exist in the end of the last century, in 1888, and all sorts of life are projected for Blacks other than that of the plantation, but these already existed and they pre-existed abolition (Nascimento, B., 1977, pp. 3–4).

For her, the concept of the Quilombo took on the meaning of ideological instrument against forms of oppression at the end of the 19th century, which, in 1970, will nurture the Black movement. It hence became a symbol of resistance and the struggle for recognition of the social role of Blacks in Brazilian society. The Quilombo was recovered "as a code that reacts to cultural colonialism, reaffirms African heritage and seeks a Brazilian model capable of strengthening ethnic identity" (Nascimento, B., 1985, p. 47). In November 1974, for this same reason, the Palmares Group of Rio Grande do Sul proposed the 20th of November (the death of Zumbi and the end of the Palmares Quilombo) as the Day of Black Consciousness, replacing traditional celebrations of the day of the abolition of slavery.

---

[25] Beatriz Nascimento, an important figure in the Brazilian Black Movement, took part in various associations, groups, and research centres on racial relations in the country. These include the International Brazil-Africa Society (SINBA,), the Brazilian Centre of Afro-Asiatic Studies (CEAA,), the Black Cultures Research Institute (IPCN,), and the André Rebouças Working Group (GTAR,). On further aspects of Beatriz do Nascimento's thought, see Ratts (2007).

In the end of the 1970s and the beginning of the 1980, the "Quilombo" thus became a symbol of Black resistance. In 1980, Abdias Nascimento published *Quilombism* (*O Quilombismo*), seeking to define the new political role that the historical term was assuming. He is responsible for first defining Quilombism as "a concept emerging from the historical-cultural process of the Afro-Brazilian population". In his words, "Quilombism is a political movement by Brazilian Blacks aiming for the implementation of the Quilombist National State, inspired by the model of the Republic of Palmares in the 16th century and in other Quilombos which existed in the country".

Based on cultural experience, the historicity and collective praxis of the Black collectivity, Abdias Nascimento, through the idea of Quilombism, questioned the basis of the model of Brazilian development and the racial dispositifs which excluded Black women and men from the benefits of development, elaborating a theoretical-practical proposal for political, social and economic transformation linked to a communal model influenced by the historical Quilombos. Its basic aim was to promote human happiness through a free, just, egalitarian and sovereign society, via a communitarian-cooperative economic base involving the collective use of the land and the means of production, and harmonious living with nature in equilibrium with all forms of life. The Quilombist proposal anticipates what is today known in "buen vivir" in Latin America. With Quilombism, Abdias Nascimento thus provided an ideological ground for the MNU, one of the main ideological matrices which will unite political and cultural radicalism. It was a political proposal for the Brazilian nation, not just for Blacks:

> A state dedicated to the egalitarian coexistence of all of the components of our people, preserving and respecting the diverse identities, as well as a plurality of cultural matrices. The construction of a true democracy necessarily demands multiculturalism and the effective implementation of compensatory policies or affirmative action that make possible the construction of full citizenship for all discriminated groups (Nascimento and Nascimento, 2000, p. 222).

In a pioneering fashion, the proposal is a first effort at registering concepts and experiences of the Black Brazilian people and their worldview. Abdias Nascimento recovers the Quilombo ideal of the commons, recognizes the political, social, and economic knowledges and practices of Quilombos, and identified the need to find again the social organization of Quilombos as a political platform for the construction of alternatives to development based on an anti-racist, anti-capitalist, anti-neocolonial, anti-imperialist, and anti-landowning model. Nascimento takes the lead in the edification of the historical-humanist science of Quilombism and its epistemological base.

One of the signs of the growth and vigour of the Black Movement at the time was, according to Abdias Nascimento, the institution of the National Day of Black Consciousness, a proposal which gained momentum and gradually came to be recognized by the media and society-at-large. The burgeoning strength of the Black Movement became evident during the re-democratization process, which began in 1979. In 1982, during the first elections for National Congress and state governments, there was a growing organized Black participation, including nuclei linked to political parties. The Democratic Worker's Party (PDT), for example, was created with the explicit aim of dealing with issues of the Black community. In other parties, such as the Worker's Party (PT), which had many Black militants as members, nuclei were also created with the same aim. However, according to Abdias Nascimento, as a sign of the immaturity of the Black Movement at the time, party commitments created a number of unnecessary divisions, ultimately proving prejudicial to the unity of the struggles of the Black cause, which was meant transcend party divisions (Nascimento and Nascimento, 2002, p. 221).

Clóvis Moura, a collaborator with the MNU, is an important intellectual in this context. Though he is not often remembered by contemporary researchers of Brazilian social reality, and remains relatively unknown considering his stature, intellectual contribution and political activity in the recent past, he moved through various fields of activity in the intellectual and political arenas. Born in the city of Amarante, in the Northeastern state of Piauí in 1952, and deceased on the 23rd of December 2003, Moura was a Black man who established theoretical resources which firmly place him among the pioneers of the deconstruction of the coloniality of knowledge and power in Brazil.

Moura noted that the Black subject, submitted to what Milton Santos (1996) called "mutilated citizenships", was considered to be a "bad citizen when he became aware of the "sifting barriers" created by Brazilian society, barriers which impeded class mobility and created de-identified subjects. This de-identified subject, a member of the minoritized majority (Santos, R, 2020), upon finding himself in the core of this device for social jettisoning, rebels and seeks, through organized civil society or even in an individual manner, to denounce the forms of exclusion and extermination of his body and his intellectual effacement. He then comes to demand of the hegemonic elites that they reconfigure the social codes that he has decodified (Moura, 1977). Moura's extensive work presents us with the paths that must be traced for Black people to access the spaces of power, to act for the reconfiguration of the system imposed upon them, and to be able to re-identify – that is, to recognize themselves and to be recognized by others as subjects constitutive of politico-social decision-making processes that transform historical reality. By contemplating the slaveholding economy, and the reality enacted after the 14th of May 1888, Moura worked tirelessly, throughout his career, to understand and make public the processes of Black resistance in Brazilian society, and of the contribution of this mass, which has been rendered invisible, to national composition.

In the field of Brazilian Social Thought, intellectuals who were subsumed to hegemonic interests, and reproduced the colonialist view, were harshly criticized by Moura in "The Injustices of Clio" (Moura 1999), and in other work, for having contributed to the creation of a racist social imagery, binding Black subjects and/or relegating the creation of a colonialist and subalternizing ideology, associating Blacks with evil, with what is not beautiful, what is undesired and can be eliminated. With his propositions, Clóvis Moura presents what came to be known as Black Praxis, a nucleus of Moura-influenced though that, in broad strokes, constituted a radical critique of academic sociology. In general, the Sociology of Black Praxis creates a double epistemological rupture in relation to studies of Blacks in Brazil: first, with the culturalist school of Nina Rodrigues, Arthur Ramos, Edson Carneiro and Gilberto Freyre (this rupture occurs through Marxism, through an analysis of class struggle in the slaveholding order); the second, operating from within Marxism, occurs when the notion of praxis is put in the foreground to the detriment of other categories (class, structure, etc.). It is from the spectre of the radical deconstruction of the fable of racial democracy, unveiling historical reality, that we see the preference for an elimination of Black bodies, knowledges, and even the Black presence from Brazilian society. This process of conscience and imagery building was classified by Moura as part of the barriers which functioned as deforming instruments of the consciousness of society concerning Blacks and their rights to full citizenship. This is how the signs and tools of what has come to be conventionally called 'structural racism' are now presented to us. Codes and political and social interjections which consecrate social alienation, violence of the imagination, and the tolerated murder of Black subjects, so that all "invisible" hurdles and impediments, those which remain unheard, and which have been historically experienced by the Black community, are transmitted to the next generation as an archive of negative signs related to this very community.

II Historical predecessors of Black protagonism

As we have been stressing since the Introduction to this book, the multicultural turn is at the core of our reflections on Afro-descendant populations. It is within the framework of this period that the political, social, and cultural processes bearing on these populations have developed most fully. However, despite our emphasis on a proximate history that begins in the late 1980s, it is necessary to first take a panoramic view of certain elements of the long-term history that links up, in myriad ways, with a contemporary dynamic. We focus on all of Latin America and the Caribbean, beginning with the late 19th century, a time when national societies became consolidated in the region. The development of characteristics of this process in Brazil will be dealt with in specific parts, but always referring the Brazilian situation to Latin America and the Caribbean. In this section, we will introduce elements, actors and thought currents that seem to us to be of the utmost relevance, both as protagonists of history itself and as ongoing influences on contemporary processes concerning Afro-descendants. Indeed, many of these elements are increasingly "relived" and reclaimed by contemporary studies and in the rhetoric of the Black movements that have become consolidated in the context of the multicultural turn.[26]

Black protagonism in the Americas since the end of the 19th century

The Afro-Trinidadian lawyer and writer Henry Sylvester Williams (1869–1911), organized the first Pan-African Conference in July of 1900, promoted by the African Association, which he founded. A further five meetings were held between 1919 and 1945, but the concept of Pan-Africanism transcends these events. The idea emerged from intellectuals of African origin in the United States, Great Britain, and the Caribbean at the end of the 19th century. One of its originators was the prominent socialist Afro-American intellectual William Edward Burghardt Du

---

[26] A good illustration of this is the work of the Afro-Puerto Rican intellectual Agustin Lao-Montes (Lao-Montes 2008, 2011, 2020). Decolonial studies have also been interested in recovering these histories. For instance, the CLASCO seminar: "Black Marxism: Race and Class in Afro-Descendant and African Thought", convened by Ramon Grosfoguel, Jacqueline Laguardia Martínez and Daniel Montañez. 2020. https://www.clacso.org/marxismos-negros-raza-y-clase-en-el-pensamiento-afrodescendiente-y-africano/ See also references later in this book.

Bois (1868–1963)[27]. Although there have been many different uses of this concept throughout history, it stems from a defence of the right for Africa and her descendants to enjoy civil and political rights, and for their countries to become independent in order to reconstitute the necessary unity of Africans, those in the continent and those who hail from the diaspora. It is, in short, a critique of the commerce of slaves, colonisation, and racism. A great many Latin-American and Caribbean intellectuals actively participated in the construction and development of the idea of Pan-Africanism (Decraene, 1970; Adi, 2018).

In his book, *Black Marxism. The Making of the Black Radical Tradition*, Cedric Robinson (2000) depicts the historical trajectory and perspective of these Black intellectuals and activists in the Americas and the Caribbean, denominating them a "Black radical tradition", constituting a current of Black Marxism. According to Robinson, the consolidation of this tradition in the first decades of the 20th century was inscribed in a long history of revolts and resistances to slavery which found their primary reference in the Haitian Revolution and were influenced by classic Marxism. This perspective gives centre stage to Afro-Caribbean persons who were little-known outside of the studies of Afro-descendants in the region.

Another Afro-Trinidadian associated with decolonial studies, as well as with more recent work in Latin America, is C.L.R. James (1901–1989). James was a politician and Marxist intellectual whose thought articulated the challenges faced by the socialist alternative and the particularities of the struggles of Black peoples. His study of the Haitian Revolution, *The Black Jacobins* (James, C.L.R., 2003) is among the more lucid analysis of the characteristics and impact of the revolution. Scott McLemee (1996)[28] sums up its contributions:

> His attention had been focused mainly on the colonial movements of the Caribbean and Africa. But the condition and the demands of African Americans were different. He could use the same analytical tools to frame "the Negro question" in the United States: Marxism was for James the framework through which social movements had to be understood. Yet Marxist theory had almost completely omitted black history and culture from its conceptions of modern society. In the early years of the Communist International, Lenin had directed the attention of Marxists in the United States to the situation of African Americans, and his writings inspired and instructed James's thinking. But by no means did he make some cookie-cutter application of the Russian's ideas. James tried to bring together

---

[27] Considered to have been one of the foremost Black intellectuals of the 20th Century. His book *The Souls of Black Folk* is recognized as a key study of the racial problems of Black populations. (Du Bois, W.E.B., 1903/1989). For a view of this work and its relevance to the study of Black populations in Latin America, see Lao-Montes, Agustin (2020).
[28] See also Almanza, Roberto (2020).

> Marxist concepts and the history of African American movements; each must stretch to incorporate the other's insights. (Scott McLemee, 1996, p. 16)

Another relevant figure was the Afro-Jamaican Marcus Garvey (1887–1940), responsible for the organization of a wide-ranging Black association – The Universal Negro Improvement Association (UNIA) – created in Jamaica in 1914, and which had a membership of up to 5 million people from 50 different countries. Garvey offered a transnational project with an African axis. Through a vehement critique of colonial and racist policies, he asserted Black pride and proclaimed the viability of constructing an autonomous project. He defended his struggle against all forms of economic and social oppression, in all countries, but his strategic position was for the return of the diaspora to the African continent and, ultimately, create large, unified nation. Garvey was able to establish UNIA nuclei in all of the islands of the Caribbean, and in most Central American countries. However, he faced constant questioning from Black intellectuals who envisaged the struggle for the demands of Black populations through a Marxist lens. His emphasis on the construction of a nationalist project, based on the personal leadership of a royal court, distanced him from other trends in Pan-Africanism that developed in the first years of the 20th century (Kroubo, 2008).

Winds of Negritude

Like Pan-Africanism, Negritude was conceived in the 1930s. The idea was born in colonialist France and was reproduced by Afro-Caribbean and African intellectuals. Subsequently, it had wide repercussions among the innovators of the Black cause in Latin America. It evoked an appreciation of the central role of African culture in identifying its diaspora in the Americas and promoted a radical critique of the slaveholding past and colonialism. Negritude gradually became consolidated as a concept that was able to encompass various expressions for reclaiming Black identity and multiple ways of addressing the problems of racism and marginalisation in which Black populations live. At present, talking about Blackness may be a generic way of referring to Afro-descendent populations and their problems without necessarily identifying it with its original characteristics. In the intellectual production and contemporary theoretical and political exchanges of the "multicultural turn" that deal with the Black diaspora of the Americas, and especially in the context of decolonial studies[29], the term "Negritude" continues to be challenged.

In the Americas, the Afro- Martinican Aimé Césaire (1913–2008) is considered to be the most representative innovator of the conceptual movement of Negritude. However, it was conceived from exchanges between Black students in Paris who hailed from colonial French territories in the Caribbean and in Africa, concerning the historical and contemporary realities of their racial and colonial condition. Three of them – Césaire; Léopold Senghor (1906–2011) [30], from Senegal; and Leon-Gontran Damas (1988) [31], from French Guiana – created, in 1935, the journal *L'Etudiant Noir*, which became a powerful instrument for critical ideas on French colonial policies, its slaveholding past and the racism that accompanied these traumatic processes. The concept of 'Negritude' emerged within this context, stressing the importance of an African culture that was being marginalized by colonial power, and enticing the Black populations of Africa and its diaspora to reclaim the African continent as a unifying element of their identity, as an instrument against European colonial cultural assimilationism. Negritude as the reclamation of a singular and African culture is clearly present in the work of Césaire (López, 2011). His *Discourse on Colonialism* (Césaire, 1950), written after the Second World War, was a radical and powerful attacks on colonialism and Western civilization, demonstrating its articulation with capitalist exploitation and racism. Césaire denounces a colonialism founded under the banner of Western-style universal values and human rights. Césarie became a Marxist and enriched his concept of Negritude with a classist and anti-capitalist approach[32].

Negritude, as a form of Black experience that rejects colonialism and racism, and reclaims African culture as a central element of Black identity, corresponds to multiple forms of existence that pre-date the concept. Césaire had already argued that the Haitian Revolution had been an initial expression of Negritude (Césaire, 1960). The intellectual output and perspectives of the "Black Marxists"

---

[29] The work of Afro-Puerto Rican intellectual Agustin Lao-Montes "Contrapunteos diaspóricos. Cartografías políticas de nuestra Afroamérica." (2020), blends these two options, that of Afro-descendant studies and the decolonial option.

[30] Senghor, who was also a man of letters and a political leader, would become the first president of independent Senegal in 1960.

[31] Damas was a poet, university professor and politician. He was a member of the French Assembly representing French Guiana.

[32] Césaire was a militant of the French Communist Party, created the Progressive Party of Martinique, was mayor of Fort-de France, capital of Martinique, and a representative of Martinique in National Assembly of France.

that we mentioned above also came to be seen as expressions of Negritude. So did the work of Marcus Garvey, with his "Universal Negro Improvement Association", or of the doctor, anthropologist, and write Jean Price-Mars (1876–1979), who reclaimed Black history and culture as a means for countering white colonialism and racism. In *Ainse Parla l'Oncle*, written in 1928, in the midst of US intervention in Haiti, Price-Mars calls on his people to recognize themselves as the bearers of a unique culture, inherited from Africa and France. Hist historical and ethnographical work is recognized as a relevant contribution to the Black cultures of the Americas (Picard et. al., 2020). Negritude continued to spread, with its many variants.

If we relate Negritude to studies in Africanist cultural anthropology, carried out by Melville Herskovits (1895–1969) and his followers since the 1930s, we find certain convergences in their common focus on cultural aspects (Herskovits, 1941, 1952, 1965). This focus raised a series of criticisms, to the extent that, despite their considerable contributions to knowledge of Black cultures, and particularly in challenging naturalist and racist "scientific" theories, they produced a fixed, rigid, and natural view of culture which falls short of constituting a paradigm that allows us to understand current social dynamic and the changes lived by Black populations throughout their histories.

Beyond Negritude: the work of Frantz Fanon

Frantz Fanon (1925–1962) was another Afro-Martinican whose work had a widespread influence on the critical movement against colonialism and racism, as well as on debates and mobilizations for national liberation and revolutions in the Third World. Fanon was from the generation which succeeded Césaire's, who had been his teacher in middle school in Martinique. It was later, when he studied psychiatric medicine in France, that Fanon became involved in debates around Negritude, its possibilities and limitations. This was during the 1950s, two decades after it had been coined and conceived as an affirmation of identity as well as a tool in the struggle against racism and colonialism. In this context, the harsh reality of Black peoples within the colonial world left little room for optimism. Fanon's two most influential books are *Black Skins, White Masks* (1952) and *The Wretched of the Earth* (1961). In the former, Fanon adopted a social, psychiatric and psychoanalytic perspective to analyse how Blacks internalize and assimilate the cultural mechanisms of racial domination in their environment, the world dominated by whites. This reflection stemmed from his own experience in the West Indies and in the French metropolis as part of his clinical practice and his commitment to the fight against colonialism and racism.

His studies of the cultural alienation of Blacks finds many echoes in the need to affirm an African identity, as proposed by Negritude. In the context of the anti-colonial struggles that were starting to heat up in Africa in the 1950s, Fanon jointed the Algerian National Liberation Front. Through his militancy and his reflections on the alienation and exploitation of Blacks, Fanon produced one of the most famous analyses on the need for the national liberation of colonized peoples the world over. In *The Wretched of the Earth*, he argues that the only viable alternative is a process of radical rupture with the colonial structure and the exploitation of the oppressed peoples of Africa and other parts of the world. It requires a "new man" who can only emerge through struggle. In the idea of the "new man" lies an implicit critique of the "actually existing" Negritude in the African continent during this period. This critique extended to the Black man enclosed in his Blackness and the whiteman in his whiteness, a double narcissism that had to be overcome in favour of a universalism inherent to the human condition. Fanon questioned the idea of replacing the colonial elites by emergent Black or African elites without thereby altering the structure of inequalities inherent to the colonial system. It is here that Fanon criticised how Negritude was being assumed by certain Black intellectuals which were at the vanguard of the burgeoning processes of national independence in Africa, most of whom concentrated on the cultural dimension without transcending the structural problems underwriting colonial alienation (López, 2011).

As we noted at the outset, the impact of Fanon's work in Latin America and the Caribbean goes beyond his influence on Black movement and Black intellectuals. Fanon influenced liberation philosophy, both in its Mexican and Argentinian variants. Enrique Dussel in Argentina, and later in Mexico, in turn considered Fanon a direct precursor to his philosophy of liberation (Maldonado, 2005). More panoramic studies of Fanon can be found in Valdés (2017), Lao Montes (2011), Fernández (1965), among others.

Rastafarianism

Rastafarianism is considered to be an expression of Pan-Africanism (Campbell, 1988). As a political and cultural movement, it originated in Jamaica, although its influence reached across the globe, particularly in its cultural dimension. The Rastafari movement emerged during the 1930s in the impoverished periphery of Kingston, the capital of Jamaica, and took hold among young Blacks affected by exclusion, unemployment, spatial segregation, and discrimination (Brown, 1997). It developed from the ideas of Marcus Garvey. Another source of inspiration for the movement was the coronation of Emperor of Ethiopia

Haile Selassie, and his return to power in 1949 after having been deposed by the Italians. Selassie was considered to be the redeemer, and Ethiopia the promised land, according to the Biblical interpretations of Evangelical sects that exerted great power over English-speaking West Indian populations (Ahkell, 1981). The movement articulated religious discourse with the demands of the oppressed Black populations against segregation and racism.

In the 1940s, various leaders coming from different currents of Rastafarianism emerged. The movement grew significantly in Jamaica during the 1950s and was strongly repressed by government forces, which, however, failed to quell its influence. Thus, beginning in the 1960s, there were important changes both to Rastafarian militants and to the attitudes of the Jamaican state. The government began to develop social policies in neighbourhoods in which Rastafarianism was strongest, and in some cases encouraged militants to migrate to Africa. The movement, in turn, began to place more emphasis on the social demands of Jamaicans than on the idea of a return to Africa (Barret, 1997).

In the 1970s, while some sectors of the movement moved further into its religious aspects, others shifted towards secularization and political concerns. In this context, the international impact of Jamaican reggae, spearheaded by Bob Marley and closely identified with the Rastafarian movement, contributed to the latter's growing influence in the Caribbean, the United States, England and Canada. In particular, since the 1970s, Rastafarian colonies emerged in the Brazilian states of Rio de Janeiro, Bahia and Maranhão[33]. This is when Rastafarianism becomes globally recognized by cultural symbols such as dreadlocks, ritual food, marijuana, and, of course, reggae. After Bob Marley's death in 1981, the political currents of the movement began to lose strength. What remained was the notable influence of Rastafarianism in cultural symbols that blended African references with its own innovations. The movement contributed a new outlook to Black identity in the Caribbean, providing symbolic elements for various Black movements in the Americas and the rest of the world (Agudelo, 2010).

The Afromerica Journal. A bold – but fleeting – effort

An interesting experiment, which remained largely forgotten because of its fleeting character, was the Afromerica Journal, published in 1945, which aimed to

---

[33] On the Rastafarian presence in Brazil, see the documentary: Reggae do Maranhão, produced by Richard dos Santos (2013) https://www.youtube.com/watch?v=Xf1 t9NIW5K0

bring together different studies of Black populations in the Americas and the Caribbean (Fernández, 2011). The initiative emerged during the First Inter-American Demographic Congress on the Black population, held in Mexico in 1943. The project was ambitious and surpassed the organizational capacity of its hosts. The journal in fact only published three issues and stopped publication in the year it was launched. However, it corroborated that a network of exchange and contact was being constituted, based on the development of studies of Afro-American populations which had begun in the end of the 19th century.

The executive committee of the journal was made up of Fernando Ortiz, from Cuba, the anthropologist Gonzalo Aguirre Beltran from Mexico, and the Haitian politician and writer Jacques Romain. According to the roster published in the first edition of the journal, it had 150 participating members, all scholars of the Afro-descendants in the Americas and the Caribbean. Among the most well-known were Herskovits, Alain Locke, Du Bois, and Alfred Metraux from the United States; from Cuba Fernando Ortiz, Nicolás Guillen, Alejo Carpentier, Julio Le Riverand, Emilio Roig de Leuchsenring, José A. Portuondo, Loló de la Torriente, and Lino Novás Calvo; from Mexico Aguirre Beltrán, Alfonso Caso, and Alfonso Reyes; from Brazil Artur Ramos and Gilberto Freyre; from Haiti Jacques Roumain, Jean Price Mars, and Auguste Remy Bastien. From the rest of the Antilles, there were Aimé Césaire from Martinique and Eric Williams from Trinidad. Ildefonso Pereda Valdés from Uruguay, and Fernando Romero from Peru were also members. When this initiative began, its most prominent members published a large part of their scholarly work. Some examples include: "Ainsi parla l'oncle", by Jean Price Mars (1928), "As Culturas Negras do Novo Mundo" by Arthur Ramos (1937); " Cahier d'un retour au pays natal" by Aimé Césaire (1939); "Contrapunteo cubano del tabaco y el azúcar", by Fernando Ortiz (1940); "The myth of the negro past", by Melville Herskovits (1941); and "The Negro in the Caribbean" (1942) by Eric Williams (1942).

The confluence of the study of Black peoples represented preceded an important articulation effort, this one specifically linked to the incidence of Negritude in Latin America, the afore-mentioned Dakar-Senegal Colloquium, held in 1974, on the theme of "Negritude in Latin America".

The Dakar Colloquium

The international spaces of debate on issues relating to Black peoples in Africa and her diaspora, which began with a London meeting in 1900[34], initially included, alongside African scholars, mostly representatives of the United States and the Caribbean. The presence of Latin American spokespersons had been minimal[35]. It was the Dakar Colloquium in 1974 that gave priority to the ties between Africa and Latin America within the framework of Negritude as a cultural bridge. This was also the first event of this type to feature a large delegation of Latin American intellectuals. Along with delegations from Africa, Europe, and the United States, there were also invited participants from Bolivia, Brazil, Colombia, Cuba, Mexico, Panama, Peru, Uruguay, and Venezuela.

This Colloquium was an initiative of the president of Senegal, Leopold Sedar Senghor, who, as we mentioned above, was one of the architects of the concept of "Negritude". Its aim was to promote exchanges on "the contributions of Africa to Latin America in the fields of thought, literature, sociology, religions, folklore, music, and linguistics". It focused on an America that was unproblematically called 'Latin America', despite being, in fact, an Indo-African-European America, where people from Africa left their indelible stamp in certain regions, maintaining their traditions, or contributing to the formation of what José de Vasconcelos called the "cosmic race" (Vasconcelos, 1979)[36]. The congress emphasised cultural aspects. In the words of Senghor, the aim was to study "Latin American civilization…" and "the contributions of Black Africa and how its values, which we sum up in the word Negritude, fertilized Latin contributions" (Senghor, 1977, p. 18).

On Senghor's views of Latin America, and in particularly of Brazil, we draw attention to Valero's (2020) synthesis:

---

34 The first Pan-African Conference was hosted by the lawyer and author Henry Sylvester Williams (1869–1911), an Afro-Caribbean intellectual from Trinidad who founded the African Association and organized the Conference in July 1900 in London.
35 Valero (2020) provides a review of these events : Premier Congrès International des Écrivains et Artistes Noirs (París, 1956); Deuxième Congrès International des Écrivains et Artistes Noirs (Roma, 1959); Premier Festival Mondial des Arts Négres (FESMAN) (Dakar, 1966); Premier festival culturel panafricain d'Algérie (PANAF) (Argel, 1969); Colloque sur la négritude (Dakar, 1971), Colloque Négritude et Amérique Latine (Dakar, 1974), World Festival of Black Arts (FESTAC), (Nigeria, 1977). With a more explicitly political perspective, we have: the Pan-African Conferences (1919, 1921, 1923, 1927, 1945 and 1974) as well as the International Convention of the Negro People" Conference, organized by Marcus Garvey (New York, 1920).
36 Introduction to *Negritude et Amérique Latine. Colloque de Dakar* (1978), by René Durand, director of the Centre for Afro-Iberian-American Studies of the University of Dakar, the first organization of this type in Africa. My translation.

> Senghor had an idealized view of what he called Latin-American civilization, particularly in relation to Brazil, where he was paid homage on the 20th of September 1964 by the Academy of Letters. In an official hearing, the author had manifested his admiration for biological mixing, but, above all, for the "cultural symbiosis", "the complementary vertices of the three ethnicities" that make up Brazilian culture (Senghor 1977, p. 28). The Academy of Letters was a conservative environment, which propagated the ideology of a racial democracy, denying the existence of racism in Brazil, as defended by the military government (Alberto, 2011, p. 245). One year later, the country would take part in the FESMAN (Premier Festival Mondial des Arts Négres) in Dakar and the FESTAC (World Festival of Black Arts) in Nigeria in 1977, with an official delegation that, under the criterion of national integration, excluded the delegation of Black independent artists. In reaction, Abdias Nascimento wrote an open letter to the Organizing Committee of the festival, expressing his disagreement with the Brazilian government's exclusion of artists from the Teatro Experimental Negro (T.N.E., the Black Experimental Theatre) because of the racism concealed behind the image of a racial democracy: "We have sent you a delegation that cannot constitute a truly representative sample of the exact situation that Black people currently occupy in the arts in Brazil. Our exclusion is not surprising" (Nascimento, 1966, p. 218). (Valero's, 2020, p. 39)

The colloquium was also an opportunity for paying homage to the Latin American men of letters whose work proclaimed the greatness of the cosmic race to which African cultures had contributed. The Guatemalan author Miguel Angel Asturias, Noble laureate, was honoured during the Colloquium, as were other intellectuals such as Leopoldo Zea, from Mexico, and German Arciniegas, from Colombia. Many lectures included comparative considerations between Negritude and Indigenism.

Though the Colloquium gave priority to cultural aspects, as envisaged by Senghor, in the ensuing debates the cultural affirmation of Blacks in Latin America was closely linked to the persistence of different forms of marginalization and racism in Latin American societies. The political and social context could not be abstracted, as clearly expressed in the closing lecture by Alioune Sene, Senegal's Minister of Culture:

> Like any school of thought, Negritude, as with Enlightenment philosophers, precursors of the revolution of 1789, should become, both in African and Latin America, the expression of a desire for political liberation and economic development, as well cultural flourishing. Yet our focus here was on culture and not politics... However, we know that cultural actions often have political implications (Siene, 1974, p. 506).

Senghor sought to strengthen the cultural aspect of Negritude, presented as a fundamental contribution for the desired construction of a universal humanity which would take into account cultural differences. Yet Africa and the Third World waged their struggles for national liberation, and for them the political-anticolonial and anti-racist aspects were a priority. This is why the cultural emphasis of Senghor's version of Negritude drew harsh criticism from people such as Fanon (1959, 1961).

The Afro-Latin American delegates to the Colloquium were aware that culture was a central element that needed to be proclaimed in order to demand recognition; nonetheless, they could not ignore the underlying socio-economic structures of power in Latin American societies. The Dakar Colloquium was positively valued by participants as a space that enabled the confluence of national experiences and scholarship. It was also an inspiration for similar events in Latin America, giving continuity to the exchanges. However, the initiatives that were to emerge were marked by agendas based on the realities of the Black population of Latin America. This will be clear in the Congresses of the Black Culture of the Americas.

"Los negros se toman la palabra". The Congresses of the Black Culture of the Americas

Participation in the Dakar Colloquium was a determining factor for the Afro-Colombia intellectual Manuel Zapata Olivella, who decided to organize the Congresses of the Black Culture of the Americas.[37][38] His aim was to hold meetings in Latin America and to feature diverse scholars from different intellectual traditions who would, through conversation, reflect on the situation of the American populations of African origin. They were intended as events which would throw up alternatives to the problems of exclusion and racism, which, through the historical context of slavery and colonialism, continued to keep Blacks in marginal positions, their cultural and social contributions being ignored in national constructs.

Negritude was a reference point in terms of the positive value afforded to the African cultural legacy, which was considered to be a component of identity. It was also understood as a tool for resistance and mobilization. According to Valero, in the first Congress, held in Cali, Colombia, in 1977, "there were various positions on the matter, but Latin Americans tended to agree that a new conception of Negritude should emerge from the Congress, one representative of Latin America, since they understand that the historical differences of each geograph-

---

37 "Blacks take the word" is the suggestive title of the work of Silvia Valero, which we have mentioned earlier. It seems to capture well the dynamic that took hold of these events.
38 We use the following sources on the congresses: Valero (2020), Valderrama (2021) Actas del Primer Congreso de la Cultura Negra de las Américas (Léon-Gontran, 1988).

ic space bore its own vision and problems that needed solving" (Valero, 2020, p. 65). The articulation of marginality, or cultural non-recognition, and the socio-economic situation was also part of the debates. Another relevant element of the exchanges, in consonance with Fanon's writings, was the issue of the necessary de-alienation of Black populations so that that their identity could be appropriated as instruments in the struggle for rights. With delegates from Africa, Europe and the Americas, the majority of representatives hailed from Latin American countries.

This first congress encouraged the consolidation of exchanges between Black Latin American intellectuals. Zapata Olivella claims that the experience of these congresses aligned with the reflection and mobilization previously carried forth by pioneers such as Du Bois and Garvey, as well as with the perspective launched in the Dakar Congress. The second Congress was held in Panama in 1980 on the theme of "Cultural Identity of the Negro in the Americas". In this congress the articulation between culture-race and class was promoted as one of the pillars of the demands of Blacks in the Americas. It is during this congress that Abdias Nascimento presented his theoretical proposal on Quilombismo, an Afro-Brazilian political alternative that was to later morph into the publication "Quilombismo: um conceito científico emergente do processo histórico-cultural das massas afro-brasileiras" (Quilombismo: an emerging scientific concept from the historical-cultural process of the Afro-Brazilian masses) (Nascimento, 1980).

Abdias Nascimento, in fact, was responsible for coordinating the third Congress, in São Paulo, Brazil, in 1982. This congress was called "African diaspora: political conscience and African culture". One of its research lines concerned the "Relations between Africa and Afro-Latin America". This congress was notable for focusing specifically on Black women, and it dealt more than previous editions with the theme of "socio-political movements". Indeed, ever since the first congress, the organizational experiences of Black populations began to brew in various countries. They were more developed in Brazil, but were also beginning to emerge in Colombia, Ecuador, Honduras, Uruguay, Peru, and Venezuela. The fourth congress was to take place in the Caribbean Island of Granada, but the US invasion in 1983 prevented its realization. New and different factors ultimately impeded further congresses from taking place (Valero, 2020).

The 1980s witnessed the emergence of Black political and social movements. Within the framework of the "multicultural turn" that took hold in the 1990s, they would give rise to social and political movements throughout Latin America. The Congresses of the Black Culture of the Americas were a key precursor to the current dynamics of mobilization and organization, and their innovative ideas had wide-ranging repercussions, such as the concept of 'Amefricanicity' developed by Lélia Gonzalez in her work, which we will turn to shortly.

The *creolité* (*creolización*) of Eduard Glissant

Another current of thought that impacted reflections on the history of societies with a marked presence of Afro-descendants in the Americas, and particularly those in the Caribbean, is what is known as *creolité* or *creolización*. This perspective emerged in the Antilles, and, as with Negritude, is notable for its nuances. Its main exponent was the Martinican writer and activist Eduard Glissant (1928 – 2011). Like Césaire and Fanon, Glissant left Martinique to go to university in Paris. In the end of the 1940s, he participated in the anticolonial struggle. Although his work was influenced by Negritude thought, it developed into an in-depth analysis of the character of Antillean culture conceived as an "interactional aggregate" (1981, p. 26) of African, European, Asian, Levantine, and Caribbean elements. The Caribbean identity is a "kaleidoscopic totality" (1981, p. 28), a multiple, complex, ambiguous, and contradictory mosaic. Glissant propounds a dynamic and interactive conception of culture (Glissant, 1981). His starting point was the situation of the Antilles, but his analyses revealed a much wider dimension, becoming a relevant analytical tool for understanding identity-construction among Afro-descendant peoples. Reclaiming the work of Glissant, Agustin Lao-Montes claims that:

> The identification processes that constitute Afro-diasporic identities can be interpreted as dynamics of crealization which, as such, are ambiguous, open, and fluid, articulating Afro-diasporic identities with its own spaces of cultural creation, intellectual production, and political action. In this key, the creolization dynamics that constitute the diaspora are counterpunctual insofar as they do not make up a systematic and coherent whole, but rather a constellation of networks, relations and pathways; articulating ideas, collective action, cultural and aesthetic practices, ideologies and political projects, and forms of co-existence that join up in discontinuous and contradictory ways while, nonetheless, retaining their power. Our "Afro-America" is a translocal space, a heterogenous and contradictory whole, the complexity of which we seek to analyse... (Lao-Montes, pp. 22–23).

El Discurso Antillano is a compilation of Glisant's work (1981), in which he traces his framework for thinking about *creolization* at the intersection of anthropology, sociology and literary studies[39].

---

39 See also Glissant (1990, 2008).

Certain tendencies of *crealization* are expressed in the French overseas départments (ex-colonies that remain under French control) as literary and cultural movements, although not devoid of a political dimension. The socio-political context for the construction of the discourse on *creolization* is the frustration caused by the process of departmentalizing the ex-colonies in 1946, by means of which these territories would be treated like the départments of the mainland[40]. But what actually occurred was a crisis of the productive system, a rise in unemployment, an increase in emigration, high school dropout rates, increase in delinquencies and in drug addiction, as well as the devaluation of indigenous cultural expressions by way of a super-valuation of the "culture of the metropolis". Tackling these problems was part of a political discourse in which metropolitan France was held responsible (Barnabé et. al., 1990).

The impact of Paul Gilroy and his "Black Atlantic"

After Melville J. Herskovits's *The Myth of the Negro Past* (1941), and, possibly, Sidney Mintz and Richard Price's *An Anthropological Approach to the African American Past* (1976), Gilroy's (1993) work marked a turning point in the anthropology of Afro-American societies and cultures. He founded a new discourse and established the basis for contemporary debate, forging his key-concepts: "anti-anti-essentialism", "hybridity", "diaspora", "changing same", "double conscience", etc. (Agudelo, 2009 p. 14).

Paul Gilroy (1956) is a British sociologist and along with Stuart Hall, he is one of the most prominent figures in British cultural studies. He was influenced by Black authors such as W.E.B. Du Bois, Frantz Fanon, and Édouard Glissant[41]. Gilroy stressed the primordial role of Black populations in the construction of modernity in the Americas (Agudelo, 2009). Indeed, *The Black Atlantic*, in particular, but his wider work as well, became a very powerful instrument for understanding the complex and dynamic processes of geographical, economic, polit-

---

[40] On March 19, 1946, the French National Assembly passed the law proclaiming the "departmentalization" of France's "vieilles colonies," including Martinique, Guadeloupe, French Guiana, and Réunion, with the support of Gaston Monnerville and Aimé Césaire.
[41] Along with *The Black Atlantic*, Gilroy's most important work includes *There Ain't no Black in the Union Jack: The Cultural Politics of Race and Nation* (1987); *Between Camps: Nations, Culture and the Allure of Race* (2000); *After Empire: Muticulture or Postcolonial Melancholia* (2004).
Além de "Black Atlantic", entre suas obras mais importantes estão: There Ain't No Black in the Union Jack: The Cultural Politics of Race and Nation (187); Between Camps: Nations, Culture and the Allure of Race (2000); *After Empire: Melancholia or Convivial Culture* (2004).

ical, social, and cultural relations between Africa, Europe, and the Americas that was produced through slavery. Western modernity found in the Black Atlantic one of the central elements of its own genesis and of the continuity between colonial relations and contemporary social relations. The Black "hybrid" "diaspora" of the Americas, to use two categories central to Gilroy's work, became the protagonist, rather than a mere victim, in the construction of rhetoric and practices that constitute social relations in our societies.

The Black Atlantic, as generic and hybridized cultural field, which produces a diasporic identity rich in creative fusions. It is also the place and time (a chrontope) of memory of the slave trade in the construction of modernity, of the duty to reclaim mobilization and struggle against racism and forms of exploitation of populations of African origin. The categories and concepts associated with it enrich our understanding of the complex realities of the Black populations in Latin America. Most contemporary studies agree on the hybrid character of the cultural, social, and political constructs of the Black diaspora as noted by Gilroy. However, it must be remembered that, in the Latin American context, in which nation-states become essential interlocutors for Black movements in the process of seeking the recognition of their rights, the national anchoring of these political, ethnic or racial processes is a crucial element. In Latin America, the articulation between the national/local and global in processes of Black identity is a reality that cannot be ignored.

For a profitable use of Gilroy's conceptual tools, it is decisive that they be framed contextually and according to their historical, local, and national situation. In the preface of *The Black Atlantic*, he reminds us that his claims were not to be definitive. The characteristics of the cultural and political processes of the Black populations in Latin America should continue to be investigated, both in their transnational and local/national dimension.

What the Black cause of the 1970s bequeathed to the Afro-descendant movement of the "multicultural turn"

In the 1970s, Negritude inflected various currents of Pan-Africanism (Davis & Williams 2007), which in Latin America was reflected in the Dakar Colloquium and the Congresses of the Black Culture of the Americas. However, these influences blended with events such as social and civil rights movements in the United States, Black Power, and the anti-apartheid struggle in South Africa, Rastafarianism or *creolization* in the Caribbean. Issues related to Black peoples became issues that affected public opinion throughout the world. In Latin America, discussions around Black identity at the time were reflected in the emergence of movements such as the Unified Black Movement in Brazil and in the significant increase in the numbers of political and cultural Afro-Brazilian organizations (Paschel, 2016, 2018). Various organizations emerged in other countries in the region, although with less intensity, displaying varied strategies for action and ideological affinities, such as the Afro-Ecuadorian Study Centre, the Colombian Foundation of Folkloric Studies, and the Cultural Association of the Peruvian Black Youth. There was a drive to shine a light on the vitality of the culture of Black peoples, their African heritage and contribution to national cultures; but these cultural claims were accompanied, to a greater or lesser degree, by the condemnation of racism and the marginal status of most Black people. This activism was fundamentally the work of intellectuals and cultural brokers to which young Blacks who had accessed university education gradually became linked. An example of this is the Soweto Study Circle movement, created in 1976 by Black university students. In 1982, this institution was at the origin of National Movement for the Human Rights of Black Communities in Colombia – Cimarrón (Agudelo, 2005).

These experiences and their protagonists come to occupy an expanding space for the dissemination of their research and publications. This space has grown exponentially since the 1990s and constitutes the context we have referred to as the 'multicultural turn'.

Without any pretence at being exhaustive, we take the opportunity to mention some of the protagonists of this period of the 1960s and 1970s. Abdias Nascimento in Brazil; Juan Manuel Zapata Olivella and Delia Zapata Olivella, siblings from Colombia; Nicomedes Santacruz and Victoria Santacruz, siblings from Peru; Juan García and Adalberto Ortiz from Ecuador; Gerardo Maloney, George Priestley and Alberto Barrow from Panama; Walterio Carbonell, Juan Rene Betancourt and Carlos Moore from Cuba; Lucía Dominga Molina from Argentina; Isabelo Zenón from Puerto Rico; Crisanto Meléndez and Salvador Suazo from Honduras; Palácio José from Belize; Quinze Duncan and Eulalia Bernard from Costa Rica. An important editorial project gathers 2050 biographies of Black personalities in Latin America and the Caribbean in 6 volumes. It includes reviews of the work of the people referred to above[42].

---

42 Dictionary of Caribbean and Afro-Latin American Biography (Knight & Gates Jr., 2016).

III Multiculturalism and new ethno-racial identities in Latin America

The advent of multiculturalism and its interpretations

This political movement of identity claims in Latin America which we have described reflected the spread of multiculturalism in the global context. Just over three decades after the beginning of the "multicultural turn", it is now time to present a retrospective of our reflections on multiculturalism in Latin America. In the mid-1990s and early 2000s, we analysed a burgeoning multiculturalism which was reflected in the constitutional changes and public policies that were being elaborated for the benefit of Indigenous and Afro-descendant peoples in the region (Agudelo, 2002; Igreja, 2005). At that time, our studies sought to understand the theoretical proposition of multiculturalism and its practical implementation as policy in Latin American states, many of which were undergoing (new) processes of democratization. As we claim in the Introduction, the transformations of this process remain ongoing, and we would like to resume the theme and its most prominent characteristics in relation to Afro-descendant populations.

In general, the discussion of multiculturalism was based on the realization that the ideal of equality among individuals proposed by the republican universalist paradigm, while remaining an unavoidable theme in discourse on citizenship, was not fully actualized as social reality. The view of an equilibrium between the rights of culturally differentiated social groups to express themselves in common spaces and the safeguarding of the rights of individual citizens could also be considered in terms of a referential ideal that served to generate a normative and behavioural framework that would allow conflicts related to identity politics, affecting distinct societies, to be resolved. The "social contract" of a multicultural citizenship should play to the interests not only of groups, but also of individuals within and without collective identities. Furthermore, the multicultural character implied transcending the limits of ethno-racial differentiations, reaching the rights of other social groups that claimed recognition in the public sphere on the basis of cultural particularities. In this sense, we see the concept of "multicultural citizenship", proposed by Kymlicka (1996) or Castells (2000), as more pertinent than that of "ethnic citizenship", as proposed by Guillermo de la Peña (De la Peña, 1999). Although the "presumption" of the legitimacy of an identity claim was a regulatory benchmark, there remained, nonetheless, elements to judge whether a collectivity had the right to recognition in the public sphere.

There is no doubt that the issue of the rights of ethnic minorities came to occupy a main place in the world in the end of the 20th century. There are many reasons behind this movement. Among them are the end of the Cold War and the fall of the Communist bloc, and, consequently, the end of the opposition between Capitalism and Communism; the migratory and refugee crisis in Europe; the threat of national secessions in countries in the North, such as Canada, Belgium, and Spain; and the re-emergence of Indigenous peoples and their political mobilization (Kymlicka, 2003, p. 30). These factors reached breaking point in the 1990s, making it evident that Western democracies had been unable to overcome tensions of ethnic and cultural diversity.

Interpreting this moment, the Jamaican scholar Stuart Hall (2003, p. 55) claimed that multicultural societies were nothing new, and that displacements of people has always been the rule rather than an exception. Colonialism was the very foundation of multicultural societies. Nonetheless, Hall believed that, since World War II, multiculturalism had not only changed, but also intensified. A key moment, as the author notes, was the fall of the old European imperial system and the emergence of decolonization struggles and drives for national independence. With the dismantling of empires, new multi-ethnic and multicultural nation states were created, but continued to reflect a situation similar to that which they had experienced during colonization. They are countries created from an undeveloped civil society, constituted by a variety of ethnic, cultural, and religious traditions, lacking the conditions for conforming the new basis of a national society. This formation-process of new nations furthermore took place in a global context of extreme inequality and poverty, in a new world neoliberal order. The crises these new nations faced became increasingly multicultural and ethnic. Thus, multiculturalism is seen to result from a series of decisive changes – a strategic reconfiguration of social forces and relation throughout the globe.

Is it in fact globalization, however, that is the main factor in the emergence of identity claims throughout the world?[43] Globalization works through contrast.

---

[43] For Stuart Hall (2003) "globalization" was not a new phenomenon, since its beginning could be identified in the exploration and conquest promoted by European colonization; however, from the 1970s on, globalization assumes new forms. This globalization is associated to unregulated emerging financial markets, global capital, and the flux of currency, voluminous enough to destabilize the economic measures, transnational forms of production and consumption, exponential growth of new culture industries buttressed by information technology, as well as the emergence of the "economy of knowledge".

On the one hand, it conforms a global system, operating within a planetary sphere, since few corners of the globe lay beyond its destabilizing interdependences. This system would then significantly weaken national sovereignty and the "range of action" of affected states, without completely undermining them. On the other hand, it is not really global, since it continues to rest on a system of increasingly wider inequalities and instabilities over which no power detains control. If the dominant cultural tendency of globalization is homogenisation, it nonetheless caused extensive differentiating effects within societies or between them. Explanations of the emergence and strengthening of cultural identities tend to coincide with more general causes, yet they also reflect the vantage point from which analysts approach the issue. We thus have authors based in Europe who explain the phenomenon by way of massive migration towards the continent, interpreted as an invasion of the ex-metropolises by the ex-colonized and as a rupture of cultural differences; or, mostly from the Americas, we have explanations that privilege the growth of Indigenous and Afro-Latin American and North American movements.

Multiculturalism took on diverse theoretical, philosophical and political interpretations. The liberal culturalism of Will Kymlicka (2003, p. 63) gained importance as his ideas became the basis for public policies and multicultural constitutional reforms, particularly those backed by international agencies. His perspective was based on the view that liberal-democratic states should not only respect the familiar set of usual political and civil rights of citizenship, upon which liberal democracies were erected, but also adopt various rights specific to groups, or policies aimed at recognizing and accommodating the identities and needs of different ethno-cultural groups which would, otherwise, grow unsatisfied with a state straightjacketed by ethno-cultural neutrality (Kymlicka, 2003, p. 38)[44]. Liberal culturalism nonetheless resisted the idea that such groups could restrict the civil or political rights of its members in defence of the purity of authenticity of the group's culture and traditions. It recognized rights exclusive to minorities vis-à-vis majorities in order to reduce the vulnerability of the former before the economic and political clout of the latter.

Kymlicka's proposals remained firmly within liberalism, and they were criticized by alternative views. Many authors showed concern with the risk that a

---

[44] According to Cardoso de Oliveira (2002:66), it is difficult to see how the citizens of modern liberal democracies could feel represented by the political institutions of the societies to which they belong, or how they could internalize some conception of civic duty, by means only of a "cultural policy" or of a Constitution that remained absolutely impervious to the values of the group or the community, where citizens recognize themselves not only as individuals, but as people worthy of consideration, bearers of moral substance and a singular identity.

larger expenditure of efforts toward the recognition of cultural differences would result in the relegation of the problem of social inequalities. It was impossible to ignore the fact that policies of recognition were being put into practice as neoliberalism was expanding throughout the world. Multiculturalism would thus benefit only transnational financial capital, supporting the process of weakening, or even doing away with, the frontiers of nation states (San Juan Jr., 2002, p. 18).

Nancy Fraser (2004, pp. 151–164) articulated both strains of thought by amplifying the concept of multiculturalist policies of redistribution. Redistribution is here seen to be not only a problem of class struggle, but, indeed, of all forms of feminism and anti-racism that sought out solutions for injustices regarding gender, ethnicity, or race in socio-economic transformations or reforms. Likewise, the paradigm of recognition is not only applied to movements which re-evaluate identities that had been unduly disparaged, and which fund their expression in cultural feminism, Black nationalism or homosexual identity movements. It also applies to deconstructionist tendencies, such as the queer movement, critical anti-racism, and deconstructionist feminism, all of which criticize the essentialism of traditional identity politics.

Charles Taylor (1994), in turn, notes that the demand for "recognition" of cultural specificity is compatible with the universalism defended by liberals; in fact, the principle of equality is, in truth, basic to demands for recognition. He argues that two transformations made the modern concern with identity and its recognition inevitable. The first is the end of social hierarchies based on honour. The notion of honour is replaced by the modern notion of dignity, which is understood in a universal sense, as a right of every citizen. This notion of dignity is compatible with, and indeed proper to, democratic societies. Democracy inaugurates an egalitarian politics of universal recognition, which, undergoing various changes throughout the years, establishes the exigency of equality of status between cultures and sexes.

The principle of dignity is joined by the ideal of authenticity, also a product of the decline of hierarchical societies. Briefly, the ideal of authenticity refers to the moral importance of a being toward him or herself, his or her nature, identity, originality. It is this identity that, according to Taylor, requires the recognition of others, for this recognition is a fundamental condition for the development of the individual. This is, hence, the second transformation that gave rise to a demand for recognition: the development of a modern notion of identity. Everyone, whether the individual or a culture, should be recognized by virtue of their unique identity. If the politics of equal dignity establishes a set of rights and privileges, the politics of difference asks that the unique identity that distinguishes one individual from the next be recognized. The demand for recognition, enlivened by the idea of human dignity, implies, on the one hand, the protection of the fundamental rights of all people as human beings; and, on the other, the recognition of the proper needs of specific cultural groups. It is this distinction which, it is argued, has been ignored, submitted to a dominant or overarching identity. This assimilation, Taylor argues, is the greatest sin against the ideal of authenticity[45].

Critiques of liberal culturalism expanded, particularly in the Latin American context. Many defended an even more radical pluralization of citizenship, one which would break not only with the republican commitment to a unitary citizenship, but also with the liberal insistence on the idea that the rights of specific groups should be limited by the liberal principles of individual liberty, social equality and political democracy. This sort of position is in alignment with post-colonial, subaltern, and post-modern studies, among others. Authors associated with these currents argued that liberal justice was merely one among many cultural norms, and that it therefore should not have any privileges within a multicultural society. It was thus necessary to dodge Eurocentric liberal values (Santos, B. S., 2003; Beverley, 1999; Dube, 2001; Chakrabarty, 2002) and, indeed, to identify those human rights that are considered universal, which Kymlicka subordinated to the rights of minorities, as rights that are markedly western and Eurocentric.

According to Boaventura de Souza Santos (2003, p. 37), these currents opposed modern notions of temporality and subjectivity that, on the one hand, resulted from the intersection between the dynamics of modernity and the different types of resistance and alternatives that they elicited, and, on the other, the historical singularity of local experiences. Its foundations thus lay with a reconstruction of the "political" in terms different from those of liberal and Marxist traditions, since reference to 'culture' was a fundamental and indispensable resource for envisaging a new alternative. Politics would be rendered cultural politics, referring to a process whereby culture becomes political. Within this new perspective of political understanding, multiculturalist policies could transgressively appropriate concepts developed in a Eurocentric context (Santos, B. S., 2003). Parekh (2000, p. 109), in turn, criticized liberal thought for believing

---

45 The recognition of differences defended by Taylor (1994) should be understood as strictly linked to the notion of 'identity'. For Taylor, identity was formed through a process of dialogue, resulting from relations between peoples. Identity was partially formed by the recognition of its absence, frequently by the misrecognition or inconsideration of others. People or groups would thus suffer real harm by the mostly negative and depreciative image that others had of them, which they end up internalizing. In this way, non-recognition can be a form of oppression over those with a differentiated identity.

that liberal values would provide justice for ethno-cultural relations. In his perspective, liberalism was itself a historical construct, the fruit of a specific historical development.

Lastly, Boaventura de Sousa Santos promoted the idea of an emancipatory multiculturalism that would replace a monocultural perspective, and which would contemplate intercultural dialogue. In this sense, culture is seen to be an indispensable resource for elaborating alternatives to the homogenizing and oppressive forces of globalization. Alternatives for the creation of an emancipatory project could be thought through the vitality of culture; an integral part of this project is the emancipatory multiculturalism of all cultures that have been subordinated by the modernizing process of the West. The emancipatory versions of multiculturalism, identified, above all, with post-colonial strands of thought, were based on the recognition of difference and the right to difference of all sorts (Santos, B. S., 2003, p. 33). Culture difference was the force that fed globalization from subalternity, and which enabled the expression and visibility of peoples oppressed by their nation states by way of associations that transcended national borders and made viable direct resistance to the pressures of foreign-capital corporations (Segato, 1998).

Searching for alternatives within this critical context, Latin American authors, or Latin Americanists in general, repositioned themselves. In the domain of emancipatory or post-colonial strands certain tendencies, such as the decolonial, were gradually widened, gaining traction in the continent and guiding future approaches and research in the study of Afro-descendant peoples. Authors in this vein coined a new category, "decoloniality", which was used in the sense of a "decolonial turn", an idea proposed by the philosopher Nelson Maldonado-Torres (2007, p. 9).

The philosophy of decoloniality presupposes a critique of modernity itself, seeing colonialism and coloniality as inherent to it (Grosfoguel, 2006, p. 27; 2020). Colonialism and coloniality, although linked, are distinct phenomena. Colonialism refers to a structure of domination and exploitation where control of political authority, productive resources, and labour are under the control of another society, with its seat in another territory. Colonialism is linked to the political process of exploitation of the colonies. Coloniality, in turn, is a wider, complex historical phenomenon that naturalizes territorial, racial, cultural, and epistemic hierarchies, enabling the reproduction of relations of domination and ensuring that Capital can exploit subalternized populations (Restrepo & Axel, 2010, p. 16). Colonialism is evidently older, but, according to Quijano (2007, p. 93), coloniality has proved to be more profound and enduring.

"Race", as a descriptive category, gains prominence within this framework. The work of Anibal Quijano, in particular, takes race to be a structural axis of capitalist exploitation and the subjugation of Indigenous and Black populations.

> Coloniality is one of the constitutive and specific elements of the global pattern of capitalist power. It is based on the imposition of a racial/ethnic classification of the world's population as the cornerstone of this pattern of power, and it operates on each of the planes, spheres and dimensions, material and subjective, of everyday existence and on a social scale. It originates in and globalises from America (Quijano, 2007, p. 93).

For Quijano, race is certainly the most effective instrument of domination known to man. Imposed as a basic criterion for a universal social classification of people, it served as the basis for the creation of new social and geocultural identities throughout the globe. The author defines 'race' as an ideological construct that has nothing to do with the biological structure of the human species; on the contrary, it has to do with relations of power in global capitalism (1999, p. 144). It is important to note Quijano's distinction between race and colour: the former is anterior; the first race was that of the Indigenous people of the Americas and there is no register of their identification based on "colour". The idea of 'race' thus emerged with America, and originally referred to differences between the continent's Indigenous peoples and their conquerors. The idea of colour, in turn, was not applied to them, but, later, to enslaved Blacks brought to America. It is a later construction of Europeans, who come to define themselves as 'white' (1999, p. 47). By situating the differences between race and colour, Quijano refers to the divisions that have already been mentioned regarding castes and the notion of purity of blood in colonization, before the advent of scientific racism. By focusing on colonialist/capitalist exploitation, decolonial considerations recentred the Indigenous and Black questions in Latin America through the perspective of populations that have been economically exploited and submitted to a Eurocentric order of thought and values, in which race is a structuring axis.

As we observe later in our analysis of the theme in Brazil, the distinction established by Quijano is distant from what has historically been treated as 'colour' and 'race' in that country. Furthermore, the specificities of the Brazilian debate notwithstanding, we are concerned with the author's historical displacement of the concept, and his lack of dialogue with earlier analyses by Latin American intellectuals, particularly Black intellectuals. Quijano's proposals help reposition racism as a structuring element of social inequalities and capitalist exploitation in Latin America, but they leave out a historicization of the concept. Eduardo Restrepo and Axel Rojas (2010, p. 217), for example, draw attention to the fact that the decolonial definition of 'race' does not adequately consider the historicization of the concept, nor draws the consequence of what happens when it assumes its biological classificatory character. In their view, the inferiorization of others, even in the past when these others may have been considered nonhuman, is not inevitably expressed racially, does not necessarily imply a racial taxonomy, but points to a widespread phenomenon that anthropology calls 'ethnocentrism'. Thus, although the concept of 'race' has its precursors, aspects which enables its historical construction, these should not be confused with the very conceptualization of the term. Citing Kathryn Burns (2010, p. 218), the authors stress the risks of imposing contemporary notions of race on colonial forms of discrimination, which may lead us to ignore the processes that created the differences and separations that we seek to understand. This does not mean, that the concept of 'race' must be sealed in biological determinism or scientific racism.

With the racist theorists and scientific racism of the 19th century, Black populations became associated with inferior social strata, their differences biologized and intellectual and social development demeaned, thereby justifying their subjugation. The experience of slavery, exploitation, and racism thus came to stamp these people. This observation does not deny the importance of cultural contributions, of memory and traditions that the Black diaspora brought along in its wake, which are constitutive and foundational of Latin American societies; they merely convey the historical processes that made these very contributions invisible, and that produced classificatory systems based on race and ethnicity to further subjugation.

The Mexican historian Maria Elisa Velázquez (2020), in alignment with Eduardo Restrepo's caveats, take the idea of race, and that of *mestizaje*, as concepts that are socially and ideologically constructed in concrete historical contexts, for specific economic and political ends. According to the author, these categories were a central part of the discourse that elaborated Latin American states throughout the 19th and 20th centuries, and they were used to justify the ignorance, the invisibility, the disdain, and the racism towards certain populations, including Afro-descendants.

In this sense, the author also roundly criticizes the renewal of the 19th century concept of race by contemporary intellectuals and research projects as a means to understand societies that were recognizes as diverse and complex. For her, the study of the emergence of "racial" categories to classify human beings and the construction of the nation, state rhetoric, and identity in Mexico, the country she studies, allow for an understanding of racism against Afro-descendant populations in historical perspective. This makes it possible to explain that, despite its validity and naturalization, racism emerges in a historical context, and it is the task of social scientists to deconstruct it, to question and probe it, and to thereby fight it. For the author, using notions such as 'race' in analytical explanations makes it difficult to understand the complex phenomenon of racism. It is thus a responsibility of researchers to create new concepts that help explain past and present problems, such as racism. Velázquez (2020, p. 31) nonetheless insists that disqualifying the notion of 'race' is not tantamount to denying racism, which is, precisely, a discriminatory practice based on the conception that "races" exist, considering that words and concepts are not mere form, for they also possess a historical content which, the author believes, must be questioned and changed, lest we continue to reproduce them.

Velázquez's critique stands in opposition to large-scale research projects, which we will talk about in more detail later on, such as Pigmentocracies and LAPORA. These are projects that consider race/skin colour as analytical categories for the study of racism and which condemn multiculturalism, much as they condemn the older ideology of *mestizaje*, replacing these terms with ethnic category and a rhetoric of cultural diversity, preferring to refer to racial oppression.

The discussion of the concept of race as a historical analytical category has been at the centre of the debate on racial relations in the American continent, and it has been reclaimed, in a new guise, in the context of multiculturalism. Evidently, in the context of globalization, cultural diversity is manifest the world over. Furthermore, demands for recognition and for the rights of different people have always existed. Nonetheless, the specific questions debated in the context of the multiculturalist turn were defined in other terms: should ethnic minorities be officially recognized? Should their recognition be promoted by specific legislation and institutional policies? Can ethnicity be thought of as a founding category for rights? Is it possible to construct a state of ethno-cultural intervention that is equivalent to the state of social and economic intervention? Is the ethnic question of the same magnitude of importance as the social question (Wieviorka, 2001)?[46] The main point, as far is this book is concerned, is to show how these questions concerning multiculturalism, posed by different authors, are connected to the discussion on race and anti-racist policies. Can race, like ethnicity, be thought of as a foundational category of rights and public policies? Of state intervention? As analytical categories for the study of racism and its manifestations? The Brazilian case is quite singular in this regard, and it is exemplary of our point that, in specific contexts, marked by determinate his-

---

46 According to Parekh (2000), we must define what policies of recognition we are referring to. There are many identity constructs, for instance: women, homosexuals, ethnic minorities, who come together and demand, in unison, that the state look at them; however, multiculturalism policies are directed only to what is characteristic of 'culture'. Gays, women, or other social groups do not represent a cultural alternative, but the pluralization of the culture of which they are a part.

tories and social structures, it is the case that "race" is a category that still needs to be utilized. For this reason, we will investigate, in a later chapter, the construction and resistance of the term "race" in the study of racial relations in Brazil.

Multiculturalism and the emergence of new identities

Ethnicity has emerged as an important theme in Latin American public debate, fuelled by three factors: the emergence of Indigenous political movements in national and international contexts during the 1980s and 1990s; the development of international jurisprudence that has characterized the rights of Indigenous people as part of human rights; and, lastly, constitutional reforms that were promoted throughout the region , recognizing the multicultural nature of Latin American societies (Sieder, 2002).

Studies by Gros (1997–2000) have proposed structural causes that enabled this "Indigenous awakening" to occur in Latin America. The author highlights the crisis of the peasantry, demographic expansion, the amplification of national society, and the development of formal education in Latin American countries. Such causes allowed the Indigenous world to quickly emerge from its isolation, widening its horizon. Among causes, we must also include the intervention of external actors, who, for several reasons, impacted communities, guiding them in a new direction more favourable to identity politics. These agents include missionaries, militants, anthropologists, human rights activists (and Indigenous rights activists in particular), non-governmental organizations (NGOs), and others who brought with them a new rhetoric, along with crucial financial resources, acting as intermediaries between local communities and the wider world.

There is, according to Gros, yet another important cause that must be considered: the crisis of national-populist projects in Latin America. From the 1970s, nationalist and populist integration and modernization, in their many guises, entered a period of crisis which made evident their inability to promote the integration of Indigenous peoples into national societies For their part, Latin American states, encouraged by a new global context, ceased to be interested in furthering their assimilationist policies and began to themselves elaborate new policies for attending to the "ethnic minorities" within their boundaries. The state was thus an important actor in the strengthening of ethnic identities in Latin America. These factors contributed to carving new channels of communication between Indigenous communities and dominant societies, altering older forms of social domination and political regulation, which enabled an ever-growing number of Indigenous movements to emerge throughout the region. So as to stake out this new relationship, Indigenous movements began to marshal, as a strategy, their desire for integration and modernization without assimilation, and without accepting forms of biological or cultural *mestizaje*, demanding, instead, respect for and recognition of their cultural differences (Gros, 1997).

We can thus conclude that, in general, the predominant discourse during the 1990s recognized that Indigenous rights were articulated with strategies for combating exclusion and poverty, protecting the natural environment, safeguarding Indigenous territories and their biodiversity. Under the influence of a neoliberal model, globally comprehensive approaches concerning "democratic governance", small government, and decentralization were associated with the need to make room for the representation to new social partners, among which Indigenous groups and Blacks were prominent.

Black movements in Latin America, and particularly in Colombia and Brazil, were not isolated from this process. They also sought to claim a cultural identity and stress their distinction as a part of specific peoples. They were influenced both by Indigenous Latin American movements and by ideas deriving from studies of the Black diaspora, mainly those produced in the Anglo-Saxon world (Sansone, 2004). Drawing from earlier struggles against racism and discrimination through individual strategies, there emerged a struggle centred on collective subjects. In the Brazilian case, the cultural dimension became increasingly important as a political strategy for Black organizations (Agier & Carvalho, 1994). We witness the development of a phenomenon within which an inferiorizing assimilation gives way to the idea of a positive separation, or, better still, gives way to a separation which integrates and asserts itself. Thus, Black resistance in the region sought unity with the Indigenous movement, seeking legitimacy in joint policies. This allowed similar rhetoric and claims to cross over into each other, even if their issues were sometimes distant, so that we can affirm that Indigenous people and Blacks were united in defining themselves against the state as new political subjects through their "cultural differences".

In consonance with changes taking place at the global level – changes which they partially architected – international organizations such as the World Bank (WB), the Inter-American Development Bank (IBD), the United Nations (UN), the United Nations Development Programme (UNDP), United Nations Educational, Scientific and Cultural Organization (UNESCO), the Organization of American States (OAS), and certain large foundations and NGO's focusing on cooperation and development, were, and still are, frontline actors in the public political transformations taking place in Latin American countries. Within their directives and plans they have included issues bearing on Black populations (Igreja & Agudelo, 2014).

Processes of national mobilization, or of presenting the issues faced by Blacks in public fora, were gradually strengthened at different levels in relation to the specific contexts of each country. Without delving in depth into the specificities of each process, we will now turn to a few examples, setting Brazil aside for a more careful analysis.

We begin with Mexico, a country in which African descent has historically been made invisible and its contributions to the construction of Mexican society have been denied. Changes throughout the continent during the 1990s allowed Afro-Mexican collectivities, aligned with the Indigenous movement in the country, to organize and denounce their social vulnerability and invisibility within Mexican society. However, while Indigenous people explored gaps which afforded them official recognition, in particular after the Zapatista uprising of 1994, Afro-Mexicans remained at the margins of such recognition. Nonetheless, some achieved a degree of prominence, such as the "*Nuestra Tercera Raíz*" of the Mexican National Council for Culture and Arts (CONACULTA), between 1990 and 1998; the workshop on Populations and Cultures of African Origin in Mexico (Afro-Mexican Studies) of the National Institute of Anthropology and History (INAH) in 1997; the Meeting of Black Peoples, which, beginning in 1997, have been held at the initiative of the Afro-Mexican communities of the Costa Chica of Guerrero and Oaxaca (Velázquez & Iturralde, 2019). Afro-Mexican organizations emerge and gather momentum within this context, particularly in the Costa Chica of Guerrero and Oaxaca, areas with a greater concentration of Afro-Mexicans. For historical reasons, Africans brought to these places during the colonial period remained isolated from internal commercial circuits, even after independence, thus enabling the communitarian reproduction of culturally inherited traditions (Velázquez & Iturralde, 2019, pp. 52–53). In their struggle for recognition, the movement, and the Afro-Mexican communities it represented, sought to include an option to feature, in the 2015 census (Encuesta Intercensal, 2015), a question that would register the self-description of the Black population as Afro-Mexican or Afro-descendant (denominations provided in the Encuesta)[47]. This same question also featured in the National Research of Dynamic Demog-

---

[47] The actual question in the Encuesta is: "Acording to your culture, history, and traditions, (NAME) consider yourself to be Black, that is, Afro-Mexican or Afro-descendant?". As a definition of this variable, it further specifies: "Person who descends from Africans who arrived in Mexico during the colonial period to carry out forced labour in farms, plantations, mines, manufacturing, or as sellers, cooks, wet nurses, among other activities. Includes people who arrived in Mexico in other periods of its national history and who have ancestors in Africa". See: National Institute of Statistics and Geography (INEGI), Directorate-General for Sociodemographic Statistics (DGES), Deputy Directorate-General of the Population and Housing Census (DGACPV) https://www.inegi.org.mx/rnm/index.php/catalog/214/datafile/F18/V1243

raphy (Encuesta Nacional de Dinámica Demográfica, 2018)[48], and in the basic questionnaire of the Population and Residence Census of 2020 (Censo de Población y Vivienda, 2020)[49] (Millán, 2017; Velázquez &Iturralde, 2019). The drive towards making Afro-Mexican populations visible stamps studies of these populations and their anti-racist struggle in the country, particularly up to the 21st century. More recently, new studies have emerged, focusing specifically on the inequalities and vulnerabilities of this population (Iturralde, G., 2018).

The Nicaraguan case is interesting. The country pioneered the institutionalization of the recognition of national ethnic diversity, particularly after constitutional change in 1987. We can highlight, in particular, the inclusion of legislation concerning autonomous regions and the rights of ethnic communities on the Caribbean coast which took into account populations who recognize their African origin (Frühling et al., 2007)[50]. The political mobilization of these groups was linked to the Indigenous mobilization of the autonomous regions (Hooker, 2005). The autonomous status of the Nicaraguan Caribbean region remains in place. Constitutional recognition revealed lacunae, however, which have hindered the full exercise of autonomy by these communities (Frühling et al., 2007, pp. 77–82). Recurring problems of low political representativity, significant social vulnerabilities, and violation of communal territorial rights are still common. It should be recalled that the Nicaraguan state was condemned by the Inter-American Court of Human Rights in 2001, for their failure to ensure the territorial rights of the Awas Tingi Indigenous people. The jurisprudence established in this case was used in various other Latin American Indigenous and Afro-descendant claims over territory.

In Ecuador, in the wake of the political transformations that followed the election of Rafael Correa, representatives of the Black movement participated in the National Constituent Assembly. For the first time, Afro-Ecuadorians

---

48 https://www.inegi.org.mx/contenidos/programas/enadid/2018/doc/resultados_enadid18.pdf
49 https://www.inegi.org.mx/rnm/index.php/catalog/632
50 The agreement over autonomous accord was an initiative of the Sandinista government to put an end to a period of popular resistance and of armed Indigenous movements in the Atlantic coast, which accepted that regional accord where "the only means for lasting peace" (p. 347) and promoting ethno-national unity. To this end, the National Autonomy Commission (CAN) was created in December of 1984, composed of representatives of various ethnic groups from the Atlantic coast, as well as official delegates. This Commission drew up the document "Principles and policies for the exercise of the autonomous rights of the Indigenous peoples and ethnic communities of the Atlantic coast of Nicaragua," published in June 1985. After a few modifications, this document served as the basis for the approval, by the National Assembly, of the "Statute for the Autonomy of the Regions of the Atlantic Coast of Nicaragua" also known as Law 28, in September of 1987. See: (https://www.poderjudicial.gob.ni/pjupload/costacaribe/pdf/Ley_445.pdf)

were recognized as a distinct ethnic group by the multicultural Constitution of 1998 and were counted as such in the 2001 census. The new Constitution of 2008 ensured for Black populations the same rights recognized for Indigenous people. Institutions which assist the Black population were strengthened and new venues for establishing dialogue with the state were created. Among these, we draw attention to the Secretariat for Peoples, Social Movement and Citizen Participation, first presided by an Afro-Ecuadorian leader. These changes were also at the origin of measures put into place since the mid-1990s, such as the creation of the Afro-Ecuadorian Development Corporation (CODAE). The aims of the CODAE were (1) to achieve the human and productive development of the Afro-Ecuadorian people, (2) to strengthen the organization of Black communities, and (3) to revitalize Afro-Ecuadorians' ancestral knowledge, identity, and cultural values. (De la Torre & Antón, 2018, p. 169). Despite the gains of the new Constitution, certain analyses understand them as an aspect of the promotion of a neoliberal multiculturalism. Such analyses appreciate the efforts of the left-wing president Rafael Correa (2007–2017) to revert neoliberal policies and reconstitute the state as the engine of development, but they argue that the president ultimately interfered directly in social movements, co-opting its leaders. Furthermore, although the cultural rights of the Afro-Ecuadorian population were recognized, the aftermath of this was a gradual loss of autonomy for their representatives, and a failure to implement policies that were flagships of social movements, such as affirmative action and respect for territorial rights (De la Torre & Antón, 2018).

In Venezuela, official agencies were developed to recognize the country's Black populations without resorting to constitutional changes that would strengthen these spheres and their corresponding public policies. It is within the scope of the measures through which president Hugo Chávez sought to respond to the demands of the poorer sectors of Venezuelan society that the policies for recognizing Afro-Venezuelans were taken into account. The government supported initiatives of the Venezuelan Black movement, such as meetings of Afro-descendants against neoliberalism in 2006 and *Afro-descendants for Revolutionary Transformation in Latin America* in 2007, as well as the 4th Forum on *Afro-descendants in Our America*, carried out between the 19th and 22nd of June 2011 in Caracas. Jesus Garcia, the most famous Black leadership in Venezuela, was nominated for the post of Ambassador of Venezuela in Angola. In the context of the national and regional debates between different tendencies within the Afro movement in Latin America, Afro-Venezuelan organizations clearly positioned themselves in the left end of the political spectrum.

In Colombia, the theme was discussed by the National Constituent Assembly (ANC), which was tasked with drawing up a new Constitution. The participation of Black communities in the discussions allowed for the consolidation or formation of different organizations led to unprecedented processes of social and political mobilization among this sector of the population (Agudelo, 2005). This dynamic remained in place during consultation for the regimentation and application of the legislation (the Negritude Law, or Ley 70 de 1993)[51]. It should be noted that the use of the term "Black communities" in the Colombia context is justified by several factors. On the one hand, we find the term in some of the anthropological studies of Black populations that have been carried out since the 1950s, which derives from the use of 'community' to refer to Indigenous populations and, in some cases, to rural populations. The Colombian state used the term 'community' in the end of the 1950s to refer to population groups with limited resources in general. The organization of these communities at the national level, in the "Juntas de Acción Comunal"[52], is a reflex of the assimilation of the term, which became common in the country. Later, in the 1970s, Christian activists inspired by Liberation Theology promoted the "basic ecclesiastical units". One of the areas where these forms of organization where boosted was in the Pacific coast, among Black populations. Similarly, the Black political movement Cimarrón, which emerged in the 1980s, as well as the new Black ethnic movements which have emerged since the 1990s, regularly used the term 'community'. Finally, the state institutionalized and generalized this way of naming groups through the inclusion of the "Black communities" in Transitory Article 55 of the Political Constitution of 1991, which refers to these populations.

This was an intense and palpable period of activities in Colombia, both of the state and the other actors involved in this interactional dynamic. After the 'furore' of these initial years we see a situation of 'highs and lows' manifested during the last administrations – that is, from 1998 until the present. Despite this observation, it is also evident that multicultural policies strengthened their own regulatory character and came to be internalized by state agencies.

---

[51] See English translation of LAW 70 OF 1993 https://www.wola.org/sites/default/files/downloadable/Andes/Colombia/past/law%2070.pdf

[52] Second Title, Chapter 1, Article 8 of Law 743 of 2002, regulated by national decree n° 2350 of 2003, "By which article 38 of the Colombian constitution is developed: Community action boards and community housing boards are first-degree community action bodies. The community action board is a civic, social and community non-profit organisation of social management of a solidary nature, with legal status and its own assets, voluntarily made up of the residents of a place who join forces and resources to procure an integral, sustainable, and sustainable development based on the exercise of participatory democracy".

https://www.funcionpublica.gov.co/eva/gestornormativo/norma.php?i=5301#:~:text=La%20junta%20de%20acci%C3%B3n%20comunal,para%20procurar%20un%20desarrollo%20integral%2C

The inclusion of the Black populations as the theme of public policies in ministerial agendas has been constant since the start of this process in 1991, whether in the National Department of Planning or other government institutions.

However, the ambiguity expressed in a sort of 'resistance' to the implementation and development of such policies remains. Additional factors are relevant to this, including armed conflict in the region of the Pacific, where 90% of the Afro-Columbian population lives, with attending forced displacements and barriers to organization. The collective title to territories for Black communities – the major achievement of this process – is losing its impact because of the gradual loss of lands that belong to Black populations. Another significant gain in this process was the creation of an electoral district for representatives of Afro-Columbian populations. Significant differences also exist within sectors of the Black movement, where we find positions that range from complete identification with government policies to open opposition to them. The debate surrounding the approval of a free commerce deal with the United States is an example of such divisions.

In this context, a central element in the current debate on public policies concerning Afro-Colombians are the mechanisms of "Prior Consultation" of the different people and ethnic groups in relation to any government or private sector project or initiative that is related to the interests of these populations. This principle, established by Convention 169 of the International Labour Organization, and ratified by Colombian legislation, in practice raises a number of issues concerning its effective implementation in benefit of communities. Most sectors of the Black Movement in Colombia question the legitimacy of how consultation is applied by the state, and in many cased they condemn the total absence of this mechanism.

A significant example of debates concerning policies for recognizing Afro-descendants in Latin America is the Garifuna case (Agudelo, 2011, 2012a, 2012b), formerly known as the "Black Caribs" until the mid-20th century. These people result from a process of miscegenation of Africans brought to the Caribbean by the slave trade and Carib and Arawak Amerindians which took place during the colonial period in the Lesser Antilles, particularly in the island of St. Vincent. Deported in massive numbers to Central America by the English, in 1797 the Garifuna began to colonise the Caribbean coast of four countries (Honduras, Belize, Guatemala and Nicaragua). At present, through a constant migratory process that began in the mid-1920s, a large part of the Garifuna population resides in the USA.

The Garifuna have acquired a degree of notoriety in the four Central American countries in which they reside, in what pertains to the recognition of cultural diversity and institutionalized multiculturalism. Taking into account the specificities of each country, their protagonism has brought into question their official characterization as an "ethnicity", the incorporation of their cultural expressions as a part of national identities, and UNESCO's recognition of their culture as universal immaterial heritage of humanity. This initiative had the support of the government of Belize, which was later joined by the governments of Guatemala, Honduras, and Nicaragua. The proposal was accepted in 2001, constituting a new instrument for legitimization by Garifuna movements, an element in the rhetoric of claims over cultural, political, territorial, and social rights (Izard, 2003). We draw attention, in particular, to the presence of the Garifuna and their organizational processes in two countries, Belize and Honduras, which are exemplary of the many forms of colonization, exclusion, appropriation, and territorial dispute that have existed in the history of Latin America.

In Belize, the Garifuna attained a significant level of political influence and recognition, which can be understood within the specificities of the national context. The Creole population of the country (constituted by the descendants of Africans brought to the region as slave labor) gradually constitute itself as a majority during the colonial British period. In the first half of the 1960s, when forms of self-government under British stewardship were established, Creoles gradually gained access to mechanisms for social ascension. Ultimately, they assumed control of the new independent state after 1981. Despite a tense history with the colonial administration, and later with the Creoles in the 19th century, the Garifuna obtained recognition, which allowed for social ascension and a representative role, including government positions.

Honduras is the country with the largest Garifuna population, spread along all of its Caribbean coast. Garifuna political activism, which includes their explicit social demands concerning collective identity, finds its contemporary references in the Creation of The Black Fraternal Organization of Honduras (OFRANEH) in 1977. Other movements and associations continued to emerge, almost all originating from subdivisions of the organization itself, or new tendencies within it. The most visible is the Community Ethnic Development Organization (ODECO) created in 1992. In terms of territorial rights, actual achievements are modest, but the state recognized the legitimacy of the claims and some communities have obtained property titles. The right to land gained complexity with the intervention of state interests and speculation from the private sector, which oppose Garifuna possession and use of areas of collective settlement, with an eye mostly towards tourism. In the field of forms of symbolic and political recognition, the Garifuna made headways, but considering the range of their claims these were, again, limited. Some leaders obtained government positions, such as the Minister of Ethnicity and Vice-Minister of the Culture and Arts.

These experiences do not exhaust the situation in most Latin American countries, where, to a greater or lesser degree, issues concerning Black populations are part of public debates. The Brazilian case, which we will follow below, is emblematic because of the proportion of the country's Black population and the reach of its affirmative action policies.

In a mutual feedback loop dynamic, these national processes relied on transnational demands of Black populations, all the while constituting their own singular support systems. An event which shone a spotlight on Black Latin American organizations was the role of some of them in the protests in opposition to the celebrations of "500 years of discovery" in the Meeting of "two worlds" promoted by Spanish and Latin American governments in 1992. The Indigenous movement, gathered under the slogan "500 years of Indigenous resistance", was amplified by the support of sectors of the Black movements, altering the slogan to "500 years of Indigenous and Black resistance in the Americas".

The Network of Afro-Latin American, Afro-Caribbean and Diaspora women (RMAAD) also emerged in 1992, in the First Meeting of Black Women, held in the Dominican Republic. In 1994 UNESCO launched The Slave Route Project, providing incentive for a transnational network of researchers who study the history of the traffic in slaves. This project became a further propitiating factor in the rhetoric of Black movements seeking to reclaim the history and memory of slavery and resistance as one of the elements of their political activities. During these years, transnational networks of Black movement continued to multiply. Also in 1994, the Continental Network of Afro-American Organizations was created in Uruguay. In 1995 the Black Organization of Central America emerged, and in 1996 the Afro-America XXI

In Brazil, commemorations of 500 years of "discovery" – in fact the invasion and conquest of the country – occurred on the 22nd of April 2000, considering the date that the Portuguese, and more specifically Pedro Álvares Cabral, reached the lands that would later make up the country. It was, again, Indigenous movements that organized protests against the celebration, particularly those linked to people who inhabit areas close to where Cabral made landfall. They were joined by students, activists of the Landless Workers Movement (MST,) and the Black Movement. Envisaged as a grand celebration in Porto Seguro, Bahia – a confraternization between the Brazilian Portuguese governments – the event became the stage for a conflict between public forces and social movements. It resulted in a number of people getting injured or being arrested, among them various Indigenous peoples of different ethnicities. Celebrations of the 500 years of "discovery" thus sought, yet again, to conceal the processes by which the Portuguese and Spanish empires invaded Latin America and the violence that they wrought, appealing, as always, to foundational myths of Latin American civilizations as a result of this encounter, reiterating an idea of the harmonious communion of races and cultures throughout the region. The protests against the invasion of Brazil by the Portuguese were later followed by protests against the Spanish invasion in other countries of the continent.

Also noteworthy is the impact of the 3rd World Conference against Racism, Racial Discrimination, Xenophobia, and Related Intolerances, held by the UN in Durban, South Africa, from the 30th of August to the 7th of September 2001. In preparation for the conference, a number of national, sub-regional, and Latin American and Caribbean meetings were held. These meetings brought together pre-existing national organizations and transnational networks. In this context, the "Afro-Latin American and Caribbean Strategic Alliance" was created in 2000, bringing together important organizations from the region.

The Brazilian delegation was one of the largest, composed not only of government representatives, but also members of civil society. As was reported at the time, the conference may not have had the international publicity that was expected, but it was extremely important in raising the stakes of debates on racial issues in Brazil and other Latin American countries, triggering government actions and the creation of new government and non-government institutions, and strengthening Black organizations in unprecedented ways. It likewise resulted in an instrument for protest, the "Durban Declaration and Plan for Action", which was engaged by all expressions of the Black movement in Latin America, both through its networks as well as within national spheres. This document contains commitments that the group of Latin American states present in Durban undersigned aimed at fighting discrimination and racism against ethnic groups and minorities.

This process of making visible the issues facing Afro-descendants in Latin America was accompanied by the growing role of institutions such as the World Bank and the Inter-American Development Bank, throughout the 1990s. This role continued into the 2000s, supported by the United Nations Program on Sustainable Development, the Ibero-American Secretary General, the Spanish Agency for International Development Cooperation, Economic Commission for Latin American and the Caribbean (ECLAC), the Organization of American States, US Agency for International Development, among other institutions which have continued to promote cooperation and support for Black movements.

The workshop "Afro-descendant Populations in Latin America" was held in Panamá in March of 2008, called by the Ibero-American Secretary General (SEGIB). The workshop originated from the mandate of the 17th Ibero-American Summit of Chiefs of State and Government, which took place in Santiago, Chile, in 2007, and which recommended "carrying out a compendium of information on the situation of the Afro-descendent population of Ibero-America".

Representatives of most of the Black movements from the region discussed diagnoses elaborated by ECLAC's consultants. In conformity with this workshop, the United Nations Development Program (UNDP) elaborated the regional project The Afro-Descendant Population in Latin America. The workshop "Rights of the Afro-Descendant Population in Latin America: Challenged to Implementation" held in Panama in November of 2009, delivered the results of this program.

These events and spheres provided a stocktaking of the rights of people of African descent in relation to the global agenda that gained legitimacy in the 1990s, particularly the commitments assumed at the Durban Conference. The UNDP added these concerns to the fulfilment of the Millennium Development Goals, in which people of African descent, who make up the majority of poor and marginalized people in Latin America, emerge as a priority for the United Nations.

In general, the results of this process show qualitative changes in what concerns the inclusion of Afro-Latin Americans in the policies of most of the governments of the region, sometimes through constitutional reform, at other times by way of laws or decrees or the creation of pertinent official instances. In some countries the visibility that the political expressions of Afro-Latin Americans and their associations attained represented a leap when compared to the situation in the 1980s. Nonetheless, despite these advances, even in countries such as Brazil, which has the highest incidence of public policies of the inclusion of the Black populations, little was done to overcome the social fissure which continues to maintain these populations at the base of the social pyramid, suffering a high degree of social segregation.

For Brazil, this claim is supported by solid statistical socioeconomic data. For other countries in the region there is dearth of such statistical input. The matter of censuses is always brought up in these exchanges. It is a consensus that, in order to be effective with political claims for social inclusion, it is necessary to rely on the best statistical tools specifically that track and measure exclusion. Organizations such as the UNDP or the European Union follow the movements and appeal to states through these means.

Despite the presence of activists from various organizations that emerged in the last decade in Latin America, there is a notable decrease in their participation in these transnational spaces and their larger concentration within national agendas. It is thus common for international circles to appeal nation states to fulfil the commitments of Durban Declaration and Plan for Action. In April of 2009, Black organizations present in Geneva condemned the ineffectiveness of the measures in place and demanded a more consistent involvement by the UN and by states who had boycotted the meeting by their absence. Many Indigenous and Black organizations did not receive the necessary support for their participation, and the visibility of this meeting was, in the end, negligible.

Since 2003, meetings of Black parliamentarians of the Americas have been carried out with the aim of constructing mechanisms for coordinating their work, defined as the support for and active participation in all of the demands for rights by Afro-descendant populations in the continent. The first meeting was held in Brasília. The second, in 2004, in Bogotá, in San José de Limón, Costa Rica, in 2005 and in Cali, Colombia, in 2008. One fact condemned by the parliamentarians that had participated in this process is the political sub-representation of Afro-descendant populations in the region (Agudelo, 2005).

In 2004, through the initiative of the Uruguayan organization Afro World Organization (Mundo Afro), a new network was created, the Regional Workshops for the Analysis and Promotion of Public Policies of Racial Equity (ORAPPER). It is currently present in Costa Rica, Nicaragua, Panama, Venezuela, Colombia, Ecuador, Bolivia, Peru, Chile, Uruguay, Argentina, Paraguay, and Canada. ORAPPER, in turn, promotes the creation of a new network, the Latin American and Caribbean Coalition of Cities Against Racism, Discrimination, and Xenophobia, with the support of UNESCO and the government of Ecuador. The Regional Afro-Descendant Articulation of Latin America and the Caribbean (ARAAC) was created through the initiatives of Cuba and Venezuela, presenting itself as an alliance against racism, imperialism, and capitalist neoliberal globalization.

These many networks took on a transnational organizational form with intermittent operations, based on a number of factors that conditioned their actions. The material conditions for their development depended largely on the support of international cooperation agencies, and they were therefore highly reliant on the changing priorities of these agencies. At the same time, the priorities of its members, who occasionally chose or were forced to focus on national struggles, also explains why these networks emerge and disappear from transnational spheres of mobilization (Agudelo, 2006). Currently, in 2021, ARAAC has maintained a more sustained level of activities, revealing itself as a protagonist in a range of virtual initiatives for combating the Coronavirus disease pandemic, as well as in assessing the results of the Durban Conference on its 20th anniversary.

The development of policies concerning Afro-descendants in Latin American in the international sphere

Considering the disappointing results of Durban and the pressure of Black movements for more effective measures against racism, the General Assembly of the

United Nations proclaimed 2011 to be the International Year for people of African Descendants in its 65th Plenary session. According to the resolution, the aim of this celebration is to "... strengthen national measures and regional and international cooperation in support of Afro-descendants in relation to the full enjoyment of their economic, cultural, social, civic, and political rights." The Durban commitments continue to be the fundamental structure on which this decision is based.

During 2011, fora, encounters, workshops, and summits multiplied, both at the national and international levels. Those which received most attention are, in chronological order: the 4th Meeting of Afro-Descendants for Revolutionary Transformations in America and the Caribbean, in Caracas, held from the 19th to the 22nd of June; The World Summit on African Descent, Integral and Sustainable Development with Identity, which occurred in La Ceiba, Honduras, from the 18th to the 21st of August; the Forum on Land Grabbing in Africa and Latin America, also in La Ceiba, on the 19th of August. The UN General Assembly, in New York, which met on the 22nd of September held a "High Level Meeting in commemoration of the 10th anniversary of the Durban Declaration"; the "World Summit for Afro-descendant Youth" took place between the 5th and 7th of October; the Regional Dialogue of Young Afro-Descendants on Democracy and Citizenship was held in Quito on the 20th and 21st of October, organized by the UNDP; the AFROXXI Meeting (Iberoamerican Meeting of the International Year for People of African descent), which occurred between the 17th and 19th of November in Salvador, Brazil. This event was organized by the SEGIB and the Brazilian government with UN backing. Some of the proposals approved include an appeal to the UN to declare the period from 2013 to 2023 "Afro-descendant Decade", with the aim of giving priority to the measures necessary to meet the demands of Black populations or those of African origin on a global scale. There was also stress on the need for the creation of a fund of international resources to financially support and implement public policies that would materialize these demands.

In 2013, the General Assembly proclaimed the International Decade for People of African descent commencing on 1 January 2015 and ending on 31 December 2024, with the theme "People of African descent: recognition, justice and development"[53]. Six years after its activities began, the results are mostly negative, as shown by the debates promoted by the Latin American Social Science Council

---

53 See: https://documents-dds-ny.un.org/doc/UNDOC/GEN/N13/453/67/PDF/N1345367.pdf?OpenElement

(CLACSO)[54]. Another regional instrument considered to be fundamental emerged from the decade: Plan of action for the decade for persons of African descent in the Americas, approved by the General Assembly of the Organization of American States in 2016 OAS, 2016[55]. The Plan aimed to provide incentives for the adoption of public policies and legislation for the protection of the rights of Afro-descendants and the recognition of their contributions to the economic, cultural, and social life of the region (OAS 2016).

Recently, a further initiative emerged in the context of the United Nations: the creation, in 2021, of the Permanent Forum on People of African Descent, inspired on the model of the Permanent Forum on Indigenous Peoples, which will become operative in 2022. One issue facing Black movements is how to transform this forum into a truly representative sphere for the diverse expressions and demands of Afro-descendants. Despite their merits, the creation of permanent fora and international councils has proven inefficient for advancing the policies that they discuss and announce.

In some of these activities, significant political differences were made explicit among the diverse Black movements in the region. The Ceiba Summit was promoted by ODECO. This initiative received the support of various international agencies, as well as the open support of the Honduran government which came to power after the coup of 2009, before it had been recognized by some Latin American governments. Other sectors of the Black Movement in Honduras remained opposed to the new government, considering it illegitimate. These included Afro-Honduran organizations led by OFRANEH, which organized, at the same time, the above-mentioned Forum on Land Grabbing.

Some sectors of the Black Movement in Latin America, particularly in Venezuela and Colombia, questioned ODECO's position, considering that holding the Summit in Honduras with government support served to give legitimacy to a government that had come to power through a coup. Likewise, these groups see the involvement of the United States and of various international organizations as an endorsement of neoliberal policies that deflect the Black movement from its aims of overcoming structural factors that hinder the elimination of the social exclusion and racism to which most Blacks in Latin America are subjected.

---

54 The CLACSO debates on the theme occurred within the scope of the International Graduate Schools "Beyond the International Decade of Afro-Descendant Peoples" carried out in 2017 and 2019 by a Working Group of the Institution: Afro-descendants, Counter-hegemonic proposals and Epistemologies from the South. https://www.clacso.org/mas-alla-del-decenio-afrodescendiente/ See also Campoalegre, Bidaseca (2017).

55 https://www.oas.org/en/sare/documents/res-2891-16-en.pdf

The Afro-Venezuelan movement has been at the forefront of this open opposition to both the International Summit and to tendencies within the movements which it considers to be reactionary. In this debate, the category "Afro-right wing" is used to define sectors of the Black movement that identify with the policies of funding agencies, and which were integrated into the institutions of national governments considered to be reactionary. During the 4th Meeting of Afro-Descendants for Revolutionary Transformations in America and the Caribbean, held in Caracas in June of 2011, a line was drawn within the regional Black movement. It was here that the ARAAC became consolidated as an agglutinating space for progressive and left-wing Afro-descendant Latin American and Caribbean activism.

It is important to highlight how networks of Black Latin American women played a role in these instances. According to a ECLAC (2018) report, ever since the Regional Gender Agenda, constituted throughout 40 years of Regional Conferences on Women in Latin American and the Caribbean, the theme of Afro-descendant women and ethno-racial and gender intersectionality had been included in discussions (ECLAC, 2018). The Afro-Descendants in the Americas Action Plan itself, approved by the General Assembly of the OAS, includes among its programs for the eradication of poverty, strategies, and acts to improve the lives of Afro-descendant women and to promote equality over discrimination (RMAAD, 2015). The acts of RMAAD have been fundamental in ensuring that the agenda of Black women is taken into account.

At various times, such as in the Mexico Consensus (2004), the Quito Conference (2007), the Brasília Consensus (2010), and the Santo Domingo Consensus (2013), governments showed themselves to be committed to promoting the transversalization of the focus on gender, race, and ethnicity in all policies and programs discussed and implemented (ECLAC, 2018). Lastly, the Montevideo Strategy for the Implementation of the Regional Gender Agenda in the Sphere of Sustainable Development by 2030, approved at the 13th Regional Conference on women in Latin America and the Caribbean (2016), will stimulate the leadership of Afro-descendant women, and pursue a more partisan democratic participation as a way of making politics and society more democratic (ECLAC, 2018).

All of these initiatives will be founded on the need for reparations for the Black population of the Americas because of the historical and contemporary impacts of slavery suffered by sub-Saharan populations in the context of colonization. Indeed, the issue of reparations was one of the central points of discussion in the Durban Action Plan and will be furthered by other organizations.

Reparations are, for example, one of the main agendas of ARAAC's mobilization. The abolition of slavery and the decolonization process did not eradicate racism, discrimination, social exclusion, and marginalization, all of which still affect millions of descendants of enslaved Africans in regions that suffered colonial influence. The growth of historical research and the diversity of the dynamics of condemnation have consolidated these claims.

Reparation as a mechanism for compensation or justice for the victims of a crime is a commonly used legal device, present in international law and in applied human rights. In relation to reparations for the impacts of colonial slavery and its contemporary effects, these legal perspectives are among the preferred options, but the debate around its viability and the form it should take is far from exhausted. The Community of Caribbean Countries (CARICOM), which since 2014 has developed an action plan to obtain from former colonial nations restorative justice mechanisms for the contemporary impacts of slavery and colonialism on their societies, has served as an example for segments of the Latin American Afro-descendant movements. In Brazil, reparations were on the agenda of the Black movement when the introduction of affirmative action policies and the consideration of the Statute of Racial Equality were being discussed, as we will see shortly.

International academic projects on Latin American Afro-descendants

The expansion of the debate on multiculturalism in the region and the inclusion of the racial issue within this debate opened doors for the study of the different Black populations, in a comparative and broader regional proposal. Many of these projects were developed with the support of universities and foreign funding agencies, such as foundations and international organizations, in alignment with the renewed interest in recognizing cultural differences. This interest was further fuelled by Latin American studies centres in the United States and in several European countries, which have featured the topic into their study agendas.

In particular, it is worth mentioning the Henry Louis Gates Junior project (2011), which resulted in a book and a documentary film about Latin American Afro-descendants. Gates is a Black American intellectual, professor at the Hutchins Center of African and African American Research at Harvard University, considered a reference for studies on Black culture in the United States. According to his book (Gates Junior, 2011), his interest in the Black Latin American population emerged from the discovery that there were numerous other Black populations in the America outside of the United States, and the realization of the importance of the slave trade in the region, highlighting shared connections and histories. To put the project into practice, the author relied on conversations with several renowned Latin American intellectuals who studied the theme in their respective countries. The documentary produced by Gates provided a panoramic perspective on Black Latin Americans, focusing on Brazil, Mexico, Dominican Republic, Haiti, Cuba, and Peru. Gates situated himself as a listener, a spectator of the realities he was observing, seeking, through a comparative effort, to also bring out the specificities of each country. Without dismissing the importance of the panoramic and comparative vision offered by the project, many of his analyses failed to bring to the fore the complexity and depth that the theme demands, remaining, in the end, at a superficial and sometimes folkloric level.

Importantly, the documentary produced by Henry Gates also coincided with a moment of debate in the United States regarding the country's population census, with a focus on racial classifications and the inclusion of the migrant population, particularly that of Hispanic origin. In this context, the "mixed races" classification was the main theme and the object of several studies of different trends, including conservative ones, based on the white fear of becoming a minority (Parker et al., 2015). The country was becoming 'Brazilianized' or 'Latinized,' both in terms of an increase in inequalities of social class, through a process by which class, race and ethnicity intersected, including in the mix a significant upsurge in the poor white classes, as well as in terms of an increase in multi-racial identifications resulting from a greater incidence of interracial marriages, among other reasons. Bonilla-Silva (2002) argues that the United States is moving from a bi-racial to a tri-racial regime because of this demographic change, assuming a make-up that is quite similar to some Latin American countries.

The debate in the United States has not, in general, been followed and studied by Latin American intellectuals, in large part because the flow of academic studies has usually gone from North to South, reproducing Eurocentrism and traditional academic domination[56]. Furthermore, there is, as of yet, scant contact between US and European intellectuals studying their own countries and Latin American scholars in a more horizontal exchange. In general, it is only Latin Americanists from Northern countries who have greater knowledge of and contact with our region. This fact has repercussions in the structuring and elaboration of new projects on race and racism in Latin America, which, while including Latin American researchers in their teams and analyses, have little

---

56 This is a broad debate that incorporates the analysis of the history of "area studies" in the United States and the geopolitics of knowledge, as addressed by the new Latin American critical theories, such as decolonial theories. As we have highlighted in other studies (Igreja & Rodrigues, 2019), there is very little academic and financial stimulus for Latin Americans to do field studies in other countries, especially in the North, considering their analytical and methodological perspectives.

connection with projects and analyses on the same theme under discussion in Northern countries.

Some examples of centres and projects focused on the theme in Latin America should be mentioned. An initial project to be stressed is the International Project on Afro-descendants and Slavery: Domination, Identification and Inheritance in the Americas (AFRODESC), developed between 2008 and 2012. The project brought together scholars from several countries in Europe, especially France, and Latin America. Its focus was the analysis of the processes of enslavement and their socioeconomic and cultural consequences in contemporary societies and the constructions of identities and essentialisms during the elaboration and consolidation of multiculturalist policies. The Afrodesc project was one of the first to propose large interdisciplinary teams with an eye on the region and to promote broader studies on the subject in some countries, such as Mexico, where the Afro-descendant population has been historically rendered invisible. In the growing market of discussion and the availability of recognition policies, academics and, in some cases, Afro-descendant organizations, many of which were only recently created, were concerned with making this population more visible.

The projects that emerged later focused more specifically on discussing inequalities and their relations with the category of "race", creating a field of dispute surrounding its use. It is important to here take note of the Project on Ethnicity and Race in Latin America (PERLA), coordinated by Edward Telles, which resulted in the book *Pigmentocracies, Ethnicity, Race, and Color in Latin America* (Telles, 2014). Edward Telles is a professor at the University of California, Irvine, and a former professor at the University of California, Santa Barbara. He was also the director of the Ford Foundation in Rio de Janeiro, Brazil, which was an important backer of affirmative action policies in the country. The project proposed a comparative study of racial inequalities in Latin America, focusing on Brazil, Mexico, Colombia and Peru, and involving intellectuals from these countries. It proposed to survey and collect statistical data on the perception of discrimination and social disadvantage in an attempt to prove that social distinctions and racial/ethnic hierarchies historically rest on phenotype, thereby substantiating existing racism in Latin America. PERLA made use of national surveys with questions about racial/ethnic classifications and inequality, also using a colour palette to help objectively racially identify the respondent. The measurement of skin colour through a colour scale garnered criticism for the project, including with regards to disrespect for the self-declaration of respondents. The goal of PERLA was essentially to prove that skin colour is the best predictor of ethnic-racial inequalities. The project's contributions demonstrate that social inequalities are coloured, and that Black and Indigenous populations on the continent are the most affected by it. Featuring a standard survey in comparative regional projects, it did not, however, consider important specificities of the history and race relations of the different countries, following a more homogeneous model of analysis adapted to Brazilian racial issues, perhaps influenced by the experience of the coordinator at the FORD Foundation in Brazil. It is worth pointing out that several Brazilian studies had already dealt statistically with inequalities and their links to racism and discrimination without use of the controversial colour palettes. In this sense, we have the pioneering studies by Carlos Hasenbalg and Nelson do Valle e Silva (Hasenbalg, 1979; Hasenbalg, & Valle Silva, 1988), which questioned the explanation of racial inequalities in the country as a mere legacy of slavery.

Parallel to and in alignment with the PERLA project, several other initiatives emerged in the United States and Europe. These are research projects that have also focused on comparative studies and analyses of racial categories and multiculturalism. Many researchers, among them several Latin American scholars, participate in more than one project. The Antiracist Action and Research Network (RAIAR) constitutes another important example. Founded in 2014, by Professors Pamela Calla, a co-founder of the Bolivian Observatory, and Charles Hale, then Director of the LLILAS Benson Latin American Studies and Collections at the University of Texas at Austin, the Network sought to create links with organisations focused on similar issues in other Latin American countries (Hale at. al., 2017). RAIAR's project, called "When Rights Ring Hollow: Racism and Anti-Racist Horizons in the Americas", included seven countries as case studies: Brazil, Bolivia, Guatemala, Colombia, Mexico, Chile, and the United States, especially considering the Black Lives Matter movement. An important result of the Network's research was that, after decades of recognizing Indigenous and Afro-descendant rights in Latin America, particularly in the legal sphere, we are currently observing a decline in this recognition and an advance of conservative and neo-liberal proposals that attack these rights. In this sense, RAIAR researchers conclude that the current period can be defined as a new historical conjuncture characterized by racist backlash (Hooker, 2020). We will return to this observation later in this book.

Other projects also stand out such as the Latin American Anti-racism in a 'Post-Racial' Age – LAPORA, coordinated by Prof. Peter Wade and Mónica Moreno Figueroa, University of Cambridge and the Observatory of Justice for Afro-descendants in Latin America – OJALA of the Florida International University, coordinated by Jean Rahier with the participation of several Latin American intellectuals[57]. Both projects also focus on an analysis of multiculturalism's capacity to meet the demands and needs of Afro-descendant populations. LAPORA in particular tracks anti-racism struggles in the region, in the wake of the multicultural turn, during what they now situate as a post-racial era. The team considers that multiculturalism, seen to be a new ideology that presupposes the existence of harmony between diverse cultures, complements the old ideology of *mestizaje* by the persistent negation of the existence and permanence of structural racism in Latin American societies. In this context, according to the premises of the project, which we summarise here, racism is denied, minimised, and its victims or denouncers are seen to exaggerate its effects and reactions; the terms 'racism', 'racial' and 'race' are avoided for their negative historical baggage and replaced by 'cultural diversity'; and, finally, when they are admitted, they are analysed through interactions between individuals rather than in their structural dimension. Thus, much as when under the influence of the ideology of *mestizaje*, the denunciation of the structural dimension of racism is made difficult in the context of the ideology of multiculturalism. LAPORA's proposals, as well as PERLA's, carve an important and controversial space for discussing the subject in the academic world, especially regarding the consideration of 'race' as an analytical category for the study of racism, a topic that we will deal with later on.

We must also mention the Afro-Latin American Research Institute at Harvard University, which considers itself to be the first research institution in the United States dedicated to the history and culture of peoples of African descent in Latin America and the Caribbean. It is important to highlight again that projects with more regional and panoramic perspectives emerge with financial and institutional support in the Northern countries. Even so, they suffer from a lack of interest from their own national academies, even in countries like the United States. While we should recognise the opportunities that they have promoted, particularly by the inclusion of Latin American researchers and even activists in their teams, the power relations remain in place. This is partly due to this structural difference in support and the resources available, as well as the scant possibility of integrating Latin Americans into the academic field of these countries in a more horizontal and open relationship.

---

57 OJALA (https://ojala.fiu.edu/) specifically aims to carry out a comparative observation of Latin America's justice systems for the improvement and defence of Afro-descendants' rights. Financed by the National Science Foundation (NSF) of the United States, with Jean Rahier, Jhon Antón Sánchez, from Ecuador, and Carlos Agudelo, from Colombia as main researchers, OJALA currently develops the research project "A Multifaceted Investigation of the Application of Ethno-Racial laws for Afro-Descendants in Contemporary Multicultural Ecuador".

On another front, new networks and projects emerge within Latin America, many with a body of critical theory that challenges the Eurocentrism of perspectives from the North. The CLACSO, as an international non-governmental institution that brings together research and graduate social science centres in Latin America, has been converted into a space where research projects and courses on Afro-descendants in Latin America have been developed. CLACSO has been occupied by intellectuals linked to a left-wing political agenda in the region, as well as representatives of civil associations and social movements that together produce an important critique of the subordination of the social sciences in Latin America., however, is open to different contributions and does not constitute a systematized research project in and about the region as a whole. In the specific case of Afro-descendants, the working groups "Crisis of civilization, reconfigurations of racism, Afro-Latin American social movements" and "Afro-descendants and counter-hegemonic proposals" are currently active.

It is important to consider examples of these projects in order to demonstrate the academic power field in dispute over the interpretation of the Black "problem" in Latin America that started to become consolidated after what has been called the Latin American "multicultural turn". These regional and comparative projects were innovative for producing a broad perspective on the topic, shining a spotlight on the problems faced by Afro-descendant populations. They also produced a systematic and organized dataset on these populations, especially statistics and analyses of public and anti-racist policies. For this reason, they were able to establish close dialogue with international institutions such as the UN, ECLAC, the World Bank, among others, with their projects of intervention in the region. In the same way, they were able to establish close ties – and even promote the emergence of – Afro-Latin American leaders and militants. Alongside these actors, they made up the voices that circulated in academic environments and global discussion forums. They are the ones who put the multicultural turn in motion. However, as is common in this type of analysis, by proposing more homogeneous and panoramic analyses they leave out the various historical specificities of different localities, and even processes of resistance and negotiation constructed during the history of colonization and domination. They thus end up transfixed on denunciatory and victimizing perspectives that ultimately make the potentialities of historical resistance of these populations unviable.

IV The construction of "race" as a foundational category of rights and public policies

The identification of Afro-descendants in the Americas: the debate on racial classification

Discussions of multiculturalism and the identity politics of Black and Indigenous populations bring ethnic and racial categories back into the debate, placing them alongside important concepts such as culture, race, and identity, which are considered to be fundamental to the identification and quantification of these populations. For this reason, its introduction in Latin America stimulated an intense process of elaborating ethno-racial statistics, fuelling efforts at standardizing basic indicators to obtain a profile for these populations.

The categorization of these populations is subordinate to the historical constructions of the social place of Blacks and Indigenous peoples, and the history of data production and ethno-racial censuses for each country. Any comparison between the different data made available for the different countries should be carried out with care, because there is unevenness in how they are produced and gathered. International agencies have been at the forefront of the production of regional data on the Afro-descendant population.

According to a World Bank report (Freire et. al., 2018) based on the most recent national censuses of 16 countries, Latin America possessed some 133 million Afro-descendants in 2005, which is close to 24% of its total population. The same report also observes that this population is unevenly distributed throughout the region. Out of the total number, 91% are based in Brazil and Venezuela, and a further 7% in Colombia, Cuba, Ecuador and Mexico. Thus, discussions of Afro-descendants in the Americas, as the report underscores, is basically restricted to countries in the Caribbean (Cuba, Venezuela), on the Pacific Coast (Colombia, Ecuador) and, above all, in Brazil.

The diversity of Latin American Afro-descendant populations emerges in their histories, settlement forms and sociocultural dynamics (see map in Figure 2). They inhabit rural and urban areas, coastal or insular regions, as well as in the interior. They make up communities, but also live scattered in different settlements, particularly in big cities. Many of them have their own specific sociocultural and religious practices, but also share in the ways of life and the identities of the non-Afro-descendant peoples with whom they co-reside in towns, regions or countries (Agudelo, 2019; Bastide, 1967; Mintz & Price, 1992; Whitten & Torres, 1998).

Figure 2: Afro-descendants in Latin America. Source: Elaborated by Carlos Agudelo, with the help of the Instituto de Estudios Interculturales, Universidad Javariana, Cali, Colombia, 2016

Sociodemographic studies show that Afro-descendant peoples adopt a form of spatial mobility that is similar to that of the population as a whole, with a marked tendency to gather in urban spaces[58]. Data from the World Bank (Freire, G. et al., 2018) indicate an average of 80% of Afro-descendants live in urban areas in Latin American and the Caribbean. Thus, despite the evident importance of the rural milieu, in which communal life and cultural expressions tend to be expressed more explicitly, urban life is the tendency throughout the region. However, it should be noted that the Afro-descendant presence is higher in urban peripheries, particularly in precariously settled areas – which reflects the social condition in which this population has historically lived.

In Central American countries such as Guatemala, Honduras, Nicaragua and Costa Rica, the largest Afro-descendant presence is found in the coastal areas of the Caribbean. The way the region was settled in colonial times ensured that the Pacific coast and the interior were inhabited mainly by Indigenous people and mestizos. Panama and Belize have their own historical particularities, since Afro-descendants in these countries are dispersed throughout the national territory. In El Salvador, the role of people of African descent has only come to attention in recent years.

Afro-Mexicans (the most common term to designate the Black population in Mexico) inhabit the full expanse and breadth of the national territory, although the states with the greatest number are Guerrero, Oaxaca, Veracruz, the State of Mexico and Mexico City. There is a greater presence both in the port area of Veracruz, in the Caribbean, and along the Pacific coasts of the states of Oaxaca and Guerrero. In addition, some 1.7% of these people are not Afro-Mexicans, hailing from other countries, most of whom live in Mexico City (Velázquez & Iturralde, 2019, pp. 26–27).

As we have already mentioned, one development in the collection of data on the Afro-Mexican population was the inclusion by the Mexican government of a question on self-identification of Afro-Mexican, Black and Afro-descendant persons in the 2015 inter-census statistical survey (2015 EIC), and subsequently in the National Survey on Discrimination in 2017 (ENADIS 2017) and in the National Survey on Demographic Dynamics 2018 (ENADID 2018), as well as in the basic questionnaire of the country's 2020 Population and Housing Census. According to data from the 2015 EIC, 1,381,853 people recognise themselves as Black, Afro-Mexican or Afro-descendant, representing 1.2% of the population. Of these, 51% are women. It is also significant to note that, of the total population that responds positively to self-identification as Afro-Mexican, 64% also consider

---

[58] As an example, we have the research project "Social organization, cultural dynamics, and identity in Afro-Colombian populations of the Pacific and Southwest in a context of mobility and urbanization". For some of the results, see Urrea and Barbary (2004). Furthermore, for Brazil we have data from the IBGE.

themselves Indigenous, and that 9.3% speak an Indigenous language (Velázquez & Iturralde, 2019, pp. 26–27). The absence of Afro-Mexicans in official histories and in State policies to include cultural diversity as part of the official views on mestizaje makes it difficult to elaborate data on the contemporary presence of this population (Millán, 2017).

In the South American countries that border the Pacific Ocean, many Afro-descendants inhabit coastal regions. This is the case of Colombia, as well as the northern coast of Ecuador and the southern part of Peru. The continental Caribbean in South America corresponds to the coastal areas of Colombia and Venezuela which have significant Black populations. Furthermore, the Atlantic Ocean coasts of Suriname, Guyana and the French overseas department of French Guyana, as well as the entire coastal region of Brazil, include important Black settlements. In these regions, in fact, Afro-descendants are a majority throughout the territory. In the insular Caribbean there is a majority of Afro-descendants, constituting 95% of the population in Haiti, as well as in other islands, such as Cuba and the Dominican Republic, where, despite the importance of Black populations, there is also a significant mestizo and white contingent. The priority given to statistics on Afro-descendants is not quite matched in the Caribbean islands, since the theme, although not absent in regional debates, manifests itself differently from most Latin American countries. The national construction of these island-nations has rendered invisible the Afro-descendant presence within a discourse of miscegenation as a fundamental characteristic of the composition of their population and national culture. This is not the case in most of the Caribbean island-countries, or Belize, Suriname and Guyana where a national Afro-descendant elite played a key role in driving nation-building.

It is important to remember that the general figures on the demography of Afro-descendants are rough estimates because only a few countries include racial and ethnic variable in their censuses in a systematic way. In most cases, these are recent processes that, according to assessments, remain deficient and underreported. Within Latin America, Brazil stands out for having a consolidated tradition of ethnic-racial census statistics. For current estimates, other elements are used that allow an approximation, such as household surveys and specific initiatives by NGOs supported by cooperating institutions, and complemented by ethnographic studies (Del Popolo & Schkolnik, 2014).

The almost universal mechanism for plotting racial variables in censuses is self-identification. The long history of racial discrimination and exclusion is a factor that makes it difficult to generalize a positive ethno-racial consciousness. Furthermore, there are many terms of self-classification by colour/race in the region, such as *moreno*, mulatto, *morisco*, *cafuzos*, and others, terms that result from their invisibilization, but also from the existing historical process of mestizaje that makes standardization difficult. Along with other technical problems, these are determining factors of demographic under-registration (ECLAC, 2020 & Loveman, 2014).

It is likewise important to include information on Black women in Latin America. Black women's movements in the region seek to give visibility to data on the Black population according to sex/gender, in order to demonstrate their particular circumstances and the discrimination they experience. They also promote the dissemination of data on paid domestic work, since it is one of the most frequent professions of Black women.

The debate concerning the production of statistical data on Afro-descendants in Latin America is broad and involves a series of important discussions concerning, especially, how these populations are categorized. It was in light of this fact that members of the Project on Ethnicity and Race in Latin America (PERLA) concluded that the questions and categories used by censuses affected the racial/ethnic composition of a country and the extent of racial/ethnic inequality, recognizing that a particular classificatory method might be appropriate to explain some social phenomena better than others (Telles, 2017). Having considered that there was no single approach, they proposed exploring alternatives using PERLA surveys with multiple ways of measuring race and ethnicity, such as that which culminated in the use of colour palettes. The project chose to use respondents' colour identification, considering that in Latin America social disadvantage correlates with increasingly darker skin tones, and also that Latin Americans often assign greater value to people with lighter skin tones and less value to progressively darker people. The conclusion of the project is that skin colour tends to be a better predictor of racial/ethnic inequality than traditional racial/ethnic categories and that this is closely related to discrimination. Let us return to the Brazilian case in order to illustrate the complexity surrounding the theme.

Since 1872, Brazilian censuses have collected information on the race and ethnicity of the country's inhabitants. The appropriateness of taking these criteria into consideration, however, has regularly fuelled discussions within state institutions and Brazilian intellectual circles. The census became more complex with the beginnings of the debate over the implementation of affirmative action policies, especially racial quotas. While for Indigenous peoples, cultural categorisation is the main element for classification, for Afro-descendants the definition of skin colour takes the foreground.

The classification of the Black population in Brazil is defined in terms of race or, more specifically, colour, and not in cultural or linguistic terms. The way people categorise themselves according to their colour/race depends on the classification proposed in the censuses, which in turn is mainly dependent on how the state and its elites define the Black population and the space it occupies in Brazilian society (Igreja, 2018).

Three major classificatory systems referring to race/colour are used to categorize the Brazilian population in a continuum of colours ranging from 'white' to 'black'. The first is that of the Census, which has three categories: *branco* (white); *pardo* (brown), and *preto* (black), as we mentioned in the introduction of this book. The second is that of popular language, which uses multiple categories such as the category *Morena* (mestizo) The third, which is preferred by the Black Movement, adopts the *pardos* (brown) and *preto* (black) categories, resulting in a binary classification: blacks and whites, or non-whites and whites (Telles, 2003, p. 105). These systems obviously correspond to ways of interpreting the term race, and each reflects the ambiguity that surrounds these interpretations. In the same way, this system, especially the multiple forms of popular categorizations, has undergone changes in recent years in the face of the recognition of categories available in the censuses. In view of this, it is necessary to review the debate around the racial categories that are used by the censuses, even if briefly, as we will do below.

The distribution of the Brazilian population by race and ethnicity is based on a complex system. Earlier works by Oracy Nogueira (Nogueira, 1985) already explained that the classification of the Brazilian population based on race, or more precisely, skin colour, and not culture or language. The choice of the category 'skin colour' was justified by the author because, in Brazil, in contrast to the United States, the Black population and the discrimination of which it is victim is determined not by African or slave ancestry, but phenotype. This does not apply to Indigenous populations that are defined by belonging to an Indigenous community, speaking a native language, and who are therefore defined by cultural dimensions.

The Brazilian Institute of Geography and Statistics (IBGE) is a government agency that conducts decennial censuses and annual intercensal surveys – National Sample Survey of Households (PNAD) (except in the year of the census). The current census classification is still based on five categories *branco* (white); *pardo* (brown), and *preto* (black), yellow (people of Asian origin) and Indigenous. This last category aims to classify descendants of Japanese immigrants who arrived in Brazil in large numbers, especially at the beginning of the 20th century. Along a continuum of colour that goes from black to white, the category *pardo* (Brown) all the terms that define the mestizo in popular discourse. It would thus accommodate all those who, due to racial mixing, do not fit into the *preto* (black), Indigenous or white category. In this category we historically find both the mulatto, a term which classified mestizos of Black the white ancestry, and the *caboclo*, with a predominantly indigenous ancestry.

The racial identification method used by IBGE is based on self-identification of belonging to a racial group and on hetero-identification carried out by the interviewer. Identification through biological techniques, such as DNA analysis, is ruled out by the institution.

The first Brazilian census in 1872 already used three categories: black, mestizo and white, three categories that emerged from a widespread vocabulary used by the population to designate race or colour. There was also the category *caboclo*, for Indians, but this population was considered to be in a process of assimilation. Slaves could only be classified as *preto* (black) or *pardo* (brown) (Osório, 2003). According to this census, the Brazilian population of about 10 million was 37% white, 44% *pardo* (brown) and 19% black. The *pardo* (brown) category included a small number of *caboclos* (1.8%).

The second census, in 1890, a year after the abolition of slavery, registers the influence of European immigration, which increases the proportion of whites to 44% of the total population. In these first two censuses, the racial question seems natural and is not the subject of controversy. Although the intellectual and political elites were concerned with mestizaje and debated the place of the Afro-descendant population in nation-building, the silence surrounding the census was justified by its modest institutionalization and the lack of confidence in its procedure. The IBGE was only created in 1938 (Nobles, 2000).

The next censuses abandoned the category of 'race/colour' up until 1940. This decision was justified as such:

> ... the answers [conceal], in large part, the truth, particularly in regard to mestizos, who are very numerous throughout the States of Brazil, and typically those most refractory to the colour to which they belong ... and even individuals are not always able to declare their ascendency, considering that, in general, cross-breeding occurred during slavery or in a state of social degradation of the genetrix of the mestizo. Furthermore, the tonality of skin colour leaves much to be desired as a discriminating criterion, since it is an uncertain element... (Lamounier, 1976:18 quoted in Piza & Rosemberg, 1998, p. 125).

In 1940, a new census resumed the same categories used in 1890. The inclusion of skin colour in this census aimed the check on the consequences of European migration on Brazilian racial composition. Between 1940 and 1991, censuses revealed the mestizaje had evidently proceeded. The Brazilian population was not undergoing a process of "whitening", as some had hoped, but was instead becoming more mestizo, more *pardo* (brown) (Telles 2003, p. 61). During this time, the Black population was reduced from 15% to 5%, and the white population from 64% to 52%. During the same time, the *pardo* (brown) population increased from 21% to 43%, confirming that Brazil had become a predominantly mestizo country.

Paixão and Carvano (2008, p. 38) focus on the 1960 census, which also gathered data on skin colour. It faced a number of technical problems, which make it difficult to consider the census today. Nonetheless, as the authors stress, this census introduced important methodological and technological changes, including the fact that it was the first census to be processed electronically. They also observe that it was the first census to sample 25% of households, using questionnaires which included questions about race/colour. Yet, from this moment on, race only came to be investigated in the sampled households.

The 1970 census excluded questions on race/colour. The military dictatorship that had governed the country since 1964 emphasised the idea of a 'racial democracy', and forbade any social representation that contested it. The situation began to change, however, while the country was still governed by the military dictatorship, in the end of the 1970s, with the emergence of the Black Movement and its condemnation of the idea of racial democracy and struggle against political oppression. In this context, a rhetoric on the defence of a Black identity and culture emerged, strengthened by exiled Black politicians who were returning to the country, particularly after political amnesty in 1979. The category of 'race' reappears in 1976, though not in a census questionnaire, but in the PNAD.

The 1980 census included racial classification, resuming the same directives of the 1960 census (Paixão & Carvano 2008, p. 38). Pressure mounted on the 1991 census with the popular campaign "Não deixe a sua cor passar em branco, responda com bom c/senso" (Don't whitewash colour, use your common sens(us)), supported by members of the Black Movement. This campaign aimed to question the IBGE on the categories which were featured in the census – white, *preto (black), pardo* (brown)" – demanding the inclusion of the category "negro" (black), which would include *pardo* (brown) and *preto* (black); and, at the same time, to encourage Afro-descendants to declare their colour by reaffirming their racial identity. Pressure from a number of groups, including intellectuals, also sought to influence the development of the 2000 census, but the IBGE refused to replace both categories by the category of 'negro'. It should be noted that, in the censuses held between 1960 and 2000, the *pardo* (brown) category was used to classify everyone who was not 'white', 'yellow (people of Asian origin)', or *preto* (black).

Brazilians use a range of terms to define their colour. Schwartzman (1999) approached the issue in his research, referring to the Monthly Employment Research (PME) carried out in July of 1998 as preliminary data for the 2000 census, which included over 100 different possible answers in reply to questions of skin colour or race. *Morena* was the preferred to *pardo* (brown) to designate mestizos. However, most of the population resorts to a much more restricted set of options, and it is within this set that censuses seek to base future research. This is corroborated by the Research on the Ethno-Racial Characteristics of the Population – PCERP (2008)[59] which shows a significant reduction in the number of terms of racial identification used by the population.

The 1998 research included "origin" as a census category. Its use was considered unnecessary, since most people considered themselves to be "Brazilian", few opting for other national origins. The term "Afro-descendant" was thus not up for discussion. Indeed, only about 1.5% of answers indicated an African origin, and it was chosen by 2.1% of interviewees (Osório, 2003)[60].

The 2000 census data reveal a marked shift in the distribution of racial categories. The population was registered at 38.9% *pardo* (brown), 6.1% *pretos* (black) and the number of whites grew significantly, to 53.4%. A possible explanation for this shift is a polarization in the categories of "white" and "black" in a time of intense debate on race and when affirmative action policies were being discussed. The percentage of Indigenous people, in turn, almost doubled due to the expansion of data gathering in Amazonia. Disinhibition in self-identifying as 'Indigenous' also contributed to this growth.

Despite the term Afro-descendant being adopted for Latin America and the Caribbean as of the 3rd World Conference in Durban, in Brazil the negro (Black) category was preferred (Igreja & Agudelo 2014; Igreja 2018). Although the term "negro" was once considered pejorative, it came to be seen positively in political rhetoric, particularly through the strengthening of the Black Movement (in Portuguese the *Movimento. Negro*), and the emergence of the MNU in 1978. The use of the term 'negro' sought to underscore the recognition of racial identity and to further racial consciousness. Movements such as the Black Panthers, with their motto "Black is Beautiful", originating in the United States, helped to re-signify this term. The term furthermore took on a special significance as an umbrella term which included both "*pardo* (brown)" and "*preto* (black)", which, together, would account for the colour of more than half of the Brazilian population.

As for the *pardo* (brown) category, its dilution, along with the *preto* (black) category, in the make-up of the Brazilian "Negro" (black) population raises various critiques, emanating from different perspectives. Initially, at the dawn of the debate on affirmative action in Brazil, the *pardo* (brown) category was criticised because of the preference of the *Morena* category as more adequate for the country. Although commonly used, *Morena* can be used to describe all sorts of physical types, including whites with black hair. This tone was believed to represent

---

59 https://biblioteca.ibge.gov.br/visualizacao/instrumentos_de_coleta/doc2789.pdf
60 The question regarding origin allowed for more than one choice, which means that the set of answers is greater than that of the number of people interviewed (Osório, 2003).

the ideal of Brazilian racial ideology, which aims towards goals such as mestizaje and whitening. *Morena* emerged as an ambiguous colour, unable to provide finer precision on the social situation of *pardos* (brown) and *pretos* (Blacks) (Osório, 2003, p. 31 & Silva, N.V.1999, p. 87). Even if the *pardo* (brown) category is a chimera, which is able to include anything, as noted by the technical coordinator of the 1991 census (quoted in Silva, N.V., 1999), its replacement by *Morena* was seen, by critics, as disadvantageous.

At the same time, in seeking to include different mestizo categories, pardo (brown) included a diverse population. This category might include, for instance, Indigenous people without any recognized ethnic identity, particularly those who live in urban contexts, de-indianized Indigenous peoples to use the terminology of Bonfil Batalla (1987) in his book *Deep Mexico*, as a designation for the nonrecognition of Indigenous identities; or traditional regional populations such as those from the Northeast of Brazil who, for historical and cultural reasons, are victims to a specific form of discrimination. The struggle for having their specific identities recognized, or against the specificities of the discrimination that they suffer, was made invisible and subordinated to a racial identity, such as *negro* (Black). We will encounter this debate again when we turn to the discussion surrounding racial quotas in Brazil.

The last census took place in 2010, as the 2020 census was cancelled because of the global pandemic. The 2010 census was innovative for having introduced the matter of colour/race in the universal questionnaire, while in the three previous censuses (1980, 1991, 2000) it only featured in the associated sample. The five categories are maintained: *branco* (white); *pardo* (brown), and *preto* (black), yellow (people of Asian origin) and Indigenous. It should be recalled the Brazilian Institute of Geography and Statistics is also responsible for the PNAD, an annual ongoing survey of the general characteristics of the population, such as levels of education, social category, employment, and residence type.

The 2010 census showed that 91 million Brazilian residents are white, which is equivalent to 47% of the population. 82 million people declare themselves to be *pardo* (brown), which is 43.1% of the population. 15 million people (7.6%) say that they are *preto (black)*, 2 million that they are yellow and 817 thousand Indigenous. The proportion of Blacks and whites in Brazil varies significantly according to region. In particular, Blacks are numerous in the Northeast, Whites in the South, and Indigenous people in Amazonia.

In efforts to better define the categories, and to add greater precision to racial classification, the use of self-identification alongside hetero-identification has been seen to be a reliable method. However, despite the training that interviewers undergo, their classification, as external observers, does not seem to be

Table 1: Ethnicity and/or colour/race by Brazilian demographic census year

Ethnicity and/or colour/race by Brazilian demographic census year								
1872	1890	1940	1950	1960	1980	1991	2000	2010
Freemen Slaves								
White	White	White	White	White	White	White	White	White
Preto (black)	*Preto* (Black)	*Preto* (Black)	*Preto* (Black)	*Preto* (Black)	*Preto* (Black)	*Preto* (Black)	*Preto* (Black)	*Preto* (Black)
Pardo (brown)	Mestizo	*Pardo* (brown)	*Pardo* (brown)	*Pardo* (brown)	*Pardo* (brown)	*Pardo* (brown)	*Pardo* (brown)	*Pardo* (brown)
Cabocla	Cabocla (indigenous)	Yellow (Asian origin)	Yellow (Asian origin)	Yellow (Asian origin)	Yellow (Asian origin)	Yellow (Asian origin)	Yellow (Asian origin)	Yellow (Asian origin)
						Indigenous	Indigenous	Indigenous

Source: Características Étnico-raciais da população: um estudo das categorias de classificação de cor ou raça 2008; IBGE, Brazil. (https://biblioteca.ibge.gov.br/visualizacao/livros/liv49891.pdf). Table re-elaborated by the authors.

any more objective that the self-identification of the interviewee (Osório, 2003, 2013). The largest areas of concern are the elements that can change the racial identification of people, particularly the socioeconomic conditions of the interviewee. These comparisons, in general, show a high degree of correlation between the two. Invariably, the colour on which there is most agreement between interviewers and interviewees is 'white', and the one with less fit is *pardo* (brown). This is to be expected, since, as Guerreiro Osório (2003) notes, interviewers and interviewees largely share the same views on race, and how it is intimately linked to social conditions, which involve elements such as social status, education, and even gender and region of Brazil.

It is interesting to note that the arrow of disequilibrium tends toward the whitening of interviewees by interviewers. As Guerreiro Osório (2003, p. 17) argues, this may be a concession of the interviewers to the interviewees, in a country that values white skin colour. Referring to the studies of Oracy Nogueira, authors such as Osório (2003) and Telles (2003, p. 115) show that interviewers, buttressed by an "etiquette of social relations", were often embarrassed to ask after a person's race or t classify them as 'Black', particularly if interviewees were of a higher social level, which often led the interviewer to answer the question on the interviewee's behalf. Latter research shows an important increase in the number of people classified as 'Black', a decrease in the category of *Morena*, and that the self-identification of interviewees still tends to accord with the classification of the interviewer (Osório 2013).

At any rate, even if social status, gender, and age can interfere in how interviewers classify interviewees, a typical Black person, according to Telles, will not be classified into any other category, as may occur with *pardo* (brown) people, particularly those whose tonality is closer to white skin colour. The Brazilian region in which the census is carried out must also be take into account, since racial classification tends to differ across regions, particularly in what concerns the proportion of people classified as black or white (Telles, 2003, p. 130).

Multiculturalist policies, identity politics, and/or racial equality?

Discussions of race and ethnicity as fundamental categories of rights and public policies extends into the debate on which policies are to be applied, according to distinct ethnic and racial groups. In *Multicultural Citizenship*, Kymlicka (1996) distinguishes between the different types of cultural pluralisms that can be found in western societies. In one case, cultural difference results from the incorporation of cultures that were formerly self-governing and territorially concentrated within a larger state. These are *national minorities* who affirm their desire to continue existing as societies distinct from the majority society of which they are a part, and which therefore demand diverse types of autonomy of self-government. In the other case, cultural diversity results from the immigration of families or individuals. Migrants tend to form associations and, thus, to constitute themselves as *ethnic groups*. These groups, in general, are said to seek to integrate themselves into the societies of which they are a part.

Kymlicka related certain differentiated rights to ethnic groups or national minorities: rights to self-government (delegation of power to national minorities, for example through a form of federalism), poly-ethnic rights (rights that help groups express their cultural specificity without inhibiting access to economic and political institutions; acting, on the contrary, to promote their integration), and special rights of representation (creation of specific offices for representatives of ethnic or national groups within the central institutions of the state). These rights further the promotion of multicultural citizenship, with the aim of integrating all ethnic minorities within the dominant society of the state of which they are a part. Kymlicka's analysis omits a more in-depth study on the matter of Afro-descendants in the Americas, on the Black diaspora, on the enslavement and forced migration of these populations. His analysis is based on cultural diversity, paying scant attention to racism and race as the basis of a system of classification.

The Human Development Report: Cultural Liberty in Today's Diverse World, produced by the United Nations Development Programme in 2004 (UNDP, 2004)[61], incorporated multiculturalist proposals, widening them to include the recognition of the cultural diversity of countries as fundamental to the promotion of human development. According to the report, human development and in particular the eradication of poverty can only be promoted once the various countries face up to the challenge of constructing societies that respect and integrate their cultural diversity. Taking into account the fact that almost all countries in the world are multicultural – that is, that they are internally heterogenous – the Report recommends the elaboration of multicultural policies on a global scale, as an intrinsic need of the current globalization moment and the construction of a multicultural democracy. These are, the Report proclaims, the only actions that can promote respect and the protection of diversity and pluralism, under threat by the process of globalization.

---

[61] See: https://www.un-ilibrary.org/content/books/9789210576932#:~:text=Cultural%20Liberty%20in%20Today's%20Diverse%20World%20argues%20that%20states%20must,%E2%80%93%20religious%2C%20ethnic%20and%20linguistic.

The report consolidates, particularly at the international level, the recognition of ethnic identities as constitutive of new political and social actors; consequently, ethnicity is placed at the centre of debates on the formulation of public policies in various countries. More specifically, the Report outlines the sorts of policies that should be implemented to rectify inequalities between peoples and to promote cultural diversity. These are: Policies for ensuring the political participation of diverse cultural groups; Policies on religion and religious practice; Policies on customary law and legal pluralism; Policies on the use of multiple languages; Policies for redressing socio-economic exclusion.

Among the latter policies for redressing socio-economic exclusion, the Report also includes the recognition of the territorial demands of traditional, autochthonous, societies, such as Indigenous peoples, in respect of Indigenous and Tribal Peoples Convention n° 169 of the ILO (1989). Furthermore, it appeals for measures that protect the redressing of inequalities between minorities. Lastly, it recommends the introduction of affirmative action – measures which are not considered to be "multiculturalist". Affirmative actions are defined as public policies that seek to redress social inequality between distinct groups. They can assume various forms, such as the establishment of specific quotas for members of these groups. Examples of how these measures were applied in countries such as India, Malaysia, and the United States are used to demonstrate their benefits for redressing inequalities between different groups in these societies, although they did not result in changes in social inequalities of income between members of the discriminated groups. Affirmative action, defined as public policy to reduce group inequalities, takes different forms. In South Africa over the past decade and Malaysia over the past three decades, affirmative action has increased the designated groups' representation in the elite and middle classes, but progress has not prevented increasing inequality between rich and poor, both within the formerly disadvantaged groups, as well as generally throughout society (UNDP, 2004, p. 9).

In a more recent report, produced by the World Bank, 'Afro-Descendants in Latin America: Toward a Framework of Inclusion'[62], a similar model for analysing policies for the Afro-descendant population in Latin America is taken into account, although they are no longer presented as being 'multicultural' (Freire, G. et al., 2018). The report identifies the following as ethno-racial policies in Latin America (Freire, G. et al., 2018, p. 26).

---

62 See: https://openknowledge.worldbank.org/handle/10986/30201

Table 2: Ethno-racial policies implemented in the region

	Ethno-policies	Policies of racial equality	Territorial Development
Referent International Frameworks	ILO Indigenous and Tribal Peoples Convention, 1989 (No.169)	Committee on the Elimination of Racial Discrimination, Durban Programme of Action	Intersectoral policies and agreements
Dominant discourse	Ethnicity, right to difference	Race, right to equal treatment	Development of lagging regions
Target Population	Rural Afro-descendant communities, enclaves, and Afro-Indigenous minorities	General Afro-descendant population facing structural disadvantages	Afro-descendants living in lagging regions
Type of reforms promoted	Protection and promotion of collective rights	Policies of social inclusion and equal treatment	Multisectoral development
Examples of policies promoted	Territorial rights, political autonomy, community-driven development, ethno-education, consultation, and consent in decision making (inclusion of free, prior, and informed consent), cultural recognition, recovery and protection of historical memory, safeguards from development, protection of traditional livelihoods, political quotas for representation, etc.	Affirmative action in education and labor, political engagement and representation, revalorisation of Afro-descendant contributions to society, awareness raising, enforcement of antiracist legislation, statistical visibility, access to justice, crime and violence prevention	Development of infrastructure, inclusion in national education and health systems, connection to markets, housing, etc. (policies aimed at better integrating lagging regions irrespective of race.

Source: World Bank Report 'Afro-Descendants in Latin America: Toward a Framework of Inclusion. Washington, DC: World Bank License: Creative Commons Attribution CC BY 3.0 IGO. (Freire et al. 2018: 26)

The multiculturalist turn in Latin America began in the 1980s through a series of legislative and political changes que foram se consolidando pouco a pouco em políticas focalizadas no âmbito da luta contra as desigualdades sociais. Indeed, more recent human development reports are written with different wording from the 2004 Report. No longer is there a recommendation for creating a multiculturalist democracy; in its place we find an extensive analysis of social inequalities, scaffolded by a new bibliography on the theme and its transversalities (UNDP, 2019[63]). The focus is on the promotion of equality and inclusion. Furthermore, it introduces discussions around climate change and the Anthropocene, incorporating more current debates (UNDP, 2019, UNDP, 2020[64]). There is evidently an ongoing effort on the part of international agencies to remain up to date, and to appropriate new debates that emerge within the social sciences.

In this landscape of changes, a number of scathing criticisms emerge, proclaiming the end of multiculturalism as a political proposal. We are witnessing its demise. At present we find that many of the laws and policies of recognition that were announced have never been put into practice. On the contrary, Indigenous and Afro-descendant populations in Latin America have watched the increasing invasion of their lands, backed by capitalist interests and large multinational mining and energy conglomerates, accompanied by growing social inequality and an increase in the discrimination and racism to which these populations have always been subjected. Multiculturalism, it seems, was appropriated by neoliberalism and has lost any possibility of being put into practice (Hale, 2020).

But which multiculturalism are we referring to? When we speak of a "multicultural turn" we are not only speaking of State policies, of norms of institutionalized rights and their limits. We can widen the analysis to a "multicultural framework" which constitutes a context of interactions that have developed since the 1990s, involving various dynamics: the commemorations of the 500 years of 'discovery' in 1992, the UNESCO Slave Route Project, the pre-conference of Santiago and the Durban Conference in 2000, the new national constitutions, territorial rights, the new discussions on affirmative action (even if they are considered to be policies for integration and equality), the multiplication and visibility of social, cultural, and academic leaderships, the collective experiences that, manifest socio-economic, environmental and political demands, whether these are organized by Afro-descendant movements or in alliances with the aspirations of other populations. Within this framework, individual or collective leadership and activism was situated in all points of the political spectrum. We see openly left-wing alignments, such as those of ARAAC, as well as those in tune with positions on the political right, and even those which defend a more eclectic posture. This variety of positions, and the diversity of protagonists that they imply, is what we situate in the field of the struggles and dynamics that make the "multicultural turn" a possibility. The contemporary dynamic of anti-

---

63   See: http://report2019.archive.s3-website-us-east-1.amazonaws.com
64   See: http://hdr.undp.org/en/2020-report

racist struggles, and the far-right offensive that strikes, precisely, at the recognition of diversity and the rights of minorities, is also made viable by the accumulation of political and organizational possibilities that were constructed within this multicultural context (Hooker, 2020).

Defence strategies against racism, but also the struggle against the limits of multicultural policies, or against the non-observation of recognized rights, or even the revolutionary structural transformations, all start from the ground gained by legal benchmarks that foster legitimacy and the possibilities for action. For these reasons, we are wary of the "prediction" that multiculturalism is reaching its demise (Hale, 2020). Hale himself affirms that:

> This does not mean an abandonment of legal struggle or of other efforts to defend multicultural rights achieved, but it does point to a marked change in emphasis, or perhaps a newly emphasized articulating principle of struggle: more-forceful refusal of political solutions garnered from dominant institutions, greater impetus for self-determined bases of political-economic power. (Hale, 2020 p. 623).

In fact, what we observe in the in the activism currently being implemented by Afro-descendant movements is the ratification of the demands of states and multilateral organizations to put into practice the multicultural rights that have been recognized, particularly those enshrined in international conventions but never realized. We here resume our discussion of multiculturalism as a wide historical-political process that marked the end of the 20th century, and which is not only circumscribed by a public-policy model.

We return, however, to the debate on policies targeting Afro-descendant populations, seeking to identify how reports, and the different public sectors and strands of civil society, differentiate between policies that are multiculturalist, ethno-cultural, and those that further racial equality. It is important to stress how this set of actions likewise takes on an air of "identity politics" by demanding an ethnic and/or racial identity to those who would benefit from them[65]. The case of Brazilian racial relations turns out to be very indicative.

---

[65] It is in this sense that authors such as Michel Wieviorka (2001) assert that a policy directed at a segment of the population, whichever segment, needs to establish a clear and stable definition for it, which will allow it to be identified, its boundaries to be recognized, and what is, and is not, specific about this particular segment of the population. It must necessarily rest on a categorization. Wieviorka thus arrives at the central questions of the debate, particularly when he approaches multiculturalism: Is it desirable for the state to act on the basis of categorizations based on cultural distinctions? Is it desirable for the state to continue to intervene as a producer of cultural categorizations?

Multiculturalism is rejected, as a political model which presupposes the recognition and protection, in the public sphere, of different socio-cultural groups, through legislation and specific institutional instances. In its place, official discourse, propounded by Brazilian militants and academics, shifted its focus to the promotion of laws and policies of "racial equality", which were seen to be more adaptable to the Brazilian racial context. These actions would be accompanied by ethno-cultural legislation and policies, as well as those of territorial recognition, a terminological proposal that would later be present in the 2018 World Bank report.

Tianna Paschel (2016), resuming the distinctions between different public policy proposals, helps us to understand this fact. The author acknowledges that, initially, after the Durban Conference, discussions centred around the cultural and territorial recognition of Black populations, drawing them closer to the demands of Indigenous people, and that new policies veered towards the language of equality and inclusion. By comparing Brazil and Colombia, she observed that this sets a new path, following the beginning of multicultural policies, which is more closely aligned with Black organizations in urban settings. At the same time, she also stresses that these new policies of racial equality remained remarkably limited in their capacity to attend to all of the historical demands of organizations linked to the Black movement in every country. Nonetheless, they amount to the institutionalization of a Black political subject that is defined not exclusively by culture, but also through his or her experiences with systematic discrimination and disadvantage. Paschel defines this phenomenon as a new moment in, or an amplification of, a rhetoric of ethno-racial policies in Latin America from 2000–2010: the alignment of racial equality.

According to Paschel, as we will see shortly when we turn to affirmative actions in Brazil, at first the territorial question of quilombo communities was the focus of Black associations in the country. However, gradually, the agenda of the Black movement shifted back toward the struggle for racial equality, as it had done in former times, in favour of quotas and against discrimination and racism. This change is related to the victories obtained with the Brazilian state, particularly legislation for establishing affirmative action throughout the country.

We agree with Paschel that policy differences in Brazil and Colombia have to do, most of all, with how the movements in each country politicized the theme, whether the populations were mostly rural or urban, and their role in the construction of the nation state. In this sense, academic knowledge on Black populations in Colombia contributed to an image of a rural and culturally distinct negritude, while in contemporary Brazil they produced an image of an urban negritude, defined by common experiences of inequality and discrimination[66].

Thus, in order to situate multicultural and affirmative action policies, we must go back to their very definition. In a general sense, we may define affirmative action as public or private policy which aims to confer specific resources or rights to members of disadvantaged social groups, typically referred to the classificatory and delimiting dimensions of ethnicity, race, social class, gender, religion, caste, among others (Feres Júnior, 2018, p. 16). Its implementation can extend to different social domains, such as access to education, culture, health and employment. It can also be geared towards the promotion of cultural recognition and the anti-racist struggle (Feres Júnior et al., 2018; Igreja, 2005). In this way, it is understood to be an instrument of struggle against racism, and as a reparation for suffering inflicted on the populations which are victims of discrimination.

Beyond this general definition, and in agreement with Daniel Sabbagh (2004),)[67], affirmative action policies differ significantly from country to country, in relation to the identity of those who benefit from them, the form that programmes take (e.g. quota/no quota), the level of the legal norms from which they derive (constitutional, legislative, administrative), and the domains to which they apply. Following Sabbagh classification, in what pertains to the first of these parameters, the most common categories are ethnic, racial, national origin, and other minorities considered to be economically or socially disadvantaged, such as women, people with special needs, among others. The requirements and the legal bases for implementing affirmative action programmes also vary between countries. Thus, we have on the one hand, cases such as that of Malaysia, referenced by the author, of the Brazilian case, which we deal with in this book, in which quotes or reserved places are obligatory; or, on the other hand, goals and schedules for meeting them, as with North American policies. They can also be distinguished in terms of their field of application, which can cover the public sphere as much as the private. Finally, they can be structured as a reserve of positions programmed in different parliaments or legislatures, as well as usually as quotas in the educational system or the labour market. To Daniel Sabbagh, it is not surprising that the widest and most radical affirmative action is found in countries were the disadvantaged groups that benefit from these policies make up a majority of the population, such as

---

[66] The social science literature on Afro-Colombians clearly expresses this Black/rural/cultural alterity bias. For a review see Restrepo (2008); for a critical analysis see Agudelo (2004).
[67] This study by Daniel Sabbagh was presented as an 'occasional paper' which supported the elaboration of the Human Development Report Office Background Paper for HDR 2004, accessed via: http://hdr.undp.org/sites/default/files/hdr2004_daniel_sabbagh.pdf

in Malaysia and South Africa and, we may include, Brazil. Affirmative action are focalized policies, meant to redress exclusion and the discrimination of disadvantaged minorities, but, as in Brazil, they are aimed at Blacks, who are a Minoritized Majority (SANTOS, 2020).

Although India is a pioneer in the implementation of these policies, it is the example of the United States that serves as a reference for the Latin American debate. Claimed in the Civil Rights Movement, affirmative action was considered as a counterpoint to the 'colour-blind' paradigm, the latter based on an abstract individualism, blind to ethno-racial differences, based mostly on an idea of meritocracy that renders discrimination, and the racism and social exclusion of African Americans, invisible (Skrentny, 1996, p. 7). In this sense, they function as insurance of an effectively equal treatment through the consideration and inclusion of representative of excluded minorities. In principle, they do not imply in cultural recognition or in the racial consciousness of African Americans, since it is a policy that integrates representatives of these groups in spaces form which they had largely been excluded, particularly in the workplace[68]. Yet, in the context of the discussion of multiculturalism, affirmative action begins to take on a different format.

In their analysis of affirmative action for African Americans in the United States, Feres Júnior et al. (2018, p. 31) seek to demonstrate this evolution through three arguments that justify affirmative action: reparation, distributive justice, and diversity. If, at first, during the Lyndon B. Johnson administration in the early 1960s, their foundation was the demand for reparations due to historical discrimination and the desire for social justice, this changed in the context of Executive Order 10.925, dating from the John F. Kennedy administration in 1961, and the Civil Rights Act of 1964, in which only the issue of social justice was present, applied to different groups that suffered discrimination. The justification for reparation thus loses out as a rhetoric of social justice comes to be adapted to 'welfare state' politics and market interests. With the resurgence of neoliberalism in the Ronald Reagan government, it is the idea of social justice itself that will be eroded, restricting further affirmative action policies and creating the terrain for a rhetoric of diversity within the context of multiculturalism. According to Feres

---

[68] Like other authors, Wieviorka (2001, p. 90) claims that affirmative action should be understood within the context of social inclusion, of integrating groups that, by virtue of race or gender, are discriminated. These policies do not, of themselves, carry with them cultural recognition. It is evident, the author continues, that the social should not be dissociated from the cultural. However, affirmative policy aims to ensure equality of opportunity or egalitarian redistribution to members of groups that are victims of social injustice, without being concerned with the impact of this redistribution on the cultures of these groups.

Júnior et al., the promotion of diversity comes to be seen as a virtue not only for discriminated groups, but for society in general, which has much to gain by promoting cultural, ethnic, and racial diversity in different domains, such as education and the workplace.

Social justice and diversity are debated ideas in multiculturalism, as are recognition and redistribution, which we have mentioned previously. The theoretical reference for the theme of social justice within the sphere of affirmative action has often been the work of John Rawls (1971). As Thomas Nagel (2003) explains, although Rawls never directly discussed affirmative action, his ideas are related to the theme, particularly his views on the equalization of opportunities and the promotion of equity. Nagel (2003, p. 84) explains that, in Rawls's terms, the injustices that affirmative action seeks to rectify is a particular example of the failure of equality of opportunities. However, in consonance with Feres Júnior et al (2018), Nagel notes that the focus on promoting diversity benefits a wide array of groups, and not only those defined in ethno-racial terms. They thus minimize the main aim of affirmative actions for African Americans: to overcome the ongoing stratification of US society along racial lines, using education as a means for bring Blacks into the dominant economic, professional and political spaces.

Historical reparation, social justice, and diversity will be fundamental themes in discussions on the implementation of affirmative actions. They also feature in the context of the "multicultural turn" in Latin America, being appropriated as an alternative, and often complementary, policies to the multicultural policies aimed at the Indigenous and Afro-descendant population. It should be stressed that, in this context of defining adequate policies, and discussing the role of the minorities and majorities that will benefit from affirmative and multiculturalist actions, one fact stands out: to be effective, such policies need to define their target-populations. In the history of debates surrounding affirmative action, this has been the main theme of discussion: who is Black and/or Afro-descendant in Latin American countries? An analysis of affirmative action in Brazil will allow us to probe this discussion.

The Latin American multicultural turn, new constitution and reclaiming the debate on colour/race in Brazil

As in other Latin American countries, the struggles for recognizing the rights of Indigenous peoples and Blacks in Brazil gained ground during the process of drafting the new Constitution of 1988 (Brazil Constitution, 1988). The period between 1985 and 1995 was one of rebuilding the nation after years of military dictatorship. It was also the time to convene the National Constituent Assembly to draft a new Constitution more attuned to the new democratic winds that were blowing throughout the country. This period opened doors for the discussion of actions aimed at eliminating the historic inequalities between Blacks and whites and combating the discrimination and racism present in the country. These actions emerged in response to the demands of social movements, especially the Black movement, and gained momentum during the period of the country's re-democratization.

Briefly, we can, as an example, refer to the process of conferring heritage status on the Serra da Barriga, on 31 January 1986, as recognition of its historical value. This is the site where the Palmares Quilombo was established. This act was complemented by two decrees in 1988, one making Serra da Barriga into a National Monument and the other expropriating more than two hundred hectares for anthropological and archaeological studies and for the reforestation of natural areas (Decree nº 95,855, 1988; Decree nº 96.038, 1988).

In 1987, the government of President José Sarney installed a Centenary Commission to start preparing for commemorative activities related to the abolition of slavery. This was the start of the National Program for the Centenary of the Abolition (PROCEM)), the embryo of what was to later become the Palmares Foundation. In 1988 "abolition" was discussed as part of the national conjuncture; in counterpoint to the official activities, the Black Movement took to the streets to mobilize society and protest.

The official commemorations of the Centenary of the Abolition of Slavery sought to stress the contributions of Afro-descendants to Brazilian art and culture, and to promote Brazil as the country of racial democracy, of harmony among all races. But the Black Movement used the opportunity to denounce the myth of racial democracy by demonstrating against the overall conditions of the Black population in Brazil and condemning racism and racial discrimination. The centenary celebrations were an opportunity to confront the Brazilian state, to demand measures that improved the lives of the Black population. The 13th of May, the date in which the abolition of slavery in Brazil was commemorated, was itself criticised by Black movements, who preferred to establish November 20th, the Day of Black Consciousness, as the new Day of Black Pride.

At various moments throughout 1988, Black activists were present. It was a very complex time, and the discussion of race was one among the many that were part of this moment of political openness. Black mobilization was diverse, including, for example, the militancy of the Zumbi Memorial[69], with the aim of

---

69 The Zumbi Memorial, founded in 1980, gathered intellectuals, community organizations,

consolidating the Black Movement's proposal to celebrate November 20 as the National Day of Black Consciousness[70]. From the articulation between the Zumbi Memorial and the Commission for the Centennial of the Abolition of Slavery within the Ministry of Culture, the Palmares Cultural Foundation (FCP) would be born (Law 7,666, 1988).

The new Constitution would also bring about important transformations in anti-racist legislation. In the 1986 elections, Black representation in the National Congress was already greater than before, and the 1987 Constituent Assembly included Black parliamentarians such as Benedita da Silva, Carlos Alberto de Oliveira Caó and Paulo Paim. It is important to note the participation of Black intellectuals and activists in the debates of the 1987 Constituent Assembly, especially in the "Sub-committee on Blacks, Indigenous Populations, Disabled Persons and Minorities", part of the 6th Commission on Social Order. Among these intellectuals, Lélia Gonzalez sought to emphasize the role of Blacks in Brazilian society, marked by a social hierarchy that marginalizes the Black population, especially Black women, and that devalues the cultural contribution of this population (Garrido, 2018). Lélia Gonzalez shared with other Black intellectuals, such as Abdias Nascimento, Joel Rufino, Beatriz Nascimento, as well as antiracist whites, such as Florestan Fernandes and Octavio Ianni, the idea that the only way to overcome racism was to overcome the myth of racial democracy, and that it was important to establish of a true political democracy in the country (Rios & Lima, 2020, p. 12).

Although many demands of the Black population were lost in the parliamentary debates (Pires, T. R. O., 2013; Santos, N.N.S., 2015), the new Constitution finally pronounced itself in defence of respect for the country's cultural diversity, recognizing popular contributions and manifestations, including those of Blacks and Indigenous peoples (Art. 215, §1º), defined racism as a non-bailable and indefeasible crime (Art. 5º, XLII), and recognized the definitive ownership of the land occupied by the descendants of former maroon communities, charging the state with granting their respective titles (Transitional Constitutional Provisions – Art. 68).

The Constitution innovated by abandoning a minimalist liberal normativity focused on merit, making inroads toward a more substantial and less procedural

---

and entities of the Black Movement from all of Brazil, as well as universities and other public agencies such as the Serviço Nacional do Patrimônio Histórico e Artístico Nacional (National Agency of Historical and Artistic Heritage, currently the National Historic and Artistic Heritage Institute – IPHAN) and the Federal University of Alagoas.

[70] It was only in 2011 that date was officially recognized as the National Day of Zumbi and Black Consciousness, by Law nº 12,519 (2011).

citizenship, one, therefore, more sensitive to the recognition of difference and affirmative discourse. It should be noted that, in what concerns the struggle against racism, the Black movement has historically relied on the law, particularly criminal law. In this way, we recall the importance of the "Afonso Arinos Law", already mentioned by us, which seen to be the most important law on the theme prior to the ratification of Convention n° 111 of the ILO (1960). The Law characterized the incitement of racial hatred or discrimination as crimes against national security (Law 6,620, 1978). In the civil area, the Public Civil Action Law (Law n° 7,347, 1985), which authorised the Public Ministry to propose public civil actions in defence of ethnic minorities, stands out.

Likewise, the Caó Law, Law n° 7.716 (1989), established new criminal types related to racial discrimination. It typified conduct involving the previous misdemeanours, but expanded and established higher penalties: imprisonment for three months or up to one year was changed to confinement in all cases, with minimum penalties of one to three years and maximum penalties of two to five years. This Law was modified by Laws 8.081(1990) and 8,882 (1994) and was then repealed by Law 9,459 (1997), which proposed an end to impunity. It is important to stress the relevant modification brought about by this law, with the revision of article 20, which promotes a more generic characterisation of the crime of racism, described as "to practice, induce or incite discrimination or prejudice based on race, colour, ethnicity, religion or national origin". The law also reinforced article 140 of the Criminal Code, introducing an aggravated form of insult (with a prison sentence of one to three years and a fine), when the insult consists of the use of elements related to race, colour, ethnicity, religion, origin, or the condition of elderly or disabled people (Machado, 2009). These changes did not curb the enormous difficulty in punishing racism, as these crimes were, in many cases, declassified as 'racial insult,' which carries a much lower penalty and is subject to prescription (Santos, G., 2015). Thus, many crimes prescribed before conviction. Recently, in November 2021, in the judgment of Habeas Corpus HC 154,248 (2022), the Brazilian Supreme Court equated the crime of racial slurs to that of racism, which nullified the issue of prescription. This equation aligns with the approval of the text of the Inter-American Convention against Racism, Racial Discrimination and Related Forms of Intolerance, adopted in Guatemala on the occasion of the 43rd Ordinary Session of the General Assembly of the Organization of American States on the 5th of June 2013[71]. It is a meaningful change in the approach to the crime of slander and libel, which had always

---

[71] The approval, through the Legislative Decree 1/2021, was published in the Official Journal of the Federal Senate on the 19th of February 2021.

been criticized for permitting exceptions to the crime of racism and was hence considered a victory for Black movements which had long denounced the lack of investigation of, and, particularly, punishment for crimes of racism.

What we thus see is that the anti-racist struggle was mainly focused on the symbolic role of the law, in its capacity to repress and finally punish racism. However, the diagnosis at the time was already that the laws were insufficient and ineffective, especially in the criminal field, as evidenced by the few convictions registered. This ineffectiveness is also generally explained by the lack of sensitivity or understanding of the dynamics and logic involved in these cases by the agents of the legal system (Machado, 2009). According to this view, other interpretations are adduced, related to the complexity of the treatment and identification of discriminatory acts based on race, colour or ethnicity, when such acts intersect with situations of discrimination and social segregation such as those existing in Brazilian society.

The establishment of the constituent assembly and the new Constitution which it produced enjoyed the close involvement of social movements and benefitted from the effervescence of the discussions on ethnic and racial diversity in the country which were ongoing at the time. The most important change was in official discourse, which shifted from defending racial democracy to recognizing the multicultural and multi-ethnic nature of the country. In addition, there was a change from the assimilationist perspective of previous years to a demand for recognition and affirmation of "Black" culture and identities as opposed to "Western" and "white" ones. The construction of a common Black racial/ethnic identity assumed a special focus. These were changes of perspective regarding how to combat racism, reinforced by the transnationalisation of the Black movement itself (Tavolaro &, Igreja, 2015, p. 450). We can claim that this was a multiculturalist moment in the debate, which was gradually giving way to another moment focusing on racial equality policies, which we will deal with below.

In this context, the Brazilian Black Movement (which we will return to shortly) sought to implement a new internal strategy, reordering its actions. Until 1991, the organizational process of the Black Movement generally established regional meetings: North/Northeast, South/Southeast and Centre-West. There were no defined criteria of representativeness (Santos de Paulo, 2002, p. 46). At the end of 1991, the 1st National Meeting of Black Entities (ENEN) was held in São Paulo. This was an innovation for the Black Movement, establishing criteria for definition, participation and representativeness of the entities that comprise it, in addition to promoting a profound revision of the movement's organisational bases and the definition of the criteria that made it explicit: the set of entities and groups, with a Black majority, that had the specific objective of combating racism and/or expressing cultural values of African origin and that were not linked to government or party structures.

After the 1st ENEN, a series of entities in the Black Movement attained national prominence: The Unified Black Movement itself, as well as the Black Pastoral Agents (APNs), the Black Union and Awareness Group (GRUCON), the Union of Blacks for Equality (UNEGRO). State-level entities, with different segments involved in mobilization and Black awareness and culture, also participated in local fora, including a range of entities linked to religions of African origin, such as the National Centre for the Articulation of Afro-Brazilian Religions (CENARAB). Finally, there are entities with different organizational structures which played a crucial role in widening the domain within which the Black movement could act by promoting the professionalization and specialization of actions, establishing a greater spectrum at the national and international level: the Centre for the Articulation of Marginalized Populations (CEAP/RJ), the Institute for the Black Woman (GELEDES), the Centre for the Study of Relations of Work and Inequality (CEERT/SP), Criola/RJ, Fala Preta! Black Women's Organization/SP, among others.

Other collective Black political expressions also emerged in the country. The National Coordination of Black Entities (CONEN), created in 1991, harboured other entities linked to political parties, churches, and international agencies. A number of NGOs worked in the field of education, culture, and the well-being of the Black population. The theme of quotas and reparations was, at the time, the subject of an ambiguous discussion in the entities that make up CONEN.

The existence of this agglomeration of Black entities raises the issue of whether initially there was one Black Movement or several in the country. This was a question posed by Lélia Gonzalez in a book co-authored with Carlos Hasenbalg, *Lugar do Negro* (Gonzalez & Hasenbalg, 1982). For the author, treating the Black Movement in a unitary manner makes analysis far too complex, since there are many variants which result from the different origins and experiences of Black people. As an explanation of these variants, her analysis includes the different cultural values brought by African peoples; the different responses to slavery, such as the quilombos revolutionary movements such as Malês, the brotherhoods, the mutual aid societies, etc., all of which would give rise to differentiated experiences. She also adds to these variations the different responses to distinct economic and political cycles, as well as the diversity of associative experiences and proposals, recalling that, since abolition, Blacks have been involved in various associations, called Black entities, split according to two alternatives: assimilationism and cultural practice. In the face of this diversity, can we speak of the Black movement in the singular?

> Of course, if we adopt the perspective delineated above, we cannot. Much as we would not be able to speak of a Woman's Movement, for example. Yet we do. Precisely because it points to that which differentiates it from all other movements, to wit, its specificity. But within this movement, the specificity of which is the signifier *Black*, there are more or less deep divergences concerning how this specificity is to be articulated (Gonzalez & Hasenbalg, 1982, p. 19)

We may adopt the concept of an organized Black movement from the perspective of Nilma Lino Gomes (2017, p. 22), for whom it is understood as a political subject, with its own historical trajectory, as well as being an integral player in the current context of the organization of social movements and a participant in the transnational articulation with other movements and non-governmental organizations in the struggle for the construction of a democratic society. Innovatively, the author considers the Black movement to be an educator due to its important role in producing emancipatory knowledge and systematizing knowledge concerning the racial issue in Brazil.

Many of the organisations that made up CONEN consisted, in fact, of specific NGOs linked to the racial issue. According to Heringer (2000, p. 344), in the 1990s Brazilian NGOs were undergoing a glorious period, encouraged by the re-democratization of the country, court victories, and the international experience obtained mainly in the wake of the cycle of UN conferences. At the same time, a crisis was unfolding with regard to the resources allocated to these institutions, which forced many of them to redefine their objectives.

On the political level, the activities of these NGOs were intertwined with the political activities of the Black Movement, with similar strategies of denunciation and intervention. Some stood out through the presentation of specific proposals in the field of public policies and legislation and more incisive action in forwarding questions to the Judiciary. Others promoted initiatives for access to education and insertion in the labour market, which, in some cases, were carried out through partnerships with private entities, city halls, universities, cooperatives, trade unions and others. It must be considered, however, that the NGOs located in the large urban centres were those with the greatest structure for such actions.

In the period after the constituent assembly, particularly during the 1990s, Black NGOs came to prominence, especially in relation to the Brazilian State and international organisations. Divided according to their specific focus, such as: the recovery and preservation of African cultural values; forms of religious expression that use the *terreiro* (Afro-Brazilian religious shrines) as the space of resistance *par excellence*; or even choices for political action and the anti-racist struggle based on the awareness of a particular racial identity, as resistance to a hegemonic Western culture that uproots Black people (Adesky, 2001, p. 157).

These differences are amplified when we take into account the regional division of the country and the various expressions of Black problems and resistance.

An important parcel of these NGOs was dedicated to the promotion and protection of Black women, based on a three-dimensional relationship that articulated race, class and gender. They differed from other feminist NGOs in their greater focus on the racial issue and discrimination, and they also differed from other Black organizations that did not consider the oppression of women to be on par with racial oppression. According to Edna Roland (2000, p. 251), against the conception of the idea that the Black feminist movement should organise itself autonomously, defining its own political agenda based on its political needs, there were sectors that urged it to tackle a specific issue while remaining part of the Black movement, and that it should therefore be subordinate its agenda. This discussion is carried into the movement, especially by women from more traditional Black movement organisations.

Sônia Beatriz dos Santos (2009, p. 277) states that Black women's organizations were not the only way Black women engaged in the collective struggle against oppression. Many black women are organised in neighbourhood associations, political parties, trade unions, cultural, artistic and literary groups, and religious organisations, such as those of African origin, Catholic Church pastorals, and even in some sectors of Protestant churches – for example the Methodist Church. Citing various authors, dos Santos (2009, p. 276) notes that we can point to the 1970s as the period in which Black women leveraged their organizational process and began to forge the basis for contemporary Black women's organizations, which had as one of its first expressions the organization of the Meeting of Black Women Aqualtune, in the city of Rio de Janeiro, in 1978, followed by the unprecedented creation of these organizations in the 1980s, 1990s and 2000s. The author also points out that prior to this movement of 1978, the historiography of Black women's movement records the existence of the national council of Black women, also founded in Rio de Janeiro.

Among the many organizations of Black women, it is worth drawing attention to the creation of NZINGA: The Black Women of Rio de Janeiro Collective. Established in 1983 as the first Black feminist organization, including figures such as Lélia Gonzalez, Jurema Batista, Sandra Bello, Rosalia de Oliveira Lemos, Elizabeth Viana, Jane Thomé, Miramar Correa, among others (Lemos, 2016). Rosalia de Oliveira Lemos claims that:

> what was at stake was the right to speak, to take part, and to make history with our own voices and hands. Black Brazilian women demanded to be allies in the struggle against racism, against sexism, against prejudice, and against the exploitation experienced by the women of the favelas and a repudiation of the normatization of sexual mores – for

when these aims were proclaimed by Black women they were considered neither important nor relevant, much less were they articulated to the specificities of the autodetermination of Black women (Lemos, 2016, p. 22).

Lélia Gonzalez was the first coordinator of Nzinga, a collective that emerged from "the need to build an autonomous group, free from a dependency on the Black movement" (Ratts &, Rios, 2021, p. 97). It is important to understand Lélia Gonzalez's thoughts on how class exploitation and racial discrimination constitute basic elements of the common struggle of men and women belonging to a subordinated ethnic group (Rios &, Lima, 2020, p. 200). In this sense, the Black women's movement would be an ally of the Black Movement. However, she highlights that economic crisis and the impacts of capitalism do not affect all social sectors equally. Quoting Virginia Vargas, she explains that it is by participating in the movement through its popular expression that African American and Amerindian women, who were concerned with the survival of the family, sought to organize themselves as a collectivity; and, at the same time, their presence in the informal labour market redirected them toward other demands. These women were most affected by the crises, considering their positions and the racial and sexual discrimination that they suffered, (Rios &, Lima, 2020, p. 200).

In her scholarly and activist career, Lélia Gonzalez sought to move beyond the role of Blacks in Brazilian society by understating them in the American context, conjugating their experiences with those of Blacks in the American diaspora with an eye toward building a Pan-African world. She innovated in her written work and speeches by contributing an anti-colonial proposal, critical to colonialism and eurocentrism, built from an Afro-centric position and elaborated on the diasporic experience and its commitment to break with imperialist colonialism (Santos, M. C. R. C. F., 2020). Gonzalez's political and cultural category of 'Amefricanity' restores a specific unity, historically forged within different societies that come-to-be in a particular part of the world. Therefore, Amefrica, as an ethno-geographical system of reference, is a creation of African ancestors in the American continent, inspired by African models. Therefore, the term 'Amefricans' designates descent: not only that of the Africans brought by the slave trade, but also of those who arrived in America long before Columbus (Gonzalez, 1988, p. 77). For Lélia Gonzalez, the Amefrican experience is different from that of Africans who remained on their continent. It is built on a history of suffering, humiliation, exploitation, ethnocide, and loss of identity, without thereby concealing processes of resistance and creativity in the struggles against slavery and racism.

Her influence across Latin America, the United States and Africa situates her within this transnational movement of Afro-descendant intellectuals and militants, and in the roster of Black intellectuals who have provided significant contributions to renewing Black Latin American thought. Lélia Gonzalez participated in various events and congresses in the United States alongside Abdias Nascimento. She was likewise in contact with Latin American intellectuals during several of her trips across the American continent, incorporating their Pan-Africanist ideas, as well as the perspective of "negritude" in her relationship with the French-speaking Caribbean. Lélia Gonzalez also followed the regional ethnic autonomy movement that was taking place in Nicaragua. From Africa, she is influenced by anti-colonialism, emanating from the contributions of Amilcar Cabral (Rios &, Lima, 2020, p. 10). For her, in addition to the similarities that united Amefricans from different parts of the Americas, including, of course, their African roots, they were brought together by another historical experience: racism (Santos, M. C. R. C. F., 2020).

> Although they belong to different societies in the continent, we know that the system of domination is the same in all of them, that is: racism, this cold and extreme elaboration of the Aryan model of explanation, which is a constant presence, in all levels of thought, as it is part and parcel of the most varied institutions of these societies (Gonzalez, 1988, p. 77).

In the same vein, Sueli Carneiro (2003), founder and director of Geledés – Instituto da Mulher Negra (The Black Woman's Institute), stands out as a Black Latin American intellectual and militant. Sueli Carneiro used the idea of "blackening feminism" to critique of the feminist movement, pointing toward a means of designating the trajectory of Black women within the Brazilian feminist movement. The author sought to, on the one hand, stress the white Western identity of the classical feminist formulation, and, on the other, to reveal the theoretical insufficiency and political practice required to integrate the different expressions of woman constructed in multi-racial and pluricultural societies. Her intention was to contribute to a specific agenda for Black feminism that would add gender inequalities to the anti-racist struggle.

Giving prominence to the historical processes of Black women's organization and resistance, Jurema Werneck (2009), co-founder of the Criola Organization and executive director of Amnesty International in Brazil, recuperated the figure of the *Ialodê* – originally a title of female leadership which, according to fragmentary historiographical records, existed in pre-colonial Yoruba cities – so as to indicate her links to public associations. The author assumed *Ialodê* as an interpetative key, a metaphor for leadership and self-government, shining a light on the capacity of agency-ing embedded in the ways that different Black women disputed, and still dispute, their role in different moments of political struggles.

> It is not a matter of providing, as a counterpoint to the patriarchal foundation myth or the bourgeois whiteness of feminism, another one that symbolises its radical opposite, that is, one that reiterates essentialisms and stereotypes with mixed signals. By proposing an interpretation from and through the ialodesis and the different identity repertoires that we use, what I intend to do is to show the contingent character of the patriarchal and racist account, naturalised and reiterated in the historiographies of culture, anti-racism and feminism. Mainly, I intend to put Black women and the impact of their action back in their place in the constitution of the Black diaspora. And, likewise, for disputes that are still ongoing, which may, even, have an impact on global culture (Werneck, 2009, p. 14).

The national organization of Black women gained momentum by participating in international conferences on women. They acquired a lot of social visibility within certain sectors, such as the government, international organisms, the media, and other social movements. However, according to Edna Roland (2000, p. 253), they were unable to process their internal differences in order to penetrate legitimate spaces of representation. Antagonisms have thus always been a part of the history of the Brazilian Black movement and, specifically, of the Black women's movement. In this specific context, the clash involved organisations that were constituted as NGOs, those that were more closely linked to the state and international organisations, and those that often considered themselves more independent.

By way of conclusion, the periods following the new Constitution were marked by new legislative and policy proposals for the Black population, accompanied by major demonstrations and resistance from Black entities. In his inaugural speech in 1995, President Fernando Henrique Cardoso announced his aim to energetically ensure equal rights among equals, including minorities and near-majorities – Blacks, mainly – who hoped that equality would be more than a word, the portrait of a reality. For the first time in Brazilian history, the president of the republic accepted the existence of racism in the country and the fallacy of Brazilian racial democracy.

In the first year of the Fernando Henrique Cardoso administration, which was also the year in which the Tricentennial of Zumbi dos Palmares was commemorated, the Black Movement held the "Zumbi dos Palmares March Against Racism, for Citizenship and Life" on the 20th of November – an event which became an important landmark for the new political strategies that would be assumed by the Movement. This year was marked by various meetings, seminars, festivals, public acts, and national and international congresses throughout the country that dealt with the racial issue, many of them stimulated by the federal government. It was this effervescence which made the March possible, and which generated great expectation among the militants of the MNU.

A historical journey made up of uprisings, silences, and rearticulations. It is possible to say that the Zumbi March enshrined an agenda that had been in gestation since May 14th, 1888, the day after the "false abolition", when countless human beings were deprived of any right and recognition of their work, remaining without access to education and only the bare possibility of survival, the vast majority having to "re-enslave" themselves by subjecting to the return to degrading work without prospects of a long life, or the freedoms and integrities due to human beings. As Wlamyra Albuquerque and Walter Fraga (Albuquerque & Fraga, 2006) observe, the experiences of slavery, in varied and creative ways, were projected onto the daily lives of the ex-slaves in the post-abolition period, guiding organizational strategies, experiences and idealizations of freedom. Projects of integral citizenship for the Minority were built and processed in the long term based on the expertise of the experience between masters and enslaved.

The March consecrated at least a century of struggles that go back to the creation of the Black Brazilian Front in the 1930s, and the reappearance of the organisational capacity of the Black subject with the creation of the MNU and the Union of Blacks for Equality – UNEGRO – and other entities during the democratic overture that followed the military dictatorship. Many experiments, several efforts, and different strategies of political action were necessary for the Brazilian Black movement to achieve national projection and to succeed in getting racism recognized as a structural aspect of Brazilian society. As pointed out by historian Amílcar Pereira (2013), the words of sociologist and President Fernando Henrique occurred within a specific context: the tricentenary of the death of Zumbi of Palmares, who, since the early 1970s, had been recovered by the contemporary Black movement as the greatest symbol of the fight against racism in Brazil. Thus, this last great uprising of the organised Black movement in the 20th century did indeed pave the way and open paths for the agenda of this new century that "officially" begins with the Durban Conference in 2001. Let us see what the note from the Organising Committee of the Zumbi March said:

> This year we celebrate three centuries of the immortality of Zumbi of Palmares. The March to Brasília is therefore based on the deepest references of our collective memory in Brazil: the struggle against the dehumanizing oppression of racism. Only the continuous and perennial strength, through successive generations, of our militant action can guarantee the cohesion, the agglutinating elements necessary for the success of a political initiative with the dimension of the March that we are impetuously unleashing. Good news travels through all corners of the country: Blacks are preparing to go to Brasilia. It is no longer a question of saying that the state is silent, that the state does not do anything. We are going to Brasilia to tell the state what it should do. We have already made all the denunciations. The myth of racial democracy has been reduced to ashes, like the burnt-out

> dummy of Princess Isabel. We now want to demand effective actions from the state – a demand of our political majority. Conceived by the Black Movement, the March is being built as a unified action involving new partnerships, which attest to the growth of our social base and the widening of the fronts in the struggle against racism: trade unionists, popular sectors, women, students, non-governmental organisations, rural communities. The March is thus a kind of bridge between this moment, which is extremely fertile but remains under the predominance of pulverised actions, and another whose initiatives will be based on a broad political programme, outlined in the effervescence of a mass movement and projected from a Black perspective. Let's all go to Brasilia, on November 20th! All those who wish to participate in some way in the construction of the March may do so. We will celebrate Zumbi, reaffirming our willingness to fight against the misery and marginalisation to which we are subjected by racist exploitation. Cheers Zumbi!

Articulated by Black organizations with national reach, the March has been enshrined as an uprising of the Black masses who walked to the nation's capital in a rare moment of unified action and coordinated demands at the national level. Agendas are typically regionalized, instead of being federally organized, which curtails the construction of a strong network that can reach every corner of the country. It may be said that, starting with the victory of the organization and realization of the Zumbi March, we begin to see a series of political acts that would thrust Brazil into assuming a starring role in the Durban Conference.

The role of Trade Union Centres and the main union sindicates in the build-up to the March should be recognized. In contrast to previous years, between 1990 and 1995 these organizations included in their agendas discussions of racial discrimination and inequality, creating room for reflection and debate, as well as internal committee concerned with these themes, such as the Secretary for Research and Development of Racial Equality of the Union Force or the National Committee against Racial Discrimination of the Workers' Central Union (CUT) (Jaccoud, 2009, p. 32). Luciana Jaccoud notes that this mobilization of trade unions reached its peak with the creation of the Inter-American Institute for Racial Equality (INSPIR) in November of 1995.

In subsequent activities related to the March, Black leaders were received in Parliament, carrying the letter/proposal of the Movement for Reparations, and received by President Fernando Henrique Cardoso. The organizers handed President Fernando Henrique a document in which they highlighted the conditions of the Black population in Brazil and proposed actions to overcome racism and racial inequalities. These demands were organized as a program: Program for Overcoming Racism and Racial Inequality[72], organized along thematic axes

---

[72] Programa de Superação do Racismo e da Desigualdade Racial, p. 15. Available via: <http://www.leliagonzalez.org.br/material/Marcha_Zumbi_1995_divulgacaoUNEGRO-RS.pdf>

that characterized the situation of racial inequality existing in the country: the democratization of information, labour market, education, culture and communication, health, violence, religion and, finally and quilombo land (Lima, 2010).

On the same day of the March, President Fernando Henrique signed the decree that established the Inter-ministerial Working Group for the Valorisation of the Black Population (GTI), coordinated by the Ministry of Justice, through its National Secretariat for Human Rights. The proposal for the GTI was forged within the government itself in articulation with sectors of the Black movement which "demanded more direct action by the federal government in the establishment of public policies, without the culturalist stamp that generally prevailed in the state when the Black segment was considered" (Jaccoud &, Beghin, 2002, p. 19). One of the most important discussions that took place within the scope of the GTI was the implementation of affirmative action for the Black population.

Hélio Santos (2000, p. 72) claims that, with the March and the establishment of the CTI, the racial issue was ineluctably inscribed within the national agenda. By creating the GTI, President Fernando Henrique Cardoso had finalized institutionalized the issue. However, the members of the Black Movement who took part in the Group themselves claimed that the government lacked boldness in implementing policies. In the end, political proposals and working groups were born but lacked depth and remained isolated.

In this context, discussions around Convention 111 of the ILO were resumed. In the early 1990s, unions complained to the ILO of the existence of racial discrimination in the labour market. The Ministry for Work and Employment (MTE) therefore proposed a series of measures that aimed to tackle the problem. In 1995, it established a partnership with the ILO with the aim of putting into motion the Program for the Implementation of Convention 111. It included the Brazil, Gender and Race Programme, based on the principles and directives of the Convention, which aimed to raise conscious of discriminatory practices in the workplace and to replicate and expand on successful policies for the promotion of equality of opportunity, such as the creation of nuclei for promoting equality of opportunity and fighting discrimination in the workplace and in careers in the regional police stations for work (Ferreira & Santos, 2000). The programme targeted the end of the *vicious cycle*, fed by discrimination that was entrenched in the daily lives of Brazilians, and which cast a permanent blight in the labour market.

In 1996, President Fernando Henrique Cardoso signed a presidential decree creating the Working Group for the Elimination of Discrimination in the Workplace and in Careers (GTDEO). The New National Human Rights Programme (PNDH), instituted by Decree n° 1,904 (1996), also included a topic specifically geared towards the Black population, including government proposals for meeting their demands in the short, middle, and long term. The PNDH also recommended gathering data on colour/race in all public agency forms. Many of the recommendations were presented as 'proposals', 'stimuli', and 'promotion', but the middle-range measures also included :the development of affirmative action for granting Black students access to professional courses, universities, and areas of advanced technology; the requirement that the Brazilian Institute of Geography and Statistics (IBGE) determine that Browns and Pretos (dark skinned) make up the Black population; and, finally, the adoption of the principle of criminalizing racism, in the Penal Code and Penal Process.

This government overture to discussing human rights and, specifically, the rights of the Black population, remained ongoing. The 10th report of the International Convention on the Elimination of all forms of Racial Discrimination, elaborated in 1996 by the Ministries of Justice and Foreign Relations, and sent to the United Nations, recognized the existence of discriminatory practices with repercussions in all social spheres. Despite racism being considered a crime (Law 7.716, 1989), it was clear that a causal relation between colour and inequalities remained in place.

On the 2nd of July 1996, the seminar on Multiculturalism and Racism: The Role of Affirmative Action in Contemporary Democratic States, promoted by the Brazilian government, was held at the Palácio do Planalto (the Presidential Palace). Based on the recommendations of the Seminar, the GTI proposed measures to promote greater access to jobs and education for Blacks, which came closer to affirmative action. These measures were synthesized in the Building Racial Democracy document, which presented the plan of actions that were being developed in terms of public policies. This document, together with the National Plan for Human Rights, expressed the governmental guidelines for combating inequalities in Brazil in various spheres such as health, education, human rights, work and employment, communication, etc.

The debate concerning affirmative action has since gained traction, particularly in government sectors and among representative organizations of the Black movement. This debate became more intense after 2000, as Brazil prepared to take parting the Durban Conference.

The National Committee for the Brazilian Participation in Durban was created to prepare for the Conference. This Committee was chaired by the Secretary of State for Human Rights and composed of governmental and non-governmental representatives. The atmosphere in the Committee was quite tense; even the lead up to its composition was the subject of harsh disagreements. There were also problems among the representatives of the government, such as conflicts with the representative of the Ministry of Education, a fundamental agency in discussions on the racial issue, which was contrary to the implementation of affirmative action, particularly as racial quotas. Curiously, the report that was sent to Durban, in which the application of affirmative action measures in education is discussed, was released without the endorsement of the Ministry of Education. Affirmative action will be discussed in a separate chapter.

A series of seminars, promoted both by the Human Rights Secretary and the Palmares Foundation, were held in preparation for the conference. The Black Movement, in particular through Black NGOs, also mobilized intensely in anticipation of the conference. By this stage it was obvious that the policies promised by the Federal government were mostly ineffective and that greater pressure from militants was necessary. As a member of the stimulating committee, Geledés, with the backing of the Ford Foundation, took responsibility for disseminating information concerning the World Conference and on preparing militants to take part in the process of its construction. The institution organized national meetings with representatives of the international human rights organization Law Group and organized that delegation for the conferences that took place before travel to Durban. At the international level, Geledés, The Zumbi dos Palmares National Office (ENZP), and the CEAP participated in the creation of the Afro-Latin American Strategic Alliance and Caribbean, which aimed to organize participation the Regional Conference of the Americas and the World Conference.

The report that Brazil presented in Durban was deemed to be significantly open to the demands of the Black Movement. Among other articles, the Brazilian state committed to accepting its historic role in slavery and the economic, social, and political marginalization of the descendants of Africans; to recognize quilombo lands; to create an Afro-Indigenous forum to jointly decide on specific policies for social inclusion; and, finally, to adopt quotas or other affirmative action measures that would promote the access of Blacks to public universities.

In Durban, the National Council for Combating Discrimination (CNCD), was created by presidential decree n° 3,952 (2001) within the State Secretary of Human Rights of the Ministry of Justice. This new council was intended to create affirmative public policies for promoting equality and the protection of the rights of individuals and social and ethnic groups affected by racial discrimination and other forms of intolerance. The council worked with representatives of Indigenous organizations, as well as those of homosexuals, special needs people, etc. The National Centre for Black Citizenship (CENEG) was also created, under the auspices of the Ministry of Justice, instituted by an inter-ministerial agreement between the Ministry of Justice and the Ministry of Culture, the main aim of which was preparing and valuing the Black community, focusing on human rights.

Other initiatives were created, such as the Ministry of Education's Diversity at University programme, which aimed to implement and evaluate strategies for access to higher education for excluded groups, especially Black and Indigenous people (Law 10,558, 2002). The programme was supported within the Ministry by educational evaluations carried out by the National Education Council (CNE) which provided the basis for curricular reforms in Brazilian secondary education, and which affirmed the importance of producing an education that recognised and valued Brazilian cultural diversity and the ways of perceiving and expressing realities proper to the genders, ethnicities and the many regions and social groups that make up the country (Igreja, 2005, p. 280). The project supported alternative programs that aimed at the inclusion of students from lower social income families in universities through preparation for admission exams, the *vestibulares*. They were a novelty in the country and were seen to be a great hope against the exclusion of low-income and Black population from the university, besides being possible agglutinating domains for supporters for the anti-racist struggle.

According to Alexandre do Nascimento (2002), the idea of organizing a preparatory course for Black students was born of the reflections of the Black Pastoral, in São Paulo, between 1989 and 1992. The concrete result of this debate was the creation of two hundred scholarships by the PUC-SP Faculty for students participating in Black and Popular Movements. In 1992, in the state of Bahia, a pre-university course was created through the Steve Biko Cooperative with the aim of supporting and articulating Black youth from the periphery of Salvador, helping young people get university places. The aim of the Cooperative was to go beyond university entrance, since the *cursinho* was conceived as an opportunity to spread Black awareness and to promote the fight against discrimination and racism. With this goal, it included as a discipline 'Citizenship and Black Awareness.'

These courses spread through the country, though the 500 or so existing courses were concentrated in Rio de Janeiro (150), São Paulo (100), and Belo Horizonte (around 30). It is difficult to obtain exact figures for the number of courses since their representatives provided discrepant data (Igreja, 2005). [73] As racial quotas took hold in the public universities of the country, these courses became less important as a form of social intervention for Black militants. Educafro: Education and Citizenship for Afro-Descendants and Low-Income People and its

---

[73] Data provided by Alexandre do Nascimento, of the PVNC, in an interview, although Friar David, of the Educafro, mentioned the existence of almost two thousand courses in an interview.

manager Friar David remained one of the most influential characters in the discussions on the inclusion of Blacks in higher education.

The Diversity in the University Project remained small and had little repercussion in the Ministry for Education. It could be said that it played a significant role in bringing to light fundamental problems in the struggle against discrimination in education, as well as in training teachers, focusing on racism in education, the low quality of public schools, and the problem of the lack of scholarships to maintain Blacks and low-income whites in university. Rather than promoting a change in educational policies to take into account the inclusion of young Blacks in higher education, the Project ended up concentrating on financing a few preparatory courses for university admission offered by Black NGOs (Igreja, 2005). The Diversity in the University Project had to reckon with the complexity of the debate surrounding the racial issue in the Brazilian context, the same complexity faced during the introduction of affirmative action policies and the quotas system: the very matter of 'race' as part of the identity of those who benefitted from such policies.

Be that as it may, various policies were instituted at the state level (Ferreira, R. &, Borba, A., 2006). Key among them is Law 4,151 (2003), signed on the 4th of September 2003, which stipulated quotas at the Rio de Janeiro State University (UERJ,), a pioneer of racial quotas[74]. The decision to provide quotas at the UERJ was not the result of an inclusive debate with different social sectors, nor with universities; instead, the university had to adapt quickly to the quota system, dealing even with a number of court injunctions against it. The system was nonetheless approved, paving the way for the introduction of racial quotas for university admission in all of the public universities of the country. The University of Brasília (UNB) became the first federal institution to approve the quota system in 2004.

In 2002, the 2nd National Human Rights Plan (2nd PNDH) was also launched by (Decree n° 4,229, 2002), elaborated through national consultations, including on the issue of cultural diversity in the country in a broader way and in all spheres. Furthermore, it expanded the goals set by the previous plan with regard to the Black population, enshrining the term "Afro-descendant", derived from the Durban Declaration and Plan of Action. The 2nd PNDH had an innovative character, proposing a series of measures aimed at balancing and improving the economic and social indicators of less favoured racial groups. On the 13th

---

[74] The approved text establishes a proportion of 45% of places, distributed as follows: 20% of students graduating from public schools, 20% for Black students, and 5% for people with special needs.

of May 2002, during the celebrations of the anniversary of the Abolition of Slavery, the National Programme for Affirmative Action was created by Decree n° 4,228 (2002), under the coordination of the State Secretariat for Human Rights of the Ministry of Justice. The aim was to implement a series of specific measures within the federal public administration that would give priority to the participation of people of African descent, women and the disabled (Jaccoud &, Beghin, 2002, p. 24).

Also in 2002, the Ministry of Foreign Affairs announced other measures for the acknowledgement of the Black population. These measures include the implementation of a project to include Portuguese-speaking African Countries (PALOPs) in the National Research Network, with the aim of using the internet as an instrument for integrating Brazil with these countries, especially in activities that strengthen education, research, and scientific and technological development. The Slave Route project was also implemented, supported by the UNESCO General Conference, on the initiative of African countries and with the support of Brazil. As an affirmative measure, the MRE decided to create the Vocation for Diplomacy Scholarship-Prize Program, which granted scholarships for Afro-descendants to prepare for the competitive entrance examination for the diplomatic career[75]. Dominated by members of the country's elite and with low Black representation, the diplomatic career was the target of various criticisms from representatives of the Black movements.

At this time, Brazil witnessed a first wave of affirmative action policies targeting public service jobs, beginning in the Ministry of Agrarian Development in 2001, then gradually extending to other ministries (Jaccoud, 2009). As we have already mentioned, this process culminated in the expansion of this policy by the National Affirmative Action Program, providing percentage goals for the participation for Afro-Brazilians, women, and people with disabilities in commissioned posts. However, this norm has not been fully applied (Osório, 2006), largely due to internal resistance within agencies, as with other projects aimed at the Black population at the federal level (Igreja, 2005). In a decentralised manner, several states and municipalities also began to issue norms including proposals with similar aims (Igreja &, Ferreira, 2019).[76]

---

[75] In 2010, the Ministry of Foreign Affairs reserved places for Black candidates in the first of the four selection processes of the public tenure contest for diplomacy. It reserved 10% for the first phase until 2013. As of 2014 there is no provision for the reservation of places in the stages of the contest, but Law 12.990, signed in 2014, ensures that 20% of places are reserved for Blacks. See: http://www.planalto.gov.br/ccivil_03/_ato2011-2014/2014/lei/l12990.htm

[76] For a chronology of norms for reserving racial quotas in state and municipal public tenure contests, see Silva and Silva (2014), and the update in Ferreira (2017).

It is important to emphasize that, despite the various policies that were announced during the Fernando Henrique administration, this initial period of discussion produced no concrete proposal for a broad state-level policy on racial equity. What was observed were isolated actions in some ministries, without any intercommunication between them and even without expectations as to their implementation. Despite the President's speeches and the numerous decrees and councils that he created, there was no determination on the part of the president of the republic to apply these measures. In sum, despite showing some progress, the debate on quotas within the government did not break with the old Brazilian political structure. However, these measures were moving towards the discussion and implementation of affirmative action in the country.

The succeeding period was marked by the coming to power of a left-wing party committed to fighting social inequalities, hunger and poverty in the country[77]. Luís Inácio Lula da Silva's victory in the presidential race symbolised the beginning of a second important stage in the country's post-re-democratization renewal: the effort to end the profound social inequalities that marked the history of Brazil. However, the issue of racism and racial inequalities has always been a subject of discussion and disagreement for those on the left. The debate has always been about where the focus should be, on the struggles of social class or on the struggles against discrimination and racism. Moreover, affirmative actions were presented as focalized policies that would ultimately tend to benefit a Black middle class. Nonetheless, the Black movement took this discussion to the Brazilian left and especially to the Workers' Party, and the campaign programme for the presidency of the PT made an effort to ponder the racial issue, as demonstrated by the elaboration of the Brazil Without Racism Programme. The Programme stated that the government would have to combat economic and social inequalities as a necessary condition for all Brazilians to be ensured their status as citizens, but also indicated the urgency for a political effort to affirm the principle of equality between men and women, between Blacks and whites.

The Lula administration brings about an important transformation in the relationship between the Black movement and the State (Lima, 2010). Members of the movement were invited to participate in the formulation of policies, to assume important public positions and occupy roles in the various consultative councils created by the government. They took their demands to the government in an effort to put into practice what had been hashed out by the previous gov-

---

[77] A number of authors reported on this historical moment for the country, which saw the introduction of public policies and new legislation targeting racism and racial inequality in the country. See Igreja (2005), Ferreira (2017), Jaccoud (2009), Theodoro (2008), Jaccoud and Beghin (2002).

ernment. It is important to highlight the creation of the Special Secretariat for the Promotion of Racial Equality (SEPPIR) on the 21st of March 2003, the International Day for the Elimination of Racial Discrimination. In 2008 the Secretariat assumes the status of a Ministry. According to Marcia Lima (2010, p. 83), the creation of SEPPIR reveals the political and institutional inflexions of the treatment of racial issues by the State. The institution had the task of formulating, coordinating and articulating policies and guidelines for the promotion of racial equality in articulation with other public agencies, as well as civil society organizations and international bodies. To this end, it created its National Council for the Participation of Racial Equality (CNPIR), a collegiate body of an advisory nature. However, SEPPIR was not structured at the same time as the other organs of the federal government and did not get the recognition it expected from them. It also lacked the necessary budget for its proper functioning. In this sense, despite the importance of its creation, its first years did not represent significant progress, as it was unable to contribute to the existing policies of the previous government, many of which had been abandoned; nor was it able to develop an integrated body of policies to combat racial inequality – despite the guidelines of the National Policy for the Promotion of Racial Equality (PNPIR) and the First National Conference on the Promotion of Racial Equality (CONAPIR) (Jaccoud, 2009; Silva et al., 2021).

In 2004, at the beginning of the Workers' Party government, the Secretariat for Ongoing Education, Literacy, and Diversity (SECAD) of the Ministry of Education was also created. All of these initiatives sought to bring transversality to the racial theme, but ran into difficulties when having their importance recognized by the state bureaucracy, and gradually saw their scope of action diminish.

In addition to SEPPIR, the government launched two important educational programmes: PROUNI and REUNI. University For All Program (PROUNI) was an initiative aimed at increasing the entrance of low-income students into private higher education, targeting the insertion of Black, poor and Indigenous students through scholarships. With the same goal, the government also includes the question of race/colour in the Student Financing Program, giving priority to Black students. The Programme to Support Plans for the Restructuring and Expansion of Federal Universities (REUNI) was aimed at expanding the country's federal universities, thus increasing the number of places available, which was fundamental for the introduction of a quota policy. These programmes elaborated by the Lula government not only recognized racial discrimination, but also sought redistribution and the righting of social inequalities. The government's affirmative action policies thus gained a political and social context for their advancement, linked to social policies against poverty and inequality in the country.

These policies were accompanied by the approval of important initiatives that recognized the contributions of the Black diaspora to Brazilian society. An example is the approval of Law 10,639 (2003), which established the study of Afro-Brazilian history and culture as part of the elementary school curriculum. The introduction and implementation of this norm continues to this day, slowly, met with the resistance of the educational industry and the lack of teachers with the requisite knowledge to teach the relevant disciplines.

It is also important to highlight the approval of Federal Law 12,288 (2010) which instituted the Statute of Racial Equality – EIRA. The Statute sought to protect the fundamental rights of Afro-descendants in the fields of culture, work, land, education, communication, sports and leisure. Affirmative action and racial quotas appear as fundamental elements of the Statute, proposing reparations for the suffering of Afro-descendants as well as measures aimed at correcting the racial inequalities that persist. In the original text of the project, reference to a financial compensation as reparation for the sufferings caused by slavery led to great commotion. The Statute of Racial Equality is the project that best corresponds to the demands of the Black Movement; however, it was only approved in 2010, with major modifications. The approval of the Statute generated a series of important debates involving the academic world and civil society.

The issue of reparations was an important agenda for sectors of the Black movement. Fernando Conceição (Conceição, F., 2005), one of the exponents and pioneers of the debate on affirmative action in Brazil and consequent compensation for the descendants of enslaved African peoples, was the national coordinator of the Movement for Reparations (MPR) in Brazil. In 1994, the movement, articulated at the national level, proclaimed that the first affirmative action should be financial payment to the descendants of enslaved men and women and their recognition as workers during the slavery period. As a characteristic of transnationalised Black articulation, the professor observed that the articulation for reparative rights had coverage in the USA, Central America, Europe, and Asia. "It's the most daring thing in the present circumstances because it's going to touch on that most uncomfortable part of the human body, the pocket", he said. At the end of 1994, a group of eleven people filed a suit for declaratory judgment in the Federal Court of São Paulo, asking the court to hold the Union guilty of the slavery of Africans and the subordinate status of their descendants due to the way that "abolition" took place. Heading the list of plaintiffs was the former slave Maria do Carmo Jerônimo, at the time considered the oldest living human being on the planet according to the Guinness Book of Records. On the 20th of November 1995, the Movement for Reparations delivered a petition to the National Congress with more than 10,000 signatures proposing a law of reparations. The project was made official by the then-congressman, currently senator, Paulo Paim. It was also through the political and communicational momentum achieved by the MPR that the term "Black" began to be re-signified in Brazil as a word associated with the political perspective of human social relations rather than with a biological constitution.

The pioneering spirit of the Movement for Reparations, the shake-up of members of the traditional organized Black movement, led the MPR to suffer serious attacks and a rejection from older leaderships. However, it also made public the actions and proposals of the Black community for the new millennium that was on the horizon. The historian and professor Petrônio Domingues usefully reviews the influences of the MPR on the agenda of the Brazilian Black movement and its reflections abroad, culminating with the Durban debates in 2001. He states that: "With internal atomisation and ever-increasing political isolation, the MPR was cooling down, emptying itself, and was practically buried in the last quarter of the 1990s. Some of its militants still founded the "Committee Pro Quotas for Blacks in the University of São Paulo (USP)" and carried out a series of demonstrations in the university campus, such as the "crucifixion" of a black actor, an "offering to Exu" at the door of the Rectory, the burning of a barrier of tyres at the main entrance of the USP, not to mention the graffiti on the walls of the campus.

In its initial phase, the proposal for instating quotas (or reserving places) for Blacks in public universities also caused controversy. Yet this new form of affirmative action gradually gained support within the social movement and supplanted the rhetoric of pecuniary compensation. This was the case in Brazil, since in the global sphere, including Latin America, the issue of reparations attained an unprecedented prominence (and proportion). At the Third UN Conference in Durban, African countries demanded that the United States of America, some European countries and even Brazil pay them compensation for slavery, human trafficking and other past injustices[78]. But there was no consensus. And Petrônio Domingues concludes by relating the actions of the Movement for Reparations to the agendas of the organized black movement in the 21st century:

> We can say that today – some two decades after its extinction – it has contributed to an inflection in the racial politics of the Brazilian Black movement. Even though compensatory policies were known since the 1960s, through the North American experience, and were,

---

[78] The demand for reparations was proposed in the Africa Preparator Conference, and presented in the Durban Conference (Dakar, Senegal, January 2001). https://undocs.org/fr/A/CONF.189/PC.2/8

in a way, already part of the repertoire of the Black Movement's demands since the 1980s, it was only in the 1990s the conditions for the systematization and legitimacy of these policies were finally established. If the proposal that won the day as the axis of the Movement was not monetary indemnity for the suffering of the ancestors of Afro-Brazilians during slavery, but, instead, that of racial quotas, the latter proposal was nonetheless gestated within the struggle for reparations (Domingues, 2018)

Indeed, in what pertains to public higher education institutions, the adoption of racial quotas in public universities was considered to be a huge step for affirmative actions. On the 13th of May 2004, the president of the republic sent the proposal to the Legislative Branch, and it was included in a Law Bill that was being processed in Congress since 1999, finally being approved and sanctioned by President Dilma Rousseff in 2012. Thus, Law 12,711, the Quotas Law, assures that 50% of all places in Federal and State universities and for federal polytechnic schools for students from public schools, ensuring that places were distributed between Black, *pardo* (brown, and Indigenous students, in proportion to the populational make-up of each state of the country, according to the most recent statistics of the Brazilian Institute of Geography and Statistics (IBGE). The law was tailored to be applied progressively, for a period of ten years, during which the results would be reviewed, and targets redefined (Ribeiro, 2014).

The introduction of racial quotas in higher education in federal public universities was expanded to include graduate degrees. It is now a consolidated policy in Brazil. Racial quotas in civil servant examinations also gained ground. A new norm, applied to all civil service sectors, was established with the Statute of Racial Equality – EIRA. However, there was only one theme which directly dealt with the reserve of places along racial criteria, without establishing clear rules for this right and merely instating the possibility of its adoption by the labour market (Igreja &, Ferreira, 2019)[79].

Discussions thus began on how to regulate the theme, including a series of popular movements (Kintê, 2013; Damé, 2013). This pressure produced effects, and a bill was presented to President Dilma Rousseff in 2013, with new rules on racial quotas in federal civil service examinations, in the hope of diversifying public administration and increasing the representativity of the Black popula-

---

[79] Art. 39. The State will promote actions that ensure the equality of opportunities for the Black population in the workplace, including the implementation of measures for promoting equality in hiring practices in the public sector and incentives for the adoption of similar measures in companies and private firms.

tion in this sector. Ratified as Law Project 6738, in 2013, it was processed in the regime of constitutional urgency[80].

After 14 months of voting, none of which altered its substance in any way, it became Federal Law 12,990 (2014), thus stated[81]:

a) 20% of all places, whenever the number of places offered in a civil service examination is equal to or greater than three (art. 1º, §1º).
b) places will be reserved for Black candidates, and this will be clearly stated in the public call for contestants, specifying the reservation of places for each position or civil service post offered (art. 1º, §3º).
c) beneficiaries of the law are those who self-identify as *preto* (black) or *pardo bown* when enrolling for the examination, according to the criteria for colour or race of the Brazilian Institute of Geography and Statistics – IBGE (art. 2º).
d) candidates who make false claims will be eliminated and their admission annulled, in cases in which perjury is established after nomination (art. 2º, single paragraph).
e) contests will be organized into two lists, one with places reserved for quotas and another for all candidates. According to a candidate's classification, in what concerns the positions advertised, the list with all candidates takes precedence, thus freeing up room in the restricted list with reserved places. If a Black candidate approved through quotas does not take up his place, the next quota candidate according to classification will be called up (art. 3º, §§1º and 2º).
f) in the absence of a sufficient number of Black candidates approved to occupy reserved places, these will be devolved to the list including all contestants (art. 3º, §3º).
g) alternation and proportionality between total places for people with special needs [82] and Black candidates (art. 4º).
h) annual review of the system of reserving places (art. 5º).
i) the norm will be in place once it is published, and will expire in ten years (art. 6º)

---

80 In the regime of constitutional urgency, which may be solicited by the president of the republic for projects that he or she initiated, Congress and the Senate must, each in turn, decide on the proposition within no more than 45 days, as enshrined in art. 64, §§1º e 2º, of the Constitution of the Federative Republic of Brazil.
81 For an approach to the Law Project 6.738 (2013), see Silva and Silva (2014) and for a more detailed analysis of Law 12.990, se Ferreira (2017).
82 Federal Law 8.112 (1990), concerning the Statute of the Civil Servant, predicts the reservation of 20% of the places in federal civil service examinations to people with special needs. f

According to data from the – SEPPIR, in the first year of its application (2014–2015) 638 places in federal civil servant examinations were reserved for Black candidates (Igreja & Ferreira, 2019; Ferreira, G.L, 2017).

Likewise, in the early days of the law's application, fraud attempts were higher than expected. These attempts at fraud were dealt with in the courts, with a number of suits filed by the District Attorney's Office and the Public Defence Office, establishing, through a decision of the Supreme Court, that the practice was fraudulent. The Declaratory Action for Constitutionality (ADC) n° 41 (2017) established the constitutional integrity of the Quotas Law in the federal public service.

All of the initiative surrounding racial quotas as recognized by law have been, and still are, the subject of vast controversies in the country, involving the world of politics, academia, and society at large. Various studies seek to review the policies, particularly in the current context, when the Quotas Law is scheduled to be rediscussed. This debate is the theme of the following chapters.

This context of innovation, with the creation of new institutions and the introduction of affirmative action in Brazil, reflected back on the government of President Dilma Rousseff, of the Workers' Party. SEPPIR loses its status as a ministry. By Provisional Measure 696, sent to the Senate in October of 2015, it was incorporated into the Ministry of Women, Racial Equality, and Human Rights, fusing the Secretariat for the Promotion of Racial Equality, the Secretariat for Human Rights, and the Secretariat for Policies for Women. Lack of support for the institution led to difficulties, often reducing it to a promoter of events and seminars. Profound changes were to take place, however, in 2019, when President Jair Bolsonaro, who openly opposed affirmative action policies with a racist rhetoric, came to power.

Affirmative Action in Brazil and the identification of race/colour

The policies targeting the Black population in Brazil which have been elaborated since the 1990s focused, above all, on anti-racist legislation, in positively valuing the Black community, and, particularly, in promoting affirmative action. In this section we will discuss the implementation of affirmative action, particularly in what concerns the identification of race/colour, but it is important to mention other dimensions of Black struggle for rights and recognition, such as the fight against religious intolerance and the recognition of Quilombo lands.

As Kabengele Munanga and Nilma Lino Gomes (2016, p. 143) stress, the presence of Black people in the development and constitution of Brazil played a decisive role in providing Brazilian cultural with a rich religious legacy expressed in numerous institutions, and in material and symbolic dimensions of great importance of the country and its civilization. Candomblé and other traditional Afro-Brazilian religions took on different forms and denominations throughout the country, covering all of the national territory, despite their practice having been outlawed in various times. Historically, these religions are the target of prejudice which associates them with malign cults, and are occasionally attacked by members of other sects and churches (Santos, C. A. I., 2018). Article 5 of the Brazilian Constitution (1988) assures freedom of religion and belief, but religious persecution remains rife. Following the invasions of the Abassá de Ogum shrine in Salvador, which culminated in the death of the Priestess Mãe Gilda of heart attack, the National Day Against Religious Intolerance was created on the 21st of January. Many branches of the Black Movement in Brazil are therefore dedicated to the struggle for ensuring rights to freedom of religion, as enshrined in the Constitution.

Although collective rights to Quilombo Lands are also assured by the 1988 Constitution, the definitive title over the land remains a distant hope for the more than 3000 communities that are recognized as being descended from Quilombos in the country (Benedetti, 2021). It was only one decade after the Constitution that the first community, Boa Vista in Oriximiná, Pará state, had its titles recognized by the National Institute of Colonization and Agrarian Reform (INCRA). Benedetti observes the slow pace in which these rights are put into practice, and laments that, considering the high demand, the number of titles issued remains low. Her data show that 267 titles were issued at the federal, state, and municipal levels, referring to 171 territories, and giving legal status to 1,042,794.4895 hectares inhabited by 17,515 Quilombo families.

Even though it is not our main focus in this chapter, we would like to highlight those titular rights to Quilombo lands was the subject of an extensive debate concerning the identification of contemporary Quilombos, with anthropologists called upon to aid in identification. If Quilombos had been treated as objects of historical studies of Black resistance to slavery, it took on a new form with the Constitution and the demands for recognition and land titles in rural communities. Anthropologists were charged with attesting to the historical links of contemporary communities with Quilombos (O'Dwyer, 2002).

Within the struggle for recognition, the legal definition of a Quilombo community underwent certain changes. The Palmares Cultural Foundation proposed a definition in the 1990s, in which it defined Quilombos as "sites historically occupied by *negros* (blacks), with archaeological vestiges of their presence, including in areas still occupied by their descendants, with ethnographic and cultural content" (Arrutti 2008, p. 325). Change only came after Decree nº 4,887 (2003) by

President Luíz Inácio da Silva, in which the descendants of Quilombo communities came to be defined as ethno-racial groups, according to criteria of self-identification, with their own historical trajectory, specific territorial relations, and with the presumption of Black ancestrality related to resistance to a historical oppression. This definition accords with ILO Convention 169/1989. The Palmares Foundation was responsible for certifying the descendants of Quilombo communities, while the process of identifying, delimiting, regularizing, and titling territories fell to INCRA (Benedetti, 2021). According to Benedetti (2021), based on data from the Palmares Foundation, up until 2021 2,811 certificates of recognition were issued, covering 3,471 communities in the country[83]. As we have observed, the state is slow to provide land titles for Quilombo territories, which are involved in an extensive and historical dispute over land in Brazil.

The recognition of Quilombo communities is deal with in tandem with discussions surrounding the delimitation and demarcation of Indigenous lands, and it is anthropologists who are primarily involved in this process. It is hence framed within debates on multicultural policies and legislation linked to collective properties and the defence of these territories. As we noted above, the theme of affirmative action, in turn, came to prominence within the framework of discussions on policies of racial equality, individual integration of members of the Black population, and the introduction of racial quotas in the public sector and universities, through analyses typically carried out by sociologists. The debate around affirmative actions propitiated this division within the social sciences.

The definition of 'affirmative action' that become predominant in the public sphere in Brazil is that proposed by Joaquim Barbosa Gomes (2001, p. 40), a Black jurist and former Supreme Court Justice, who considered them as:

> a set of public and private policies of a compulsory, optional or voluntary nature, conceived so as to fight discrimination of race, gender, and national origin, as well as to rectify the contemporary effects of discrimination practiced in the past, with the aim of making concrete the ideal of effective equality of access to fundamental goods, such as education and employment.

Joaquim Barbosa's definition binds affirmative action to the main aim of antiracist and anti-discrimination struggles, which is thereby transfixed as a primordial goal. What becomes consolidated in the country are the controversial racial quota policies for access to public university and public sector jobs.

---

[83] It is important to distinguish the process of recognizing and certifying a rural community as being descendants of a Quilombo from the titling of land, which requires recognizing collective rights of property of the community over that land.

From the very beginning, these policies faced a series of allegations against their implementation, dealing with themes such as the constitutional principles of isonomy and meritocracy. However, we would like to resume the debate around racial identification and social inequality, a discussion that still permeates contemporary debates. It is in the academy that we find an unexpected debate regarding the institutionalization of racial identities and the role of scientists, particularly social scientists, in the formulation of public policies based on racial categories. Social scientists were called to the debate, which put controversial themes on the agenda, such as race, identity, miscegenation, racial democracy and the difference between social and racial inequality. Debate turned on the best political strategy for dealing with racism in the country (Igreja & Tavolaro, 2015).

In the academic world, perspectives on these policies diverged between two ways of understanding the problem. On the one hand, there was a rationale based on statistical data that confirmed the great social and economic disparities between whites and blacks i.e., *pardos*(brown) plus *pretos*(black) in the country and the urgency of applying affirmative action as measure for promoting black inclusion in higher education and the civil service with a quick turnaround. From this perspective, "racial democracy" was denounced as a myth that served to conceal the racism that exists in the country, a myth fed by racist interests that prevented a confrontation with the problem of racism and racial inequality. On the other hand, there were those who considered Brazilian race relations as being more "fluid" and "ambiguous", as a result of the high rates of miscegenation in the country, the interracial marriages, cultural syncretism and the absence of formal segregation in urban spaces, facts which would inhibit a policy based on the racial identification of Blacks and whites[84]. From this perspective, racial democracy was celebrated as a national myth, not as a reality but as a goal, an ideal to be achieved through the struggle against racial discrimination. This last perspective was especially grounded in the work of anthropologists who believed that this myth, in the anthropological sense, constituted a set of ideas and values that guided daily life, a perspective that demanded a better understanding of it, of its efficacy, and of its permanence (Fry, 2002; Schwarcz, 2002).

What we observe is a polarization between studies with a more statistical trend, which revealed the socioeconomic inequality between Blacks and whites, and those with a more qualitative trend, essentially ethnographic studies, which sought to explain everyday social relations, demonstrating the complexity of ra-

---

[84] On the divergences within the academic and disciplinary fields in relation to the introduction of affirmative action policies, see Igreja and Tavolaro (2015).

cial classifications that could not be reduced to a binary opposition between Black and white (Igreja, 2005; Igreja & Tavolaro, 2015). These studies drew attention to the importance of the social processes and to history as a determining factor in the unfavourable contemporary situation of Black people, as well as to the risks of the racialisation of Brazilian society. In addition, they reiterated the idea that race is a concept whose meaning is constantly renegotiated, experienced according to the social and historical context (Schwarcz, 2001).

Marcelo Paixão (2014) sought to deconstruct this discrepancy between qualitative and quantitative studies, criticising what he saw to be an apparent epistemological duplicity in the field of Brazilian race relations. It is via the deconstruction of this epistemological duplicity that the author arrives at his definition of the *legend of enchanted modernity* that, in its contemporary version, would validate the myth of racial democracy. This perspective assumes that all peoples have origin myths, and that, in the Brazilian case, this myth predicts an underlying generosity in the construction of a social world, one based on tolerant and egalitarian principles, even if in daily life the socioeconomic inequalities between whites, blacks and mestizos prevail. The author draws attention to the fact that, insofar as this distant dream of human relations or equality serves as an efficient reason for the denial of the implementation of measures that move in its direction, such an idyll is nothing but a legend. In other words, for the author, if the legend narrates the dream of fraternity and equality among the bearers of different racial characteristics, it would be compelling to say that, as this plot is constituted, it is precisely this idyll that is at the mercy of an extremely unjust, authoritarian and violent model of society (Paixão, 2014, p. 438).

Paixão, however, warns that there are more similarities than one might imagine between statistical historical-structural studies that focus on measuring social and racial inequalities and culturalist perspectives that present themselves as being more in-depth because they focus on symbolic elements, i.e., on the cultural plane. He recalls that even authors such as Florestan Fernandes, who denounced the myth of racial democracy, believed that with freedom from patrimonialism and with a more competitive order, racial democracy could be achieved, without the deeply rooted imprints of racist and discriminatory social practices. Thus, racial democracy would also present itself as a living myth that we could still aspire to.

At the heart of the initial debate was also the comparison with multiculturalist policies and the North American model of race relations, underscored by the idea that there is a Latin American pattern of race relations that can be clearly distinguished from an Anglo-American pattern. Hasenbalg (1996) claimed, for example, that this Latin pattern was characterized by a combination of the whitening ideal and a conception of racial harmony in which both were understood to be synonymous with the absence of prejudice and discrimination, which led to the social subordination and invisibility of afro-descendants (1996, p. 235). According to this perspective, affirmative policies aimed at well-defined racial groups, although necessary, seemed, if not improbable, quite unlikely in countries like Brazil, where this "Latin pattern" would have assumed specific and even more forceful contours through the ideology of racial democracy (Tavolaro & Igreja, 2015, p. 487).

Other approaches to the theme tended to attribute to such policies an inauthentic character, since they originated in political and social contexts in which racial classification of a binary type prevailed. We may remember Monica Grin's argument, for whom this would be the tendency of "culturalist" interpretations according to which extensive miscegenation gave rise to racial relations that were simultaneously hierarchical, inclusive, and complementary, characterized by harmony and plasticity (Grin 2001, pp. 175–176). According to these approaches, this plasticity, however, would not be a sign of the absence of racism, since it is a specific cultural trait of Brazil which must be taken into account in the formulation of anti-racist public policies. This also seems to be the tone of the article by Bourdieu and Wacquant (1999) in which the authors suggest that the influence of the binary classification system on Latin American countries is an inappropriate importation of the American model. Lília Tavolaro and Rebecca Igreja (2015, p. 487) consider that it is important to consider, however, that, although under the influence of the international institutional debate, affirmative action policies were also the result of the political struggles and claims of the Brazilian Black movement. In this sense, Tavolaro and Igreja insist that it would be wrong to say that affirmative action policies were merely a model imported from abroad, imposed from the top-down, finding no support in political-social processes and in the demands of social movements that traversed Brazilian society.

The Black Movement saw, in this new space for debate on the racial issue, an opportunity to promote effective changes in the condition of Brazilian Blacks and in the fight against racism. Recognizing the difficult in seeing social policies through in Brazil, they demanded urgency in combating racial inequality, principally from the state. This urgency allowed the demands of the Black Movement to be unified around these proposals, although at first there was no consensus among the organizations that affirmative action was the solution or even the best path. Quotas has always been part of the agenda of some Black organisations, but always accompanied by a concern for broader social measures such as the fight against poverty and violence. In general, representatives of these organisations recognised in the public sphere that affirmative action was a result of pressure from the Black Movement. However, there was a distrust of the interests that guided the state in taking on the defence of its interests and in promoting the debate on affirmative action, often with limited participation from society. There was a feeling of loss of control over the initiatives and fear of co-optation of this agenda by the State (Igreja, 2005).

The debate around racial identification in order to define the beneficiaries of these policies also brought to light the difficulty in delimiting an ethno-cultural and territorialised "Black community" in Brazil. The demographic dimension of Black Brazilians was not enough to widely and publicly bolster and legitimise a racial identity, nor to delimit a "Black community" that would bind itself to a single political institution, for example. In political rhetoric, an appeal to Quilombos and Africa has allowed Black militancy to create the idea of a community based on a common origin. The Black community has also been defined by its links with Afro-Brazilian religions. However, these elements are not sufficient for the creation of a strong Black ethnic-cultural identity in the country. Many authors refer to a "Black community" when they speak of militants and Black intellectuals who fight for the Black cause together. Sodré (1999, p. 209) affirms that the Afro-Brazilian community ethic finds in practice what, in theory, a certain Western thought about difference would call an "open project". It should not be confused with the societal subdivisions that are called "communities", which are generally forms of binding according to group or religious affinities under the conduction of social relations characterised by economic selfishness, by the rationality of juridical ties and by individualistic subjectivation. In the political struggle of afro-descendants, the community or liturgical communality could, according to Sodré, be equivalent to what some theorists of contemporary multiculturalism call "agency", that is, the concept of a collectivity capable of political action outside the grand utopian narratives and the liberal consciousness shaped by parties, something like the Wittgensteinian notion of grammar of conduct.

Much of the Brazilian Black population lives in urban areas, in an environment characterized by a greater exposure to processes of globalization. The actions emanating from these areas have paced little weight on ethnic and cultural particularities and placed greater emphasis on the anti-racist struggle. Lívio Sansone (2004) emphasises that, even if Black Brazilian cultural heritage has proved insufficient to identify an isolated sociocultural entity, considering that Afro-Brazilian culture has historically been considered a part of Brazilian culture (even if a subaltern part), it nonetheless has enabled the constitution of Black cultural spaces that are used to negotiating with "white world". It is these spaces that Blacks have used, and still use, to negotiate with the white domain, and it is in them that they circulate with greater freedom, and even with greater power (Sansone, 2002; Sodré, 1999). Muniz Sodré (1999), for his part, claims that

Black culture is part of the Black contribution to the Brazilian people (which Sodré understands to be a special amalgam of economic, social, phenotypical, and cultural heterogeneities). If "Black culture" is insufficient for agglutinating Blacks around a politicized racial identity, it has been enough to carry its expression forward – despite predictions to the contrary.

Internal frictions in the academy and the involvement of the Black Movement in wider debate in the public sphere led to formal manifestations of positions in favour of and against racial quotas. Two public manifestoes were presented to Congress in 2006, outlining the main arguments of the debate surrounding affirmative action, particularly in relation to admission to federal public universities. The first manifesto, stating the position against racial quotas, was called "All have equal rights in the Democratic Republic"; the second, "Manifesto for the Law of Quotas and the Statute of Racial Equality", defended the policy.

The first manifesto was signed by 144 people, among them renown intellectuals, was delivered to the National Congress by Professor Yvonne Maggie and by José Carlos Miranda, representative of the Black Socialist Movement. The manifesto expresses the signees concern that the nation would be divided between Blacks and whites. They argued that racial identities should not be imposed or regulated by the state; that policies targeting hermetic social groups in the name of social justice would not eliminate racism; and that, indeed, it could have the opposite effect by providing a legal basis for the concept of 'race' and fuelling conflict and intolerance. Finally, they affirmed that the widely recognized means to fight against social exclusion is through the creation and strengthening of high-quality universal public services in education, healthcare, and welfare, and particularly by the creation of jobs. In the name of a formal equality, the manifesto was openly opposed to affirmative action policies for imposing racial identities upon beneficiaries. For militants of the Black Socialist Movement, many of these positions were based on the view that the struggle should involve all workers against capitalism, and that this sort of policy was a means to control the revolt of workers, among which, of course, Black workers.

The manifesto for racial quotas, signed by a greater number of people, including intellectuals, but also by many militants and artists, argued that affirmative action policies were the only way to fight the existing inequalities between Blacks and whites in the country. It affirmed that racial inequalities have deep historical roots in Brazil, and that this inequality could not be significantly altered without specific public policies, since racism exists, is reproduced, and intensifies. The approval of a law of racial quotas would thus be an adequate response to a series of international commitments assumed by the country, and it would challenge this inescapable reality. The manifesto also criticizes the idea of 'universal equality' that opponents of a policy of racial quotas defended, believing that it could not be an empty principle but a goal to which all should strive. Affirmative action, based on the positive discrimination of the victims of historical processes, is the legal device created by the United Nations to reach this aim. Finally, it further criticized the other manifesto for the absence of a concrete alternative proposal for racial inclusion in Brazil, merely reiterating that we are all equal before the law and that we need to improve public services until such time as all equally benefit from them.

There are various points of contention in the in establishment of these policies, which must be discussion and probed, always in conversation with the concrete experiences of Brazilian Blacks. A crucial point to keep in mind is the focus on racial identification rather than social difference. Discussing race instead of social class is a historical part of the study of race relations in Brazil. For many of the perspectives linked to the idea of a "racial democracy", the difference in the social conditions between Blacks and whites in Brazil results from the huge inequality of the country. It is, in this sense, this inequality, and not racism, which explains the differences between whites and Blacks. However, as we mentioned earlier, studies promoted by UNESCO and carried out in the 1970s and 1980s by Carlos Hasenbalg and Nelson do Valle e Silva already revealed the existence of racism, showing how racial discrimination was renewed as new forms, thereby contributing to perpetuate the social inequality of Blacks. All of these studies confirm racism as a structuring element of existing social inequalities between Blacks and whites in the country, a view which has only become more robust as new studies on the socioeconomic circumstances of the Brazilian population continue to isolate 'race' as a relevant variable.

The dispute between these perspectives was a fundamental in questioning affirmative action, and, as a result, led to racial quotas initially being based on social condition. Among people with low university entrance rates, a specific sub-quota was established for *pretos* (blacks) and *pardos* (brown), particularly in the norm which set quotas for higher education[85].

The question that remains in debate is: is affirmative action the best means to combat racial discrimination, raising racial identification and classification to a requisite? It is important to give voice to people in the academy and intellec-

---

[85] According to Daflon, Feres Junior and Campos (2013), the main beneficiaries of racial quotas in education are graduates from public schools. This is because it is a structural aspect of education in Brazil that the best institutions are private schools, while lower-quality public education basically attends to low-income students. On the percentages of distribution of racial quotas in education, see: <http://portal.mec.gov.br/cotas/sobre-sistema.html>. Accessed on the 14/08/2018.

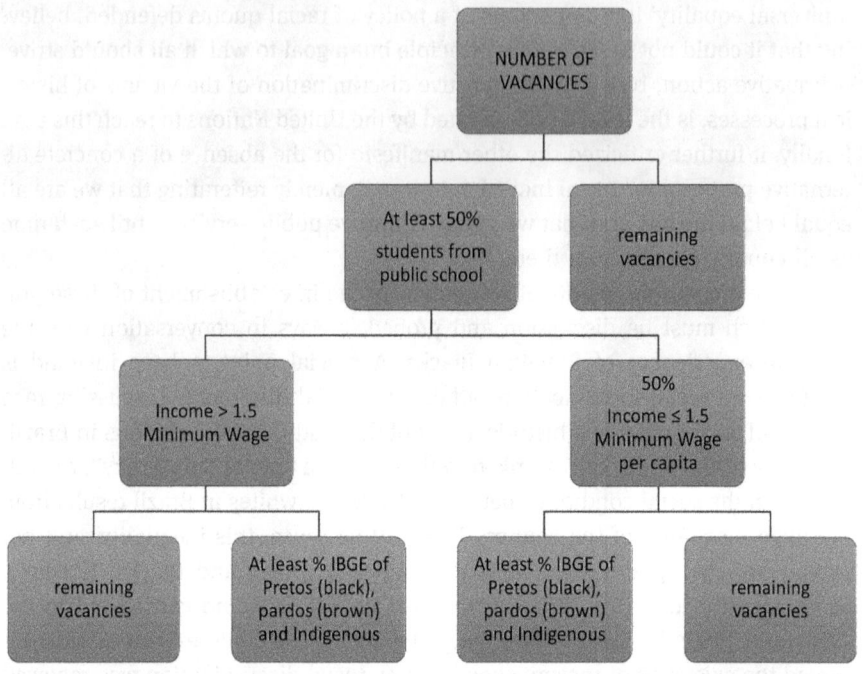

Figure 3: Racial Quota system in federal public universities. Source: Elaborated by the authors, using data from the Ministry of Education. http://portal.mec.gov.br/cotas/sobre-sistema.html

tuals linked to the Black Movements, who came to prominence during the initial context of this debate. Mário Theodoro (2014, pp. 215–217), for example, shows how the construction of a policy for promoting racial equality that is adequate for the enormity of the issue of race in Brazil needs to face five challenges, which we briefly summarize:

a) the construction of a conceptual base of support for effective action, and the delimitation of a field within which such actions can take place, since these policies should target not only the causes but also the effects of racism, and it must hence be involved in the struggle against racial prejudice.

b) the deconstruction of the idea that a policy for the Black population merges with a policy for the poor population. It is fact that the majority of the poor are Black; however, it is necessary to distinguish policies that target poverty from those that deal with racism. The two issues must be analysed and engaged in their specificities.

c) tackling institutional racism. Agencies and organizations are still dominated by the perception that the racial issue is secondary, or even supplementary,

which making putting these policies into practice an arduous and laborious task.
d) dimensioning programmes and actions, taking into account the grandeur of the racial problem in Brazil. In general, they are one-off and restricted initiatives, incapable of challenging racism.
e) the establishment of a solid system for funding programmes and actions: policies without financial resources are doomed to fail.

The consolidation of affirmative action in Brazil, in particular during the government of the Workers' Party, was accompanied by measures that allowed for their expansion, ensuring good results. One such measure was the growth in access to public universities through programmes such as the PROUNI, which was enacted alongside quota policies for higher education, and the 22 million people who left a condition of poverty, particularly between 2002 and 2012, 15 million of which were Black, according to the PNAD/IBGE (Theodoro, 2014, p. 214). A number of other policies also improve the lives of Blacks in the country. This highlights the importance of linking these policies to social policies.

Some *a priori* critiques of affirmative action stemmed from a lack of understanding of what these policies are, their possibilities and limits, as well as their benefits – a problem which persist. Confusions surrounding these understandings have been prejudicial to a wider debate, creating a series of polarizations and expectations especially in relation to racial quotas. Affirmative action, as focused policies, presuppose a limited impact. They can be useful in combating a racial discrimination that leads to a differentiated social position for Blacks and whites, as statistical data make clear, but also to promote public debate concerning racism and the role of Blacks in society. In Brazil, affirmative action generated an important symbolic shift in the image of Blacks, particularly in education and the media. They are not, however, sufficient to confront existing racial prejudice of structural racism. To this end, positive policies would have to be enacted, aimed at the recognition of the ethnic and racial pluralism that exists in Brazilian society, an anti-racist education that would make the negative effects of racism clear, and which would contemplate society as a whole[86]. Nor can they be considered to be a solution to poverty, since they cannot solve all of the problems of the Black population in Brazil, and it is probable that they are

---

[86] According to Wieviorka, these policies aim for the social inclusion of racially discriminated groups, and cannot be defined as policies that, in and of themselves, provide any cultural recognition, nor do they fight racial prejudice or racism or aim poverty as such (Wieviorka, 2001, p. 90)

more helpful for a Black middle class that for Blacks at the bottom of the class structure (Igreja, 2005).

However, the debate has centred, and centres still, on how to identify those who benefit from these policies, and on the possibilities of fraud in the system. Efforts at improving methods of identification has been an ongoing part of the consolidation of the policies. A trigger for this debate was the establishment of quotas for Black students at the University of Brasília (UnB)[87]. This was the first federal public university to offer specific quotas for Blacks, with no consideration of social class, gaining notoriety for its exclusively racial approach to the issue, as well as for its methods for designating beneficiaries.

According to the UnB's "Plan of aims for social, ethnic, and racial integration", 20% of places were to be reserved for *preto (Black)* and *pardo*(brown)candidates, who must not only declare themselves to be Black, but must also be photographed upon registration of their application. Photographs were then presented to a committee of "specialists", among which anthropologists, charged with verifying the phenotype of the candidate, with aim of ratifying their application, and thereby avoiding frauds, cancelling the application of white students who declared themselves to be Black, and therefore subject to the ethnic-racial sub-quota system established by Law 12.711/2012. (Nunes, 2018). The use of photographs by the UnB was abandoned after twin brothers went through the commission at separate times, and only one of them had his racial identity recognized, which resulted in a series of attacks to the system, particularly by the large media conglomerates (Folha de São Paulo, 2007; O Globo, 2007).

In this climate of anxieties, Marco Chor Maio and Ricardo Ventura Santos (2005) published an article in which they expressed concern with the ethical repercussions of using anthropology as a privileged field of knowledge for committees of "racial expertise"[88]. This concern was based on the fact that the mechanisms adopted for identification of candidates amounted to "a restriction on the individual right, in particular to the right of self-identification". This system, furthermore, disregards "the conceptual framework of the social sciences and, in particular, of social anthropology and biological anthropology". For Marco Chor Maio and Ricardo Ventura Santos (2005), the ambiguous characteristics of racial perception in Brazil made it impossible to reproduce such classifica-

---

[87] The university was not the first to create a commission for racial verification, since the University of Mato Grosso do Sul had done so previously. However, it was the first top-tier university to do so and being based in the capital gave it greater visibility (Feres et al., 2018).

[88] The authors' views were the subject of debate in a special issue of the journal *Horizontes Antropológicos*, published by the Graduate Programme of the Federal University of Rio Grande do Sul (Horiz. antropol. v.11 n° 23, Porto Alegre January/June 2005).

tions in the "eyes of society" (an expression used by one of the members of the committee that installed quotas at the UnB). Other authors pointed out that, while the use of photographs at the UnB may have been an error, the issue of identifying those who would benefit from racial quota in Brazil should not be an impediment to the implementation of urgent policies that seek to aid a discriminated group (Guimarães, 2005; Sansone, 2005). Racial quotas at the UnB were the basis for Claim of Non-Compliance with a Fundamental Precept (ADPF), n° 186 (2010), a suit entered by the Democratas (DEM), a right-wing political party, in the Supreme Court. The Court, in turn, was unanimous in dismissing the suit on the 26th of April 2012, claiming that the system was constitutional and ratifying it, including the procedure of alter-identification alongside ethno-racial self-identification

As well as being a forum for academic and political debate, the UnB became a privileged field for understanding not only how the racial issue is debated, but also the political and social dynamics by means of which racial signifiers are constructed, discussed and renegotiated. The discussions which followed therefore represented a privileged moment for sociological and anthropological analysis on the social phenomena of race and racism. In effect, they allowed social science researchers to access the structural dimension that conditioned the need for affirmative action policies, and the contingent and situational characteristics of the process of racial categorization (Igreja & Tavolaro, 2015).

It is now more than ten years since the Statute of racial equality was approved and affirmative action implemented. Within higher education, accusations of racial fraud, made mostly by representatives of social movements and Black students – that is, that various white students were declaring themselves to be Black to benefit from quotas – added weight to demands for more efficient mechanisms to verify self-identification. As part of the obligations of the state in administering affirmative action policies, the elaboration of these mechanisms befell to institutional administrators (Nunes, 2018). This is when commissions for ethno-racial alter-identification are established and expand in various Brazilian universities.

Sales Augusto dos Anjos (2021) stresses the importance of distinguishing between existing committees, charged with verifying purported fraud and which are constituted to this end, and the committees which validate the ethno-racial self-identification of students. The former is provisional, created to investigate formal accusations involving students who are suspected of having acted fraudfully to gain a place at university, while the latter are permanent and have the preventive function of ratifying the self-identification of candidates during the selection process. According to Sales Augusto dos Anjos (2021, p. 28), there are 94 Commissions for ethno-racial alter-identification in federal public universities in Brazil[89]. These are divided into 44 Commissions for the Verification of alter-identification and 50 Commissions for the Validation of alter-identification; 5 federal universities did not respond the questionnaire, and among respondents nine had not implemented any commission. Commissions in Brazilian universities are quite varied in the criteria they apply and in their composition, but most follow the indication in the afore-mentioned ADPF nº 186, from 2009, which determines that "evaluation should be based on phenotype and not ascendency"[90]. In his comprehensive bibliographical review, the author concludes that ethno-racial alter-identification has been effective against fraud or attempts at fraudulent use of the ethno-racial sub-quotas. Its success lies largely in how it inhibits fraud. Data from university shows that students asked to appear before an alter-identification commission often do not show up, which results in a high rate of ratification of those who self-identify as Black by the commission. Appeals often confirm the commission's decision.

There has not been any regimentation by the Brazilian Ministry of Education of the formats and criteria for ethno-racial identification by the commissions. The norm which has been followed has thus been Normative Ordinance nº 4, passed on the 6th of April 2018, by the Secretary for People Administration of the Ministry of Planning, Development and Management (MPDG), which is charged with overseeing the commissions for alter-identification in public tender for civil service positions, as laid out in law 12.990, as we have mentioned previously.

Although it is not the main aim of this book, it is important to recall that racial quotas for higher education are also applies to Indigenous candidates. Debates surrounding quotas for the Indigenous population take a different direction in what concerns the identification of beneficiaries, raising questions of cultural recognition and diversity through projects of individual inclusion of its members (Souza Lima, 2018)[91]. This issue merges with wider debate on the

---

[89] There are 69 federal public universities in Brazil, according to the Ministry of Education.
[90] On examples of commissions in public universities, see, along with the recent work of Sales de Augusto dos Anjos (2021), the Special Section "The importance of commissions of alter-identification in ensuring affirmative action for Blacks in Brazilian public universities", in the ABPN Journal, June – August 2019, | v. 11 n° 29 (2019); https://abpnrevista.org.br/index.php/site/issue/view/33
[91] In her study of the Diversity in the University Programme, Rebecca Igreja (2005) explain that the inclusion of Indigenous peoples was, initially, part of the Ministry of Education's search for recognized cultural difference as a means of making the policy legitimate. The debate had involved only the Black population, but it was increasingly polarized because of the issue of racial identification. Within the project itself there was little dialogue with specialists on Indigenous people, although there were manifestations from Indigenous leaders.

Indigenous question in Brazil, which would take us far beyond the aims of this book. Briefly, affirmative action enables a fairly large contingent of Indigenous people to gain university places, without, however, making provisions for projects of Indigenous higher education, which would be conceived collectively and in accordance with the demands of different peoples. Nor does it bring to the university a discussion of Indigenous culture, the place of Indigenous people in Brazilian society, or of the importance of intercultural higher education (Souza Lima, 2018). The challenge is to enable higher education institutions to validate, and to disseminate, other types of knowledge, anchored in other cosmological, philosophical, and epistemological bases (Baniwa, 2013).

Gersem Baniwa (2013) explains that while affirmative action is very important for Indigenous peoples, since the contribute to their full and differentiated citizenship in dialogue with the state and national society, as well as giving them access to an important multicultural space, certain measures remain to be implemented. One concern is with the individualization that these measures impose, since:

> The principal marker of Indigenous rights is difference and equivalence, not equality or similarity, which is why Indigenous peoples have demanded a differentiated treatment through policies that value and recognize difference and diversity, rather than inclusion in homogenization, even in the sphere of policies that target diversity or social minorities. In many cases, policies of inclusion, though well-intentioned, can result categorically in socio-political exclusion (2013, p. 20)

In this way, self-identification compromises an Indigenous commitment to collective rights. According to Baniwa, communities often fight for collective rights, but Indigenous people who benefit from quotas are not committed to their communities. This is exacerbated by the fact that many of those who benefit come from urban contexts, being less involved in community values. Although Indigenous people in urban contexts certainly have the right to university places through quotas, Baniwa (2013, p. 20) proposes that there is a need to find an equilibrium between their participation and that of residents in traditional communities. This would also mean conceiving of policies that ensure that students remain enrolled in university, and programmes to help them adapt to the academic context, with particular attention to bilingualism. The critique targets the homogenization of policies that focus on diversity.

While accepting Gersem Baniwa's considerations, it is important to stress that inclusion in academic contexts has been difficult even for Indigenous people associated with urban contexts, mostly because of their poor social conditions and the racism and ethnic discrimination that they face in the city. Furthermore, they face yet another hurdle: the recognition of their identities considering that they live outside of Indigenous communities (Igreja, 2019; Souza Silva, 2022). Many Indigenous people who arrive in urban contexts, usually as workers inserted in the city's dynamics, cease to present themselves as being Indigenous and are included in the *pardo* (Brown) category, and consequently considered to be "Black". Thus, many associations point to the phenomenon of *pardismo* (Brownisn), which makes invisible Indigenous people in urban contexts.[92]

The discussion concerning affirmative action for higher education targeting Indigenous students also brings us relevant questions concerning Black students. The policies carry an individualized dimensions which must be taken into account. The admittance of Black persons in the university setting is not guarantee that this people will develop greater commitment to the anti-racist struggle. The debate has often focused on the individual responsibility of quota students; but racism is a structural problem, and the responsibility must fall to entire society. Furthermore, affirmative action is also unable to transform what is a Eurocentric, and often racist, educational environment. This change must come about through more inclusive educational projects, such as the ones outlined in Law n° 10,639 (2003), which focuses on the teaching of Afro-Brazilian history and culture, stressing the importance of Black culture to Brazilian society, although the law has been applied slipshod in the country. We can likewise include the critique of the homogenization of politics, which often fails to consider the local contexts and regional diversity of the country. What, then, can we deduce from these policies?

At the time of writing this book, there are ongoing discussions for the revision of affirmative action policies in higher education. As per law n° 12,711 (2012), quotas are temporary policies that need to be reviewed ten years from the date of their publication. The review is taking place during an election year, in which a new president will be voted in, and also during a troubled political period, in which the country is being governed by a far-right politician, openly opposed to the policy. In this scenario, an evaluation of the results obtained during the decade proves more than necessary.

---

92 Between the 11th and 18th of April 2022, Brazilian Indigenous organizations held an event called "I'm not Brown, I'm Indigenous: Debating *pardismo* (Brownism), to which they invited a range of leading figures and intellectuals to discuss the ethno-racial classification *pardo* (Brown). See: https://www.correiocidadania.com.br/brasil-nas-ruas/14590-nao-sou-pardo-sou-indigena-o-pardismo-em-debate . Contesting Brownism and its association to the ethno-racial category "Black" has been particularly important for Indigenous identity claims in urban contexts, and even for Indigenous peasants who struggle to be recognized for their cultural difference.

Many studies that seek to evaluate affirmative action have focused on the history of the policy, considering the evolution of the debate and the legislation that supports it. There are few qualitative studies that trace the experience of quota beneficiaries and the perceptions of non-beneficiaries regarding quotas in the academic field. In general, the majority of studies are based on surveys of quantitative data. From this perspective, they seek to account for the expansion of the policy, spelling out the number of public and private universities that apply it and the criteria that are followed, as well as the number of Black students who are beneficiaries. Measuring these policies using the isolation of quotas as an explanatory variable is difficult as it involves a series of complementary elements, much like the strengthening of educational policies and the expansion of Brazilian public universities in previous governments. Affirmative action, as we have mentioned, reinforces a series of social policies that have been implemented and that have contributed to its successful operation. How, then, can we verify their success?

An initial conclusion of several studies is that there has been an increase in the inclusion of students from public schools, including Black and Indigenous students, in federal public universities, for which the Quotas Laws are more strictly regulated (Godoi & Santos, 2021; Machado et. al., 2017). As Godoi and Santos (2021, p. 18) observe, the most recent surveys indicate a major transformation in the social and ethno-racial composition of newly admitted students in universities: in 2019, 40% of freshmen were graduates from the public network, and Black and Indigenous freshmen made up 25.2% of the total, compared to only 6% in 2010.

An IPEA study (Silva, T.D., 2020, p. 16) also shows that the racial composition of students at public universities is constantly changing, as a result of the increase in the number of places and policies to democratise access to public higher education. The average number of years of formal education of the Brazilian population increased between 1992 and 2015 from 5.2 to 8.2 years. The Black population, which averaged 65.3% of the number of years studying when compared to the white population (4 and 6.1 years, respectively), now has indicators which show an average of 82.5% years of study when compared to the white population (7.4 and 9 years). Silva points out, however, that although average schooling has gone up for both groups, it is important to highlight the elevated level of inequality that nonetheless persists. The study also shows that if Blacks previously represented only 22% of students in higher education, in 2015 this figure reached approximately 44%. In this sense, the study also shows that, throughout this period, there was also a significant increase in people who declared themselves to be Black or mixed race, a phenomenon that comes closer to racial identification than to specific demographic components. Despite these gains, the Black population in 2017 still corresponded to 32% of people with higher education degrees. When only the population aged 25 years or more is taken into account, as little as 9.3% of blacks had completed higher education, while in the white population this figure had reached 22.9%.

Many of these young quota holders are the first people in their family to have access to higher education[93]. It is important to remember that, in general, they access university through racial sub-quotas set within the scope of social quotas that establish maximum family income for beneficiaries and a public-school education; that is, they are young people from the poorest social strata of the country. It is also worth remembering that Brazilian public universities are of the highest quality in the country, with difficult admission exams, while public schools are considered to be of the lowest quality and constantly subject to underfunding. The origin of these students and their trajectories are a crucial variable for considering the policy in a country where social inequalities and differential access to education are marked. Furthermore, access to universities is not enough; measures must be taken to prevent these students from dropping out, which requires providing institutional support, including material resources and special counselling.

This is a theme addressed in several manifestations of quota beneficiaries in universities. They need scholarships to dedicate themselves to their studies, without needing to work regular hours to maintain their own livelihood and often that of their families. Furthermore, assistance with transportation, food, technological equipment, books, among other necessities, are essential demands for ensuring the success of these students, inhibiting them from dropping out of their courses. Affirmative action in Brazil is linked to the struggle against social exclusion and inequality.

It is not just material resources that these students need. How the institution receives and hosts them is also fundamental. Access to a highly elite space, historically white and Eurocentric, in a context of highly polarised debates, generates insecurity and fear. Even before the introduction of quotas, the literature on the theme warned of the dangers of structural and contemporary racism in Brazilian society, including in academic institutions. We should recall that the first quota project set up at the University of Brasília was born from an episode in 1998, when a Black doctoral student, Arivaldo Lima Alves, denounced that he had been a victim of racism by a professor in the anthropology department.

---

[93] Recent studies by Rodrigo Ednilson de Jesus (2019, 2021) show some of the biographies of these young quota-beneficiaries in Brazilian universities.

From a contrary point of view, it was often claimed that affirmative action policies called into question the meritocratic principles of access and risked the quality of education by providing access to students who are not qualified. The system would, furthermore, transfer to the university a social problem that needed to be solved at the foundation of the education system, in public schools. Although this criticism is well-founded, since in fact the problem of quota beneficiaries begins in elementary school, young Black and Indigenous people fight for their right to be enrolled in public universities. Following this contrary perspective, quotas end up being viewed as a favour, a privilege granted by the state, rather than a right of citizens to ace public university.

In this context, quota beneficiaries feel that they need to prove that they have a right to be in the academy, seeking out better qualifications for themselves, even if they lack the structure and material conditions of other students (Reis, 2007). More recent analyses show that this educational inequality between quota beneficiaries and non-quota beneficiaries does not seem to be confirmed; on the contrary, in some degree courses quota beneficiaries show a better performance than their non-quota counterparts (Cavalcanti et al., 2019; Godoi & Santos, 2021;). Once admitted to university, it their income over time becomes similar to that of non-quota students (Bezerra & Gurgel, 2012; Griner et al., 2013; Santos, J., 2012). There are still barriers, particularly the hard sciences, considered to be more difficult to access and requiring more resources to discourage students from dropping out.

An evaluation of racial quotas must take several factors into account, but we would like to focus on the process of racial identification that accompanies these policies. As already mentioned in the IPEA studies (Silva, T.D., 2020), an increase in the number of Black students in Brazilian universities had already been noted, and this increase has been amplified by affirmative action. We can highlight, then, that the introduction of affirmative action helped to renew criticisms of the myth of Brazilian racial democracy, and the condemnation of persistent racism, shining a spotlight on the problem and promoting Black pride. The presence of Black scientists in Brazilian universities is nothing new, but many occupy the peripheries of the academic system, with little visibility or recognition. For this reason, we increasingly see the creation of associations of Black intellectuals in the country, followed by stimuli for the access of more Blacks to university. In this sense, we can question accusations regarding the pernicious effect of racial quotas, which, it was argued, could generate serious racial conflict. A more critical literature attests that this is not a concrete effect of racial quotas, since there is no record of conflicts or tensions in the university context (Bezerra & Gurgel, 2012). Affirmative action revealed a social fracture that victimizes the Black population, reflected in their different socioeconomic levels, as well as in daily violence and in the complaints of racism that are brought forward. The exclusion of Blacks from higher education, from public universities, was itself clear evidence of the racial division to which they were subjected. We believe that, instead of creating racial tensions, quotas allow us to denounce a historic situation of exclusion and to ensure a Black presence in these spaces.

Higher education quotas, initially restricted to undergraduate degrees, are now being applies at graduate level, bringing themes related to the Black population and their diaspora to the heart of discussions in graduate degree programmes. In the same way, there is a growing number of new research groups on the study of racial quotas. Less attention has been paid, however, to how racial quotas are applied to public service positions, at the federal, state, and municipal levels, even though they pre-date quotas in public universities. The first cohort of beneficiaries of affirmative action for the hiring of federal civil servants were admitted to the Ministry for Agrarian Development in 2001, and the policy was gradually extended to other ministries. This first phase culminated with Federal Decree n° 4,228 (2002) which instituted the National Affirmative Action Programme within the Federal Public Administration, providing for percentage targets for Afro-Brazilians, women and people with disabilities in assuming commissioned positions. This norm, however, was never fully applied (Osório, 2006), largely due to internal resistance within agencies. It is still in force, though now greatly slackened. In a more decentralized manner, similar law proposals have been issued at the state and municipal levels. A norm seeking to apply it to federal public service as a whole only emerged years later, with the Racial Equality Statute – EIRA, which we have referred to previously. However, only one article of the Statute dealt specifically with racial quotas, without clearly regulating this right and with only suggesting how it might be adopted in the labour market. Although proposals in this direction have been submitted in the House of Representatives, it was only in 2013 that a bill dealing with the issue passed the final stage of the legislative process, being converted into Federal Law n° 12,990 (2014). This norm marked the beginning of the second generation of racial affirmative action for public positions, resulting in a significant growth of new legislation in the various spheres of the Brazilian federation. (Ferreira, 2017; Igreja et al., 2021; Igreja & Ferreira, 2019).

Racial quotas law in federal public administration positions only take ethnic-racial identification into account, without considering socioeconomic aspects. Ferreira (2017) explains that three questions were not adequately answered by the Law: "how much", "where" and "who". Such questions reflect discussion on the percentage of reserved vacancies (how much), the lack of distinction between reserved vacancies according to career (where) and the non-inclusion of commissioned positions (who). He questions the established decision of 20 % of reserved places, for even if it takes the number of Black people already in public service as a reference point, it does not adequately consider their representation in Brazilian society according to statistical data, and neither does it factor in the under-representation of Blacks in deliberative political bodies. Ferreira explains that there is an imbalance in Black representation according to different careers which has not been considered in the Law, given that those which demand greater qualification, and, as a consequence, pay higher wages, have less Blacks than those which require fewer qualifications, and hence pay lower wages. The bill does not thus adequately address the problem of the exclusion of Afro-Brazilians, especially in decision-making positions. Finally, there is no consideration of the presence of Black people in positions which are freely appointed by competent authorities. According to the author, these questions ultimately come down to a protection of white privilege in the control of State institutions.

The analysis of affirmative action in competitive examinations for admission to public careers provides interesting perspectives. Rebecca Igreja and Gianmarco Ferreira (2021) have drawn up a georeferenced map that presents a normative overview of affirmative action in the country[94], demonstrating that there has been an effective national expansion of the policy, encompassing different spheres, including temporary positions. A first element that emerges is related to the racial identification of candidates and the selection criteria. Almost all the rules establish the option for self-identification, but there is terminological variation in the selection notices that does not correspond to exclusive categories. Some laws, while maintaining the tendency to use the IBGE's colour and race questionnaires, are flexible in terms of the racial identifications of quota beneficiaries, proposing as interchangeable and non-self-exclusive the categories "Blacks" (*pardos* + *pretos*), "Afro-descendants", "Afro-Brazilians", *pretos* (Blacks), as well as others. All of these are considered to be the same in terms of the percentage of reserved places. In other words, the terminological fluidity used by legislation is compatible with the aim of contemplating the greatest possible number of people who, using one term to the detriment of another, would otherwise not feel contemplated by the policy. Thus, for example, Act 1,453, of

---

[94] It is important to take note of the breadth of the norm, which, in general, is applied to the Executive, Legislative, and Judiciary branches. In certain cases, for certain careers, it is applied to other spheres, such as the Public Prosecutor's Office and state-level Public Defence. In the sample analysed, 101 positions are in the executive branch; 14 in the legislative branch; 7 in the judiciary branch; and 9 exclusively in state-level Public Defendant's Offices. As can be discerned by the sum of these positions, with exceeds the total of 113 federal entities, some apply affirmative action to all three branches (Igreja & Ferreira, 2021, p. 23).

November 28, 2019[95], issued by the São Paulo City Council, provides that "Blacks, Negroes or Afro-descendants are the people who are *preto* (black), *pardo* (brown) or an equivalent denomination, as established by IBGE". It adds that "the expression equivalent denomination ... covers *preto* (black) or *pardo* (brown) people, that is, they will only be considered when their phenotype socially identifies them as Black" (Igreja & Ferreira, 2021, p. 299). In this case, it is worth noting that racial identification commissions were established to verify the declaration of the candidates.

The debate around racial quotas in the public service sphere has taken place in parallel with that in higher education, although the latter has received more attention from the public-at-large. Quotas in education have been prominent because of the belief that it is in this sphere that the structure of racism is tackled, not only because of the inclusion of Blacks in academic spaces, but also because of education to promote a plural, inclusive and anti-racist ideology. Focusing only on this perspective, however, conceals the potential of the application of affirmative action in public bureaucracy. This is where public policies are thought out and elaborated, where a state project is consolidated and where decisions are made.

Takin a Weberian perspective (Weber, 2004), bureaucracy is not only an administrative organisation, but a form of legitimate domination that reflects the power relations existing in society and that are rendered concrete in this space. In the analysis of public bureaucracies, we observe what has been called institutional racism, a concept defined by Stokely Carmichael and Charles Hamilton, activist members of the Black Panthers group, in 1967 (Carmichael & Hamilton, 1967). In their understanding, institutional racism reveals itself as the collective failure of an organisation to provide an appropriate and professional service to people because of their colour, culture or ethnic origin[96]. For this reason, the debate on the subject has been explored especially by Black movements that recognize the importance of promoting effective changes in institutional structures (Werneck, 2013) [97].

---

95 http://documentacao.saopaulo.sp.leg.br/iah/fulltext/atoscmsp/AC145319.pdf
96 Igreja and Ferreira seek to develop the theme in the sphere of discussions surrounding representative bureaucracy by considering affirmative action policies in public bureaucracy not only as a policy that provides jobs for Blacks, but which also has an anti-racist and transformative potential (Igreja & Ferreira, 2021).
97 In a study of the "Diversity in the University" Programme, Rebecca Igreja (2005), for example, demonstrates the obstacles inhibiting the development of an anti-racist educational policy by the institutional structure of the Ministry of Education, which tends to be conservative and inflexible to the changes that such a policy would require.

Affirmative Action and the political far-right in Brazil

President Jair Bolsonaro came to power promising a cultural and moral reform of the country and the recovery of Christian and family values. He has positioned himself radically against socio-cultural, gender and racial agendas, which he identifies as strategies of ideological domination of the international left and as a moral subversion of traditional Brazilian culture. The president's positions are based on: an anti-democratic verve; a pro-military stance, in defence of allowing citizens to carry firearms, and promoting violence and repression; ultraliberal viewpoints; moralistic opinions, with regular attacks on LGBTQIAP+ populations; radically anti-left ideology; anti-political populism, showing contempt for politics and political parties; anti-media, criticising the partiality of the press; anti-minorities, with constant attacks on Blacks, Indigenous peoples, landless peasants, women, the unemployed, the homeless, immigrants, prisoners, criminals; and anti-cultural, with attacks especially on artists (Igreja & Negri, 2020; Negri et al., 2019).

The Bolsonaro administration is identified with the rise of a new far-right that has parallel in other liberal democracies. It is associated with the contemporary context of globalisation, the domination of neoliberalism, exacerbated individualism, the growth of socioeconomic inequalities and, in specific cases, large migration flows. It is in this context that we observe the far right promote hate speech that rejects (and manufactures) "the other", composed of immigrants, the poor, Blacks, gays or other political minorities, naturalising inequalities and exclusions (Igreja & Negri, 2020).

Founded on the principles of the far right, President Bolsonaro calls for the liberation of the Brazilian people from what he understands to be a cultural Marxism that imposes indoctrination in schools and subverts traditional and family values and democratic principles. In a singular interpretation of the meanings of democracy and freedom, he considers them to boil down to the right to private property, liberalism, the possession of weapons, freedom of the family without the interference of the state, and Christian freedom in rejection of the secular state. Based on these values, he organizes his government structure to serve the "good Brazilians", true representatives of the people, as opposed to the "bad Brazilian".

According to the president, Brazilians are Christians, Evangelicals, patriots, fond of the military (as a virtue more than a profession), liberal, heads of family, honest, loyal, true, workers, incorrupt, defenders of freedom, private property, agribusiness, democracy, traditional family values, and representatives of a united people, the majority. The "bad Brazilian" is leftist, a supporter of the Worker's Party, a communist, corrupt, militant, a bum, a thief, a terrorist, politically correct, a journalist, an environmentalist, member of a minority, a defender of gender ideology (the devil itself). It is necessary to consider these categories not in isolation, but in their interrelations. In his proposal for cultural and moral reform, they go together, complement each other and are constantly re-signified. It is in this type of categorization that the government idealizes the Brazilian people and it is in this categorization that it classifies Indigenous peoples and Afro-descendants (Igreja, 2021).

Bolsonaro subscribes to this new far-right that some interpret as form of right-wing populism. Emphasising anti-pluralism, this perspective considers that the elites are immoral, corrupt and parasitic, opposed to the idea of a people seen as homogeneous and pure. Its consistent claim is that they, and they alone, represent a true people. Their political distinctions are binary, of a moral character, between the true and the false. By these characteristics, populism is synonymous with a strongly moral polarization (Müller, 2016, p. 176).

Rebecca Igreja (2021) explains that this symbolic construction of what the true Brazilian is takes place in a terrain of disputes in the public arena, opposing the conservative ideology of the government and the advance of progressive forces. This dispute is heterogenous, but it articulates around the defense of human and collective rights, anti-racist agendas, the environment and the greater involvement of the state with social policies. Faced with broad changes in recent years, including the expansion of rights for women, for the LGBTQIAP+ community and for Black and Indigenous people, with wide-ranging social policies, including the introduction of racial and ethnic quotas, and, as a consequence, a more comprehensive inclusion of Blacks and Indigenous peoples in education, the elites react seeking to guarantee their historical privileges, taking advantage of discontent with previous leftist governments which failed to fully meet the expectations of part of the population.

In his studies on the far-right, Rydgren (2007; Igreja, 2021, p. 16) explains that its resurgence in Europe takes place alongside novel social and political movements related to new parties (i.e., green parties and new left-wing parties). The author believes that, for this reason, there is a misunderstanding when analyses about this ideology are carried forth without considering approaches in the field of social movements and the analysis of ethnic networks and relations. It is in this sense that Rebecca Igreja (2021) considers this rise of the far-right in the context of multiculturalism and insurgency and of the strengthening of ethno-racial demands. It emerges in a context of fear and insecurity generated by the strengthening of other cultures, other peoples, as well as feminist demands and those of LGBTQIAP+ groups, which threaten the traditional conservative order. It relies on culturalist and identity rhetoric to reclaim its traditional ground, as Crépon (2001; Igreja, 2021) observes. In this oscillation, it seeks allies, makes concessions, and builds consensus. The extreme right thus reacts to multiculturalism, but redefines itself through its own principles.

In order to consolidate his project for a conservative government, Bolsonaro proposes a broad ministerial reform. One example of this reform is the Ministry of Women, Family and Human Rights, headed Damares Alves, a conservative woman, pastor and one of the most important personalities in the government. This ministry has a number of subordinate agencies, including the National Secretariat of Policies for Women – SNPM, the National Secretariat of the Family – SNF, the National Secretariat for the Rights of Children and Adolescents – SNDCA, the National Secretariat of Youth – SNJ, the National Secretariat of Policies for the Promotion of Racial Equality – SNPIR. There is hence a de-structuring of institutions focused on the issue of minorities.

Even before being elected, Bolsonaro already positioned himself against affirmative action. In an interview to the Cidade Verde TV, in the state of Piauí, on the 23rd of October 2018, he claimed that the racial quota policy was "completely equivocated". He considers affirmative policies to be an example of "victimism", which reenforces prejudice. Bolsonaro said that it was necessary to "end all of this"

> There is no doubt that they strengthen [prejudice]. For example, the quota policy in Brazil is completely equivocated", he claimed. "This is all a way of dividing society. We shouldn't have special classes, for questions of skin colour, questions of sexual choice, or religion, or whatever it is. We are all equal before the law. We are one people. [...] You don't need a policy for this. This can't continue to exist, everything is victimism. Poor Blacks, poor women, poor gays, poor Northeasterners, poor piauíense. Everything is victimism in Brazil. We're going to end this. (O Globo, 2018).

This opinion is complemented by many other statements made by the president, showing disdain for policies which target minorities, often accompanied by manifestations of prejudice. Bolsonaro collects racist and discriminatory phrases directed at Blacks, women, gays, northeasterners and Indigenous people. In August 2018, during a campaign event in Rio de Janeiro, he pronounced an infamous phrase, which led to his conviction in the first instance, but later acquittal in court: "I went to a quilombo in Eldorado Paulista. Look, the lightest Afro-descendant there weighed seven animal units. They don't do anything. I don't even think they are good enough to procreate. More than R$ 1 billion a year is spent with them". Or more recent phrases, such is one addressed to a boy with afro hair: "How is the cockroach breeding there? Look at the cockroach breeder here", he said, laughing. He also continued: "you can't take ivermectin, it will kill all your lice", citing a drug that was falsely touted as a treatment for covid-19 (Migalhas, 2021). The president considers that criticism of his speeches are merely politically correct censures, and that they are therefore meaningless.

Bolsonaro openly defends the opinion of the "majority" (defined from his very own perspective) of the Brazilian people. If, at first, the president attacked quotas directly, during his period in office his manifestations have been less common. His constant attacks on public universities, interpreted as strongholds of the left, and the massive withdrawal of resources from public education indirectly threaten the development and continuity of quotas in higher education. Furthermore, the government constantly acts to produce a counter-image of the Black man, constructing a Black man who does not need "victimisms", who is enterprising, neoliberal, respectful of conservative family values and religion. In his rhetoric, he does not emphasize racial democracy or mestizaje, but re-signifies identities based on what he considers to be the Indigenous persons and Blacks who make up the nation. Agendas related to tackling racism, poverty, and violence are not part of his government's guidelines, since they are understood to be linked to the left.

Sérgio Camargo, the new president of Palmares Cultural Foundation, appointed by Bolsonaro, is Black and conservative, aligned with the president's ideas. He is a controversial figure, who constantly speaks out against anti-racist agendas and social movements. In several of his public manifestations, in documents and internet posts, he praises what, according to him, is a dignified Black man, one who respects his history and his aspirations as a citizen. He believes that the Foundation should treats the Black man as "a normal person" with common desires like all Brazilians; a Black man who turns to entrepreneurship, who defends meritocracy and who recognises himself in the conservative values of Brazilian society. He rejects the militant Black man, the Black man of the Quilombos, exalting conservative Black historical figures, considering that the Black man of the Worker's Party governments (in reference to the previous governments) is the "eternal arrival from the slave ships, treated as a manipulable mass, fuel for the fire of victimism".

In alignment with the president, Sérgio Camargo associated himself with the ultraconservative currents of the country. He takes parts in events such as the "Conservative Congress: Liberty and Democracy", the largest even of the type in Brazil, held on the 14th of November 2021. According to the site of the Foundation Camargo, beside Dom Bertrand, the would-be heir to the Brazilian crown, stressed the importance of whites and Blacks living in unity, without resentments:

> We have to look to the future of Brazil. We are one people, and we will not be divided by the racist left. Decent and honourable Blacks in Brazil are grateful to Princess Isabel. She sanc-

tioned the abolition of slavery. Today, the Marxist Black Movement seeks to enslave and subjugate Black minds, and they try to destroy the legacy of the Redeemer. (Fundação Cultural Palmares, 2021)

Expressions such as "authentic Brazil", "decent and honoured Blacks", contain a selective moral judgement in relation to left-wing Blacks who are part of the resistance and who are redefined as the true racists. It is fundamental to observe how the concept of racism is manipulated in this context. The very discussion of racism, especially by Black movements, is said to create a separation in society between Blacks and whites, producing what several conservative currents identify as reverse racism. According to this perspective, a policy aimed exclusively at Blacks is racist because it would foster division and racial hatred. Racism is thus expanded to include a person of any colour, including whites, removing the historical inequalities and exclusions of Blacks by whites. Camargo's speech reflects Bolsonaro's thinking, as demonstrated by his recent message on racism to the national congress, in which he does not mention the Black population once, focusing only on anti-Semitism (Brasil. Presidente, 2022).

In sum, in the current Brazilian landscape, official public discussions concerning the Black population is linked to the conservative proposals of the extreme right, which include religious conservatism and neoliberal market interests. Shrewdly, the current government does not deny the existence of racism, but appropriates the concept, resignifying and expanding it to non-black citizens.

A further way of observing how discussion about racism and Afro-descendants has been repurposed is to look at how religious intolerance, a theme which is central to Black organizations because of Afro-Brazilian religions, has been dealt with by the government. Since the beginning of her administration, Minister Damares Alves has aired her concern with the persecution of Christianity. In a recent event organised by the Ministry of Women, the Family and Human Rights to celebrate the day against religious intolerance, involving the participation of conservative entities in the country, It was defended the idea that persecution and intolerance were not only an experience of Afro-Brazilian religions, but also of conservative Evangelical and Catholic churches, which no longer had the right to uphold their family values, their anti-minority agendas, especially anti- LGBTQIAP+. The event was not attended by any representative of Afro-Brazilian churches (Ministério da Mulher, da Família e dos Direitos Humanos, 2022).

This political scenario is complemented by the increase in poverty and violence throughout the country, resulting, to some degree, from the end of social policies, the empowerment of the police and armed groups, the armament policy, and, finally, ongoing discriminatory and racist manifestations. In addition, an important number of neo-Nazi cells are coming to light in the country, especially in the southern region. Bolsonaro and members of his government affiliate with ultraconservative movements around the world and, in a way, legitimise neo-Nazi groups that oppose LGBTQIAP+ groups, women, Blacks, Northeasterners, and different minorities. These hate groups had preciously remained underground, in obscure internet for a, but now they are much more visible, even organizing events and creating associations. Adriana Dias reports that, at present, the public sphere has been taken over by neo-Nazis, and that this network can already be considered a mass movement that extends across the country. According to Dias, it is estimated that there are currently about 530 extremist cells in Brazil[98].

Faced with this political scenario, Black and progressive movements in the country respond mainly by denouncing racism and genocide of young Blacks. The Atlas of Violence (Cerqueira, 2021, p. 49) shows that in 2019 Blacks were 77% of homicide victims, with a homicide rate of 29.2 per 100,000 people. This rate is 2.6 times higher than that of a non-Black people. Also, according to the Atlas, data from the last decade shows that the reduction in homicides that occurred in the country was more concentrated in the non-Black population. Between 2009 and 2019, the homicide rates showed a decrease of 20.3%, with a reduction of 15.5% among Blacks and 30.5% among non-Blacks, that is, the decrease in homicide rates of non-blacks is 50% higher than that of the black population. If we also consider the absolute numbers for the same period, there was an increase of 1.6% of homicides among Blacks between 2009 and 2019, from 33,929 to 34,446 victims in the last year. Among non-Blacks, in contrast, there was a reduction of 33% in the absolute number of victims, from 15,249 in 2009 to 10,217 deaths in 2019. These data help us visualize the immense problem of violence that the Black population, especially, young Blacks, face in the country.

Despite the persistence of violence, and even its increase, in recent years social policies, including affirmative action, enabled not only the socioeconomic improvement of the Black population through enrolment in higher education, but also expanded discussions on racism in the country, shedding light on the issue and broadening the spheres in which it is broached, particularly in the media through television programmes and newspapers with wide circulation. News reports in several newspapers in the country also point to an important increase in denunciations of racial insult and racism (CNN, 2021; Diário do Nor-

---

98 https://www.youtube.com/watch?v=OGE5-cm-qdY

deste, 2021; Periódico UEPG, 2020; UOL, 2021)[99]. The interpretation for this increase is that there is today a greater awareness and recognition of rights that lead people who are victims of racial prejudice to publicly denounce it. Although punishment for these crimes is rare and there is still little data on the subject, illustrative cases gain public repercussion quickly. This space is constantly occupied by representatives of Black associations and by Black journalists and intellectuals, especially younger ones, who also become renowned for their work in social media.

The country is currently going through a complex and difficult political period. There is a sharp polarization of political debate, and it is difficult to understand President Bolsonaro's capacity to attract supporters from the lower-middle and middle classes, which include Black people, considering his elitist and racist rhetoric. How are we to explain this phenomenon, considering the many political gains which have benefited these sectors in recent governments? Jessé Souza argues that the inclusion of tens of millions of Brazilians in the job market and in consumptive patterns promoted by the Worker's Party was not accompanied by information and political education of the beneficiaries. These inclusionary policies furthermore stirred the deepest and most repressed Brazilian social wound, racism against the "new slaves", the "caste of untouchable Brazilians, almost entirely composed of Blacks, condemned to personal, dirty and dangerous services that everyone, from all social classes, wants to exploit and humiliate" (Souza, 2021, p. 266). The author also explains that this Brazilian racism and elitism were not only restricted to the upper classes. Bolsonaro also stoked this feeling in the popular classes themselves, especially in the Evangelicals, appealing to the rhetoric of the corrosion of customs, the fight against corruption and the defense of traditional family values.

Indeed, in public debate, since the mass demonstrations of 2013 leading up to the impeachment/ coup of President Dilma Rousseff, representatives of the middle class were complaining of their diminishing quality of life, including, as an indicator, the impossibility of hiring domestic work, performed mostly by Black women, because of the new labour rights established. The social inclusion promoted by the last governments would have deeply displeased the middles classes, because it broke through social boundaries that set them apart from the popular classes, in which Blacks are over-represented. The year 2022 is an election year. Initial prognoses reveal the great likelihood of a return of the left to power. However, the crusade of conservatives and religious radicals in the country, linked especially to extreme right ideologies, will likely continue.

---

99 On denunciations of racial insult and racism in Brazil see Santos, G. (2015)

Their existence is old; they are merely returning to the public sphere with more strength and legitimacy.

The Black movement in the contemporary context

In the contemporary landscape, in which we witness the rise of the far-right in the country, new political manifestations that bring together representatives of Black associations, as well as other minorities, such as LGBTQIAP+, Indigenous people, women, and members of anti-fascist movements. These political mobilizations are considered to be associated with the ideological left and with the growing influence of identity politics in the country.

On the matter of identity politics and race, critical positions have emerged alleging that a reverse racism is being promoted in the country, that is, an anti-white racism fuelled by a left-wing identity-based fascism that equally denies criticism and difference. Such positions reject the idea of the existence of structural racism in the country; deny that racism is a system of oppression, reducing it to a consideration of interpersonal conflicts between blacks and whites. It is important to emphasize that much of this debate occurs within the context of the mainstream media, with editorials written in a superficial manner and without basis in research, in a national level in which the sciences are in discredit, stoked by the extreme right. Identity politics, a target of the criticism of the extreme right, is also part of the reflection of intellectuals and Black social movements. At present it is the focus of the debate on racism and racial identity in the country, always in correlation with socioeconomic and material conditions which subordinate much of the Black population.

In reference to the book *Mistaken identity: race and class in the age of Trump*, written by Asad Haider, Silvio Almeida (2019, p. 10) draws attention to the pitfalls of identity, which risks being seen as the sole focus of antiracist politics and, in an essentialised manner, disconnected from material determinations. Paraphrasing Haider, Almeida recalls that a Black man is Black because of racism and not because his Blackness is not valued, not recognised, in the same way that a white man is white because of racism and not because of his whiteness. And there would be no racism without political and economic structures that sustain a continuous process of transformation of individuals into Blacks and whites. Thus, to treat racism from a vague idea of "white supremacy" without explaining in what terms it is made politically and economically viable is only evidence of the confusion that identity politics currently carries. It is in this sphere that the author deals with the efficiency of the identity trap that serves both the right and the anti-revolutionary left. For the right, it is associated with the methodological individualism proper to liberalism and neoliberalism. For the anti-revolutionary left, because a Black identity disconnected from social structures can also be conservative or reactionary and serve the purposes of reproducing capitalism. In neoliberal contexts, identity politics can be a key factor in the social division and atomisations of capitalism. In conclusion, the author states that without a horizon for transforming the very "social machinery" that produces social identities, identity politics generates a straitjacket that reduces the Black, woman, LGBT "subject" to, at best, an improved and less suffered version of what the world historically reserves for him or her.

Jessé Souza (2021) is also critical of what he calls "identity neoliberalism", he also sees as emerging among younger Black intellectuals who disassociate the racial struggle from the social struggle, creating privileged standpoint speeches and confectioning authority over the antiracist agenda of the country. The author criticizes these intellectuals for colluding with the neoliberal elites' hijacking of emancipatory discourse, pushing a perspective that does not discuss the real and structural causes of poverty but focuses on the cultural and ethnic rights of politically dominated groups. The problem, as Souza sees it, is that this type of inclusion is of an individual, meritocratic and liberal nature, benefiting only an ethnic and racial elite that accepts the rules of the dominant system. It is this elite that believes itself to be the spokesperson of oppressed Blacks and that is accepted by the dominant white elites, precisely because they do not constitute a threat to them. Souza explains that his criticism does not aim to deny the existence of a scheme of oppression that affects women and Blacks in a peculiar way, but that this flag cannot be raised by concealing the structural and invisible inequalities that affect the most various types of racism, not only that of race, in his perspective of multidimensional racism (2021, p. 22).

These critiques reopen discussions on the actuality of emancipatory, antiracist and identity policies in the country and their appropriation by neoliberalism. This discussion may be revisited alongside the criticism of neoliberal multiculturalism, which we have been addressing, and which situates the theme of the recognition of cultural rights in a manner equally disconnected from the approaches on the advance of capitalism and social inequality. At a moment when there is a steep regression in social policies in the country as neoliberal policies promoted by the extreme right take hold, the debate around policies directed at Black populations cannot disregard the struggle against social inequalities. The introduction of affirmative action in the country, as we have been stating, was accompanied by social policies against poverty targeting the population as a whole, which caused great impact. They were thus applied following their aims of promoting the inclusion of Blacks in certain spaces dominated by the elites in a focused and specific manner. Without being linked to discussions on social inequalities, their continuity would disconnect them from the broader struggle against racism that permeates the history of this country and upon which these very inequalities are structured.

One way of approaching the issue is to deal with it within the framework of social equity policies, which require complementary measures when universal rights prove insufficient. Inequality is a phenomenon inherent to Brazilian society, resulting from power relations that exacerbate prejudice and racism. The demand for a reparatory justice that considers the four centuries of slavery, and social exclusion that existed and continues to exist, must be understood within the framework of the struggle for rights and opportunities for all, the search for an integral and real citizenship. The high rate of violence, social alienation and barbarism against Black bodies are examples of what happens when rights remain non-comprehensive and ineffective. This is the main criticism of Black scholars and militants to the celebration of May 13 as the day of the end of slavery, because the date did not mean the integral emancipation and reinsertion of the enslaved mass into Brazil's project of nationhood. As the last country in the West to abolish slavery, a year and a half after the law was promulgated, the Brazilian Empire fell victim to the first military coup in national history and ended up giving way to a republican project led by military participants from the "old" monarchical regime.

The collective manifestations of the Black movement position themselves in tune with these critiques, breaking with individualistic and identity-politics expressions. Reducing the Black movement to the identity debate does not do justice to the diversity of manifestations in the field of anti-racist struggle. The 2015 Black Women's March against Racism, Violence and Well-Being is an example. The Black women's movement in Brazil is as old as the struggle for human dignity of racialised subjects brought as slaves to the Americas. Black women were fundamental in the abolitionist struggle, in the organisation of the enslaved Black family and in the architecting of struggles and insurrections. However, due to a historical narrative associated with patriarchy, also present in the black milieu, the fundamentally significant role of mothers, sisters and daughters, independent and struggling women, has been side-lined and/or silenced in accounts of Black insurgency. In this way it is possible to say that the March held in Brasilia, with representatives from every state in the country, was a pivotal point for the consolidation and visibility of the struggle of these women, finally consolidated after decades of articulations and reflections on the feminist women's movement.

Other examples of these demonstrations are Black Convergence and the Black Coalition for Rights. The "Black Convergence", a political action cooperative that brings together the main black organisations in the country, which emerged in 2016, has presented a critical stance against the advance of conservatism's attacks on the hard-won rights of the Brazilian population, which directly and mostly affect the lives of Black people. Conservative capital, which uses racism, machismo, LGBT-phobia and other forms of violence and oppression to impose the continuity of privileges that are concentrated exclusively under the dominion of the landowning classes, constitutes itself as the main target of decolonization actions and confrontation to racism sponsored by the organization.

The "Black Coallition for Rights" emerged in 2020 as a result of decades of anti-racist struggles, with the aim of standing up against the genocide of the Brazilian Black population, whose deaths, trials and persecutions have increased in broad daylight in this period of right-wing extremism. The Coalition's public manifesto states that there is no democracy, citizenship and social justice without a public commitment to recognize the Black movement as a political subject. There is no democracy without confronting racism, police violence and a judicial system that disproportionately incarcerates the black population. There is no citizenship without guaranteeing redistribution of income, work, health, land, housing, education, culture, mobility, leisure for all and participation of the Black population in decision-making processes. There is no democracy without constitutional guarantees of titling to Quilombo territories, without respect for the way of life of traditional communities, and without respect for religious freedom. The manifesto also recognizes the features and meanings of the Quilombist struggle of Abdias Nascimento and the TEN project; the contributions of Solano Trindade and his life poetry; of Lélia Gonzalez and her writing for a united America under the banner of Amefricanity; among other historical contributions of important Black figures and associations. Finally, among so many other references, the insurrection proposed by the Black Coalition, which echoes from universities to unions, is a reflection of this history of struggle and living.

In the context of recent achievements, these political manifestations are an example of the comings and goings, ebbs and flows, which shape the political agendas for the community. The most recent conquest of the organised black movement, in the year 2020, happened in the scope of electoral regulation. Black men and women represented only 24% of the federal congressmen chosen by popular vote in the 2018 elections. Data from the Getúlio Vargas Foundation showed that white men represented 43.1% of the overall sum of candidates for federal congressmen in the 2018 elections and concentrated 60% of campaign revenues. The same research pointed out that Black men and Black women remain underfunded; Black women amounted to 12.9% of the candidacies and were left with only 6.7% of the total volume of resources[100].

In 2020, instigated by Congresswoman Benedita da Silva, a reknown Black activist, the Superior Electoral Court (TSE) looked into the distribution of electoral funds and television time in the country. The congresswoman filed a legal consultation with the higher court with the aim of transforming this scenario of low resources and lack of support for Black candidates by discussing the reservation of resources from the Electoral Fund – as well as radio and TV time – to make campaigns involving Black candidates viable. The public funds, which in the 2020 municipal elections totalled R$ 2 billion, would be divided according to racial criteria, obeying the proportion of Black and white candidates in each party. The consultation sought to overcome the historic dependency of Black candidates on party chieftains, who divide up the electoral pie and provide funds and support for campaigns according to the interests of their own power groups, always white. In addition to this historical electoral *coronelismo*[101] found within the most varied party denominations, another motivation for the consultation was the case of Douglas Belchior, a Black candidate in the state of São Paulo, who in 2018 denounced racism and discrimination in relation to the distribution of funds of the Socialism and Freedom Party (PSOL), a left-wing party that supports identity agendas. The case led to a lawsuit in the TSE, which, after being accepted, allocated more funds for Black candidates in 2020, by establishing proportionality in the distribution. This proportionality also requires the adoption of this same division in the free electoral advertising on radio and TV.

This example of the distribution of electoral fund recalls with the sociologist Clóvis Moura called "sifting barriers" (Moura, 1977), that is, invisible stumbling blocks and hurdles that inhibit furthering the demands and representations of the Black community, which remain unclear and hard to identify for those who are not integrally involved with the theme. They are centuries-old strategies which place the Black population in the fields of the minoritized majority – black territories, in the words of Richard Santos (2020), guettoes or pockets of invisibilities, frustration and social immobility, not due to inertia, but through gateways built by the white national bourgeoisie which silently limits the citizenship and social mobility of this sector of the population.

There are many examples of institutional spaces that create "sifting barriers" which the Black struggle faces and which generate these ebbs and flows in the

---

[100] https://bibliotecadigital.fgv.br/dspace/bitstream/handle/10438/27646/RELAT%C3%93RIO%20FINAL%202018–2019.pdf?sequence=5&isAllowed=y

[101] A system of unwritten agreements ("coronelismo") promoted special by rural oligarchies, the colonels. They used the power to control the political system in return for favors.

history of resistance. The Brazilian justice system itself portrays this reality, with a judiciary composed mostly of white judges (Igreja & Rampin, 2022). Some concrete cases demonstrate its existence, such as the lawsuit of the accusation of racism that originated in the sentence of Judge Inês Marchalek Zarpelon of the 1st criminal court of the district of the metropolitan region of Curitiba (PR), which in 2020 sentenced Natan Vieira da Paz, a 48-year-old black man, to 14 years and 2 months in prison. In recording the sentence of a case with more than a hundred pages, the Honourable Judge stated the following

> Of his social conduct, nothing is known. Surely a member of a criminal group, because of his race, he acted in an extremely discrete form in his crimes and his behaviour, like that of the others, caused the restlessness and hopelessness of the population, which must make him negative valued. (Brasil de Fato, 2020)[102]:

Now, she claims that because he is of a different race from the standard determined to be beautiful, pleasant, superior, civilised and/or free from questions as to origin, with unblemished behaviour, the citizen (?) would no longer have the rights extended to all other Brazilian citizens and regulated constitutionally by the Magna Carta of 1988, being configured as a potential criminal. On reading this news, one tends to impute guilt only and solely to the magistrate, a public servant, in the ethical deviation of the functions that govern public service and, furthermore, in the administrative deviation that governs and/or should govern the working act of the magistrature, a career that mediates that which we are led to call 'justice', and which is meant to be blind to racialized distinctions and codes. According to our reading of the case, the Inspector General's Office of the Paraná Court of Justice (TJ-PR) did not consider the act to be a practice of racism and unanimously decided to dismiss the disciplinary proceedings against the judge. This decision is related to the very way in which the meaning of what is fair and just is constructed in the country, in what is taught in law schools and in the training of Brazilian judges, a place where various eugenicist doctrines still prevail and remain reference works. These references of thought and social theory are essential for the maintenance of the colonial, Eurocentric and racist society that still exists, and they are influential in silencing black intellectuals and their productions, a process that the philosopher Sueli Carneiro (2005) has classified as racial epistemicide.

Thus, it is appropriate to say that there is no need for an idea of race legitimated by science for racism to exist, and this is what explains its resilience

---

102 Page 107, of 115, of her sentence of condemnation. The case was reported in various newspapers.

today. All that has passed is the transformation of the forms of social legitimation and rhetoric on human differences, as well as the mechanisms of domination and subalternization that maintain the positions of power between racialized whites and their "opposites", the "other". Indeed, it is not a matter of re-situating race in biological parameters, but of referring to it as a source of social constructions that function as a mechanism of privileges, demarcating and establishing a hierarchy of groups which we call 'whiteness'(branquitude) (Santos, R., 2021).

As Maria Aparecida Silva Bento (2016) comments, in Brazil, whitening is generally seen as a problem for blacks who, because they feel uncomfortable with their condition as blacks, seek to identify with whites and dilute their racial characteristics. In this whitening process, the role of white people is not questioned. Bento explains, based on his research, that the focus of the discussion is always the black, as if there were a pact, a tacit agreement between whites not to recognize themselves as an essential part of the permanence of racial inequalities in Brazil (Bento, 2016, p. 29). The author thus concludes that whiteness is a place of racial, economic and political privilege, in which raciality, not named as such, loaded with values, experiences, affective identifications, ends up defining society.

In the light of Bento's concepts of whiteness, the endogenous solidarity network of Moore's racially hegemonic group and recovering Sueli Carneiro's concept of raciality dispositif, Souza et al. (2021) propose the notion of whiteness dispositif in order to understand the resistance and adaptations against measures that aim to promote material racial equality. Now, if it is in the process of classification that we find the meaning of race; and if this category was used to subordinate some racialised people (Blacks) and legitimise the power and superiority of others (whites), also racialised; it is important to say that, once the concept of race as a relation of biological identification is overcome, it is consistent with the understanding proposed by Antonio Sergio Guimarães (2012) of race as a social classifier.

In Brazil, racism is at once produced by racial categorization and produces the category of race. Authors associated with what we call Contemporary Black Thought, such as Alberto Guerreiro Ramos, Lélia Gonzalez, Clóvis Moura, Sueli Carneiro and Muniz Sodré, among many others, hailing from distinct periods and realities, are responsible for seminal works that condemn the myth of Brazilian racial democracy, and reveal how the manipulation of the category of race serves white identity and the maintenance of its powers. With their contributions it is possible to observe the Brazilian phenomenon, in which the State has never recognized the racism experienced by the Black population official, although it is perceptible in social practices, rhetoric, demographic data and the experiences of non-white populations. From this perspective it is possible to understand the analytical tools of raciality that is the Minoritized Majority, a subversion of the category of race as a subalternizer, with roots directly fertilized by this racialized soil. Minoritized Majority is articulated as an idealized and paradigmatic image, a revelation of alienating ideological relations and social power. A productive path in the analyses and experiences of the black Brazilian population.

Finally, we return to Muniz Sodré (2015, p. 92) who predicts that "the racist social relation imposed itself with more force in the petty-bourgeois conscience of Brazil after the abolition of slavery, exactly at the moment when the old social hierarchizations felt more threatened". After years of advances in the conquest of social rights and anti-racist policies, we can affirm that, once again, using old political tools such as coups d'état, the conservative elites rise to maintain the same unequal and hierarchical structure of the Brazilian society.

V Multiculturalism and the new landscapes: Final thoughts

The panorama of multicultural policies targeting Latin American Afro-descendants contains many ambivalences. In the last 20 years there has been a transition from the official "invisibility" of Afro-descendants to their institutional recognition, but many of their social and political demands remain unanswered. Numbers continue to show that the majority of Blacks in the region live in conditions of poverty, marginalization, and social exclusion. The timid results of socio-economic measures in what pertains to inclusion denote inconsistency, by states, in carrying out the necessary socio-material transformations. Furthermore, in the most varied ways, racism and discrimination are still part of the daily lives of Blacks.

The different policies aimed at ethno-cultural and racial recognition, including multicultural policies, continue to be the product of complex interactions between the state and various actors (social organizations, political movements, NGOs, local authorities, cooperating agents for development, academics, etc.). Ethno-cultural diversity and the antiracist struggle remain their focus, even if their aims may diverge or converge, depending on contexts and power correlations. Beyond the ideological and political nuances that are explicit in Black movements in the region, we identify elements of confluence, such as the demand for the implementation of the Durban agenda, which continues to be a reference for political mobilization. Meanwhile, the ongoing commitment of states and international institutions to this agenda continues to show, on the one hand, an imbalance between declarations of principles and, on the other, the lack of will and determination necessary not only to promote, but above all to put into effect concrete measures that constitute tangible developments to overcome the exclusion of Afro-descendants. Twenty years later, the evaluation of most Latin American and Caribbean movements that took part in the Durban Conference demonstrates the validity of the goals outlined there and the challenge of adapting the forms of mobilization to achieve their fulfilment in contemporary conditions.

Thus, multiculturalism, seen as a historical-political process, is still on the agenda, even if currently under other names and conditions. Some authors claim that we are witnessing its decline. They take into account the current context in which intolerances and racism increase, and in which there is no public interest in recognizing and organizing diverse cultural and racial identities (Lins Ribeiro, 2018 & Wieviorka, 2015). We believe, however, that what we are witnessing is, in reality, a loss of control in the public management of difference due to the expansion of ethnic and antiracist demands. Even if haphazardly, popular movements of resistance arise in this global context, demanding legislative changes and new policies (Igreja, 2021). The appropriation of multiculturalism by the neoliberal state sought to promote ethno-cultural recognition, organize the different demands and propose focused policies in such a way as to control conflicts, resistance and any threats to its expansion. However, it was overtaken by the breadth of public debates around these agendas. With its many contradictions, the space promoted by multiculturalism is also appropriated by social movements and accompanied by the empowerment and insurrection of various social sectors.

It should be recalled that dealing with the demands of Latin American Afrodescendants and their struggle against racism has always been a challenge to multiculturalist policies. As the team of the LAPORA Project, mentioned in Chapter 3, has concluded, multiculturalist ideology denies, minimizes and renders invisible structural racism by focusing on the existence of harmony between different cultures, repeating, in a way, the rhetoric of racial democracy. Racism is at the base of capitalist exploitation, and fighting against it demands important structural reforms involving the state and society which seek an end to social inequality and the promotion of far redistribution. This is due to the fact that capitalism has always been based on the exploitation of bodies it considers inferior, animalized, ready for their labour power to be physically exploited. If slavery left behind the legacy of social inequality, of exclusion and violence, structural racism works to maintain it. We hence affirm, once again, that racism, in its very definition, is always structural. Violence against Blacks, the genocide revealed by the number of young Blacks who are homicide victims, and Black poverty, all attest to the continuity of this exploitation.

These issues are also observed in the academic environment, in which new theoretical and empirical perspectives for the study of gender have emerged, particularly Indigenous, Black and ethno-racial feminisms. These perspectives, in general, contribute to the critique of Eurocentric thought, which they identify as a form of neocolonialism, arguing for new epistemologies in university teaching, particularly those form countries in the Global South which have also undergone long processes of colonization. These changes stand against a revenge of conservative forces, particularly those linked to the far-right, and anti-progress positions that seek to stall this movement. The Brazilian case is exemplary.

In what pertains to the far-right, Rydgren (2007) explains its resurgence in Europe in conjunction with the emergence of new social and political movements linked to new parties (i.e., green parties and new left-wing parties). For this reason, the author believes that there is a misunderstanding when analyses about this ideology are made without considering approaches carried out in the field of social movements and the analysis of ethnic networks and relations. It is also in this sense that we highlight that need to consider the rise of the far-right in the context of multiculturalism and the insurgence and strengthening of ethno-racial demands (Igreja 2021, p. 16). It emerges in a context of fear and insecurity generated by the strengthening of other cultures, of other peoples, as well as of feminist demands and of LGBTQIAP+ groups, which threaten the traditional conservative order. It relies on culturalist and identity rhetoric, as Sylvain Crépon (Igreja, 2021) states, in order to reclaim its spaces. In this movement, it seeks allies, makes concessions, and builds consensus. Thus, the far-right reacts to multiculturalism, but re-defines itself through its own principles.

In this context of dispute between projects of power, we can say that we are becoming aware that culture and race are not only dimensions of Indigenous and Black peoples, but also of whites – whites define themselves culturally and racialize themselves in their whiteness, which is itself ill-defined because it is also fragmented, imaginary, diverse. Although we are still responding to the idea of racial democracy in Brazil, we must also admit that it has vanished from the official public scene, since conservative forces no longer hide their racism; if before it was veiled before, it now shows itself in its virulence. We could think that this reflects the introduction of multiculturalist policies and affirmative action, that it is a revenge of the elites for the introduction into their privileged spaces of representatives of the excluded popular layers, mainly constituted by Blacks. We must reflect that in this scenario a new national pact is in dispute, a new reflection on nation building and the state project that accompanies it, in which Blacks are no longer relegated to their peripheries.

We must consider, however, that despite their similarities, discussions of multiculturalism and their appropriation as public policies and legal changes differ according to regional and national contexts. The realities are different and the historical, socio-political and economic processes in which they are inserted are also diverse. In this book we have surveyed this global process in which multiculturalism was idealized as a means for the public management of diversity and its demands, and, at the same time, to establish the contours it assumes in regional contexts such as Latin America and, especially, in Brazil.

One of the central aspects of the debate on multiculturalism is how it consolidates the ethno-racial classifications and categorizations which necessary for the identification of the people to whom they are addressed. However, in the case of Latin America and the Afro-descendant population, they result from a historical process characterized by regimes of exploitation and slavery, by inequality and racism. Moreover, all these markers are transformed in this historical process, oscillating between forms imposed by the dominant elites and their interests and appropriations and re-significations that are made and negotiated by the different subordinate peoples and social movements. There is no linearity in the definitions of these classifications. For this reason, multiculturalism is based on a system of classifications which is itself in constant transformation and readaptation.

In particular, the use of "race" as a category of identification arouses quite polarized opinions in several Latin American countries. Predominant among critics is the fear of feeding back into a biological category of classification that was created in the context of the racist theories of the 19th century and which affirmed the superiority of white people over Black people, legitimizing racism and racial prejudice. In the opinion of these authors, as we mentioned in this book, it is racism that must be fought, destroyed, rather than the category itself that must be reinforced. In contrast, we have seen that the defense of "race" as a social category, re-taking and re-signifying it as part of the antiracist struggle, is to give visibility to racialization, which has historically affected Afro-descendants, and to racism.

In this sense, in an effort to contextualize these processes of classification and categorization of the Latin American Afro-descendant population, we resort to a synthetic analysis of the historical construction of the notions of race, colour and racism in the region, especially in Brazil. As mentioned in the first chapter, the genesis of the concept of race, as well as the discourses and practices that ground racism, are not unrelated to the processes of historical construction of the place of Blacks in society. This construction necessarily goes through the memory of slavery and processes of social exclusion and racialization. They are the portrait of social hierarchies that are legitimised by an elitist, patrimonialist and racist order that still exists today. This historical overview, however, also allows us to glimpse the protagonism of Black people in their struggle to resist this same order. These are accounts of continuous resistance that, although often invisible, reveal great characters and achievements that repositioned the place of Blacks in national societies. For this reason, in retelling them, we seek to give place and voice to Black intellectuals and activists.

We brought up the Brazilian experience because it seems to us illustrative of the different phases through which Blacks and their position in society were defined. An experience marked by a long period of slavery and the consideration of Blacks as belonging to an inferior race based on racist theories of the 19th century, followed by the liberation of slaves and official projects for whitening the Brazilian people through the attraction of immigrants and miscegenation, and then a period of invisibilization of the discussion on race and racism, a history of erasure in the myth of racial democracy. What seems evident to us is that the debate around race has always been at the core of Brazilian national construction. It is enough to remember that historically, since the 19th century, the country's censuses have gathered information on the colour/race of the population.

The discussion of categorisations and the best way to face racism and discrimination involves different social actors. It is important to highlight the importance that academia, especially the social sciences, assumes in this context. Discussions of public policies and legislation on the subject have always involved academics who, in turn, incorporated the prevailing theoretical paradigms into their analyses. To reopen the debate on race and racism is to rediscuss the role and influence of academics in the public political arena.

An academy that discusses the issue must itself culturally and racially representative and diverse. It must be an academy that includes the voices of those for whom it speaks. And for this reason, we convey in our work the criticism to Eurocentrism and racism that are also present in the academy and that generate what many Black intellectuals and activists have called Black epistemicide. We are equally concerned with the presentation of these Black intellectuals, their trajectories and their bibliography. Finally, we include a presentation and contextualization of the diverse international projects that have dedicated and/or are dedicated to research on Afro-descendants in Latin America, seeking to trace their perspectives and their connections with local and national contexts. The theme of racism and Afro-descendant populations in Latin America are as broad, complex and diverse the many interpretations of these phenomena. Reconstructing, even if briefly, the trajectory of the debate, and the different actors who participated in it, was one of the aims of this book.

The core of the book, however, was the discussion of public policies aimed at Afro-descendants. An important issue that permeates the differences between Brazil and other countries in Latin America is the centrality of policies of racial equality rather than the multiculturalist policies that were part of the "multicultural turn" in the region. Although these policies have emerged in a context of strengthening and expanding collective rights, policies of racial equality arise with the aim of promoting the integration of Black people into society and the antiracist struggle. They are accompanied by policies that value Black cultural heritage, especially the religious legacy of the Black diaspora, as well as policies of territorial recognition, such as those for titling the lands of remaining Quilombos. As we have explained, this choice is due to the socio-historical specificities of the Blacks in the country, their population size, important location in urban contexts, among other elements. This distinction between the two forms of policies allowed us to raise questions of them, resuming the discussion on their definitions, objectives, potentialities and limits. More than trying to make an assessment of them, we provided a broad and complex analysis, focused on the debate that has been built around them, the controversies they have raised and, finally, how they present themselves today.

Our last chapter discussed affirmative action in Brazil. Our goal was to delve deeper into the discussion of the policy in order to demonstrate the complexity of dealing with racism in the country and meeting the demands of Black populations. Affirmative action resurrected old controversies and raised new debates, new clashes, as well as new concepts, new ways of dealing with the racial issue in the country. They are currently undergoing important political changes, such as the aforementioned rise of the far-right and different forms of conservatism and racism. It is important to highlight the strength that, in a certain way, neo-Nazi manifestations have gained, fuelled by the behaviour of members of the Brazilian government.

How are we to interpret the contemporary context? What can we envisage for the future? The Latin American landscape has been marked by pessimism. Analyses of multiculturalist policies demonstrate that, in general, they have not been translated into real levels of transformation of the conditions of Afro-descendant populations, considering especially their education, health, safety, among others. Furthermore, little has been seen of effective recognition of the collective rights of the territories of Black peoples in the region. The data regularly released for the region continues to show significant gaps between Blacks and whites in terms of access to economic resources (Freire et. at., 2018). Few studies, however, contain analysis of what these policies have meant for the fight against racism and the representativeness of Black people in Latin American society. In addition, little is said about what they meant for the self-identification of this population, an identity reconstructed in the context of these policies, but always in dialogue with their experiences. The discussion of these policies gave rise to an important process of social mobilization among Afro-descendant populations, a contradictory and fragmented process with many ruptures, but which strengthened new forms of association and consolidated the role of Black intellectuals, especially in the academic context and in the public space in general. This movement made racism and violence against this population more visible. Although less effective, it also allowed legal and political instances at national and international levels to be constituted and to serve as a resource and support for their defence. The analysis of the moment is complex. The anti-racist struggle has historically been dependent on political opportunities to consolidate itself and has always had to respond to how racisms were structured, readapting itself to contexts, innovating in its actions. Multiculturalism, as a historical-political process appropriated and adopted by many countries, must be analysed within the political dispute that it originated and in through the different actors that participate in it. Black protagonism and resistance have always been present in all phases of Latin American history.

In relation to Brazil, we present an even more pessimistic scenario. However, analysis is always complex. Gender, race and class policies have been demonised and social rights have been set back. Racist manifestations, especially from the current president, are constant. Black physical features are the butt of jokes and the objects of criticism; explicit racism is often followed with violence that gains legitimacy in light of the political context. The Bolsonaro government, as we have seen, is a classic example of this regression and the use of state force to resume the project of a white, Christian and conservative Brazil. It is, again, the reaffirmation of a race that sees itself as dominant, of capital and of colonial interests recombined in the 21st century, in what Mbembe classifies as the Becoming-Black of the world (Mbembe, 2017).

We can take the rise of the far-right in Brazil and extend it to Latin American and the Caribbean, seeing it in the light of growing conservatism in several countries in the region, and interpret them as constituting what in the artistic world we call "shadow theatre". Inspired by an ancient Chinese artform, it is a theatrical staging in which silhouettes of puppets or people acquire movement on a canvass and take form according to the play of light projected onto them. The Brazilian conservative, oligarchic and racist elites once again cast shadows on the national scene, reconstructing their images and those of the nation itself, re-telling and re-signifying histories, validating their values and their representations, thus legitimating, in a grand scenario in which they project themselves as the true representatives of the Brazilian people, a discourse that pretends to be universal and inclusive, but which responds only to their interests. They thus reaffirm a speech centred on whiteness and on the Eurocentrism of their values. We can interpret this moment as a mirror of contrasts, a racial mirror in which the white man recognises himself in opposition to the Black man. It is in this mirror of alterity that the extreme right redefines itself and constitutes its own image. It is the study of this image that they project that provides us with elements for understanding the resilience of racism in Brazil. For this reason, studies of whiteness in the country today draw so much attention. These studies demand reflection on the role of whites in the production of racial inequalities, decentralizing analyses that focus exclusively on the problematization of blacks. It is necessary to continue questioning who is white in the country.

In this book, we also drew attention to how, in this process of shadows and reflections in which alterity is historically constructed, Blacks define themselves. Processes of oppression and domination cause Black self-identification to be based on response to, and in contrast with, how whites define it, and how whites define themselves. And, in this contrast, the tendency is to take refuge in essentialist perspectives, reinforcing racialisations. It is important to remember, however, that, racism cannot be seen separately from capitalism, for it is a structural basis that underlies it; it cannot be dissociated from the discussion of social inequalities, from that which underlies socio-economic exploitation and which gives it persistence. The never-ending search is to recreate oneself, to renew and innovate through resistance, to gain spaces of autonomy and power, breaking the historical cycle of subordination.

References

ADC Declaratory Action for Constitutionality n° 41. (2017, April 12). Direito constitucional. Embargos de declaração em adc. Aplicabilidade da política de cotas da lei 12.990/2014 às forças armadas. Provimento. https://redir.stf.jus.br/paginadorpub/paginador.jsp?docTP=TP&docID=14763674#:~:text=%C3%89%20constitucional%20a%20Lei%20n,e%20indireta%2C%20por%20tr%C3%AAs%20fundamentos

Adi, H. (2018). Pan-Africanism: A History. Bloomsbury Academic.

ADPF Claim of Non-Compliance with a Fundamental Precept n° 186. (2010, June 30). Arguição de Descumprimento de Preceito Fundamental. Atos que instituíram sistema de reserva de vagas com base em critério étnico-racial (cotas) no processo de seleção para ingresso em instituição pública de ensino superior. Supremo Tribunal Federal (Brazil). https://redir.stf.jus.br/paginadorpub/paginador.jsp?docTP=TP&docID=6984693

Agassiz, J. L. R. & Agassiz, E. C. (2000). Viagem ao Brasil 1865–1866 [translation and notes of Edgar Süssekind de Mendonça]. Senado Federal, Conselho Editorial (Original work published 1938).

Agier, M. & Carvalho, M. R. (1994). Nation, race, culture. Les mouvements noirs et indiens au Brésil. Cahiers des Ameriques Latines, 17, 107–124.

Agudelo, C. (2004). No todos vienen del río: construcción de identidades negras urbanas y movilización política en Colombia. In E. Restrepo, A. Rojas (Eds.), Conflicto e (in)visibilidad. Retos en los estudios de la gente negra en Colombia (pp. 173–194). Ed Universidad del Cauca.

Agudelo, C. (2005). Retos del multiculturalismo en Colombia. Política y poblaciones negras, Ed. IEPRI – IRD – ICANH. La Carreta.

Agudelo, C. (2009). Populations noires et politique en Amérique latine. L'Atlantique noire comme outil d'interprétation (et projet politique?). In C. Agudelo, C. Boidin & L. Sansone (Eds.), Autour de l'Atlantique noir " Une polyphonie de perspectives, (pp. 123–132). Editions de l'IHEAL.

Agudelo, C. (2010). Movilizaciones afrodescendientes en América Latina. Revista Colombia Internacional, 71, 109–126. https://doi.org/10.7440/colombiaint71.2010.06

Agudelo, C. (2011). Les Garifuna. Transnationalité territoriale, construction d'identités et action politique. Revue européenne des migrations internationales, 27, 47–70. https://doi.org/10.4000/remi.5215

Agudelo, C. (2012a). The Afro-Guatemalan Political Mobilization: Between Identity Construction Processes, Global Influences, and Intitutionalization. In Jean Rahier (Ed.), Black Social Movements in Latin America. From Monocultural Mestizaje to Multiculturalism. Palgrave Macmillan

Agudelo, C. (2012b). Compilación bibliográfica sobre el pueblo Garifuna. Cuaderno de Trabajo No. 15 Afrodesc-Eurescl. http://www.ird.fr/afrodesc/spip.php?article441

Agudelo, C. (2019). Paradojas de la inclusión de los afrodescendientes y el giro multicultural en América latina. Cuadernos Inter.c.a.mbio sobre Centroamérica y el Caribe, 16(1). https://doi.org/10.15517/c.a.v16i2.37746

Agudelo, C. & Igreja, R. L. (2014). Afrodescendentes na América Latina e Caribe: novos caminhos, novas perspectivas em um contexto global multicultural. *Revista De Estudos E Pesquisas Sobre As Américas*, 8(1), 13–28. https://periodicos.unb.br/index.php/repam/article/view/18475

Ahkell, J. (1981). Rasta: Emperor Haile Selassie and the Rastafarians Port of Spain, Trinidad. Black Star Line Inc.

Alberto, P. (2011). Terms of inclusion: Black Intellectuals in Twentieth Century Brazil. University of North Carolina Press.

Albuquerque, W. & Fraga, F. W. (2006). Uma história do negro no Brasil. Centro de Estudos Afro-orientais; Fundação Cultural Palmares.

Almanza, R. (2020). Panafricanismo afrocaribeño en George Padmore y C.L.R. James. Insumos para ampliar la genealogía de la teoría descolonial. Tabula Rasa, 35, 59–87. https://doi.org/10.25058/20112742.n35.03.

Almeida, S. (2019). Prefácio. In A. Haider (Ed.), Armadilha da identidade: raça e classe nos dias de hoje (Coleção Baderna). Veneta.

Andrews, G. R. (2004). Afro-Latin America, 1800–2000. Oxford University Press.

Antón, J., Bello, A., Del Popolo, F., Paixao, M. & Rangel, M. (2009). Afrodescendientes en América latina y el Caribe: Del reconocimiento estadístico a la realización de derechos. Serie Población y Desarrollo 87. CEPAL. https://www.redalyc.org/journal/4769/476958952009/476958952009.pdf

Arruti, J. M. (2008). Quilombos. In O. Pinho & L. Sansone (Eds.), Raça: perspectivas antropológicas (pp. 315–350). EDUFBA.

Azevedo, C.M.M. (2004). Onda *Negra, Medo Branco: o negro no imaginário das elites do século XIX.* ANNABLUME.

Bailey, F. (1969). Stragems and Spoils. A social Anthropology of Politics. Blackwell.

Bailey, S. R. (2009). Legacies of Race: Identities, Attitudes, and Politics in Brazil. Stanford University Press.

Banco de la República. ([1856] 1958.). Comisión Corográfica. Geografía física y política de las provincias de la Nueva Granada (Soto, Santander, Pamplona, Antioquia, Medellín; Córdoba, Cauca, Popayán, Pasto y Túquerres).

Banton, M. (1987). *Racial Theories*. Cambridge University Press.

Barbary, O. & Urrea, F. (2004). *Gente negra en Colombia: Dinámicas Sociopolíticas en Cali y en el Pacífico*. Editora Lealon; CIDSE/Univalle; IRD; COLCIENCIAS.

Barret, L. E. (1997). The Rastafarians. Beacon Press.

Barrows, W. (1976). *Grassroots Politics in an African State. Integration and Development in Sierra Leone*. Africana Publishing Company.

Bastide, R. (1961). Variations sur la negritude. Presence africaine, 36(1), 7–17.

Bastide, R. (1967). Les Amériques Noires. Les civilisations africaines dans le Nouveau Monde. Payot.

Benedetti, A. C. (2021). Entre avanços e bloqueios: uma análise da política de titulação de territórios quilombolas. Estudos Sociedade e Agricultura, 29(3), 699–726. https://doi.org/10.36920/esa-v29n3-8

Bento, M. A. S. (2016). Branqueamento e branquitude no Brasil. In Carone, I. & Bento, M. A. S. (Eds.), Psicologia social do racismo: estudos sobre branquitude e branqueamento no Brasil (pp. 25–58). Vozes. http://www.media.ceert.org.br/portal3/pdf/publicacoes/branqueamento-ebranquitude-no-brasil.pdf

Bernabé, J., Chamoiseau, P. & Confiant, R. (1990). *Éloge de la Créolité/ In Praise of Creoleness*, *13*(4), 886–909. The Johns Hopkins University Press.

Beverly, J. (1999). *Subalternity and representation: arguments in cultural Theory*. Duke University Press.

Bezerra; T. O. C. & Gurgel; C. R. M. (2012). A política pública de cotas em universidades, enquanto instrumento de inclusão social. Revista Pensamento & Realidade, 27(2), 95–117.

Bicudo, V. L & Maio, M.C. (2010). Atitudes raciais de pretos e mulatos em São Paulo. Editora Sociologia e Política.

Bicudo, V. L. (1945). Estudo de atitudes raciais de pretos e mulatos em São Paulo. [Master Dissertation]. Escola Livre de Sociologia e Política de São Paulo.

Bicudo, V. L. (1955). Atitudes dos alunos dos grupos escolares em relação com a cor dos seus colegas. In Bastide, R. & Fernandes, F. (Eds.), Relações raciais entre negros e brancos em São Paulo: ensaio sociológico sobre as origens, as manifestações e os efeitos do preconceito de cor no município de São Paulo (pp. 227–310). Anhembi.

Bonfil Batalla, G. (1987). *México profundo: una civilización negada*. Grijalbo.

Bonilla-Silva. (2002). We Are All Americans!: The Latin Americanization of Racial Stratification in the USA. Race, 5(1), 3–16. https://doi.org/info:doi/

Bourdieu, P. (1980). Questions de sociologie. Éd. De Minuit.

Bourdieu, P. (1994). Raisons pratiques, sur la théorie de l'action. Seuil.

Brasil de Fato (2020, August 12). Juíza declara em sentença que homem negro é criminoso "em razão da sua raça". https://www.brasildefato.com.br/2020/08/12/exclusivo-juiza-diz-em-sentenca-que-homem-negro-e-criminoso-em-razao-da-sua-raca

BRAZIL. [Constitution (1988)]. Constituição da República Federativa do Brasil de 1988 Constituição (planalto.gov.br).

BRAZIL. Presidente (2022). Mensagem ao Congresso Nacional, 2022 [online] 4ª Sessão Legislativa Ordinária da 56ª Legislatura. – Brasília: Presidência da República. https://www.gov.br/mdh/pt-br/assuntos/noticias/2022/janeiro/liberdade-religiosa-e-de-crenca-sao-temas-de-evento-on-line-nesta-sexta-feira-21

Brown, S. (1997). The Foundation of the Rastafari Movement. In Barret, L. (Ed.), The Rastafarians (pp. 148–150). Beacon Press.

Campbell, H. (1988). Rastafari as Pan Africanism in the Caribbean and Africa. African Journal of Political Economy / Revue Africaine d'Economie Politique, 2(1), 75–88. http://www.jstor.org/stable/23500303

Campoalegre Septien, R. & Bidaseca, K. (2017). Más allá del decenio de los pueblos afrodescendientes. [Colección Antologías del Pensamiento Social]. CLACSO. http://biblioteca.clacso.edu.ar/clacso/se/20171006013311/Mas_alla_del_decenio.pdf

Campos, L. A., Feres Júnior, J. & Daflon, V. T. (2013). Administrando o debate público: O Globo e a controvérsia em torno das cotas raciais. Revista Brasileira de Ciência Política, 11, 7–31. http://dx.doi.org/10.1590/S0103–33522013000200001.

Cardoso de Oliveira, L. R. (2002). *Direito legal e insulto moral – Dilemas da Cidadania no Brasil, Quebec e EUA* (Coleção Antropologia da Política). Relume Dumará / NUAP

Cardoso, M. (2002). O Movimento Negro em Belo Horizonte: 1978–1998. Maza Edições.

Carmichael, S. & Hamilton, C. V. (1967). Black Power: The Politics of Liberation in America. Random House.

Carneiro, E. (2001). Singularidades dos Quilombos. In C. Moura (Ed.), *Os Quilombos na Dinâmica Social do Brasil* (pp. 11–20). UFAL.

Carneiro, S. (2003). Mulheres em movimento. Estudos Avançados, 17(49), 117–133. https://www.revistas.usp.br/eav/article/view/9948

Carneiro, S. (2005). A construção do outro como não ser como fundamento do ser. [PHD Thesis]. Universidade de São Paulo.

Carvalhaes, F., Feres Júnior, J. & Daflon, V. T. (2013). O impacto da Lei de Cotas nos estados: um estudo preliminar. Textos para Discussão GEMAA, 1, 1–21. http://gemaa.iesp.uerj.br/wp-content/uploads/2018/03/TpD-gemaa-1.pdf

Castells, M. (2000). *A Sociedade em rede*. Paz e Terra.

Cavalcanti, I. T. do N., Andrade, C. S. M., Tiryaki, G. F. & Costa, L. C. C. (2019). Desempenho acadêmico e o sistema de cotas no ensino superior: evidência empírica com dados da Universidade Federal da Bahia. Avaliação: Revista da Avaliação da Educação Superior, [S. l.], 24(1). http://periodicos.uniso.br/ojs/index.php/avaliacao/article/view/3623

Cerqueira, D. (Ed.). (2021). Atlas da Violência 2021. FBSP; IPEA. https://www.ipea.gov.br/portal/index.php?option=com_content&view=article&id=38836&Itemid=432

Césaire, A. (1939). Cahier d'un retour au pays natal. Volontés, 20.

Césaire, A. (1950). Discours sur le colonialisme, Edition Réclame. Présence Africaine, 1955.

Césaire, A. (1960). Toussaint Louverture. La Révolution française et le problème colonial. Présense Africaine.

Césaire, A. (1978). Discurso Sobre o Colonialismo. Livraria Sá da Costa.

Chakrabarty, D. (2002). *Habitations of modernity*. University of Chicago.

Chaves, M. E. (2015). Los "otros" de las independencias, los "otros" de la nación: Participación de la población afrodescendiente e indígena en las independencias del Nuevo Reino de Granada, Chile y Haití. Universidad Nacional de Colombia.

Chivallon, C. (2002). La diáspora noire de Amériques. Réflexions sur le modèle de l'hybridité de Paul Gilroÿ. L'Homme, 161, 51–74.

CNN (2021, November 20). Ministério dos Direitos Humanos recebeu 1.019 denúncias de injúria racial em 2021. https://www.cnnbrasil.com.br/nacional/ministerio-dos-direitos-humanos-recebeu-1-019-denuncias-de-injuria-racial-em-2021/

Conceição, F. (2005). Como Fazer Amor Com um Negro Sem se Cansar e Outros textos para o debate contemporâneo da luta anti-racista no Brasil. Terceira Margem.

Conceição, F. (2017). O negro na academia brasileira: o sujeito insurgente. In Jesus, D., Conceição, F. & Margarida, M. (Eds.), Racistas são os outros: contribuição ao debate lusotropicalista em África, Brasil e Portugal (pp. 18–34). Afirme-se.

Convention n° 111. (1960, June 15). Convention concerning Discrimination in Respect of Employment and Occupation. International Labour Organization. https://www.ilo.org/dyn/normlex/en/f?p=NORMLEXPUB:12100:0::NO::P12100_ILO_CODE:C111Costa, S. (2002). A construção Sociológica da Raça no Brasil Estudos Afro-Asiáticos, 1, 35–62. UCAM

Cotes, M. (2018). Sincretismo religioso en América Latina: Una visión desde da Santería y otras religiones de origen africano en Cuba desde la Conquista hasta el Siglo XXI. *Revista UNAULA*, *38*, 143–192. https://publicaciones.unaula.edu.co/index.php/revistaUNAULA/article/view/1153

Crépon, S. (2003). L'extrême droite sur le terrain des anthropologues. Une inquiétante familiarité, Socio-anthropologie, 10. https://doi.org/10.4000/socio-anthropologie.164

D'Adesky, J. (2001). Pluralismo étnico e multiculturalismo-Racismo e anti-racismos no Brasil. Pallas.

Damas, L.G. (1988). Actas del Primer Congreso de la Cultura Negra de las Américas. UNESCO; Fundación Colombiana de Investigaciones Folclóricas; ECOE.

Damatta, R. (1987). *Relativizando: uma introdução à Antropologia Social*. (6th ed.). Editora Rocco.
Damé, L. (2013, 22th April). Movimento negro cobra de Dilma cotas raciais no serviço público. O Globo. https://oglobo.globo.com/politica/movimento-negro-cobra-de-dilma-cotas-raciais-no-servico-publico-9105293
Davis, D. J. & Williams, J. M. (2007). Pan-Africanism, Negritude, and the Currency of Blackness: Cuba, the Francophone Caribbean, and Brazil in Comparative Perspective, 1930–1950s. In Davis, D. J. (Ed.), Beyond Slavery: The Multilayered Legacy of Africans in Latin America and the Caribbean (pp. 143–167). Rowman & Littlefield.
De la Fuente, A. & Andrews, G. R. (2018). *Estudos afro-latino-americanos uma introdução*. Harvard University; CLACSO.
De la Peña, G. (1999). Territorio y ciudadanía étnica en la nación globalizada. *Desacatos*, *1*, Centro de Investigaciones y Estudios Superiores en Antropología Social.
De la Torre, C. & Antón, J. (2018). Afroecuadorian Politics. In Johnnson, O. & Dixon, K. (Eds.), *Comparative Racial Politics in Latin America*, (pp. 163–183). Routledge.
De Oto, A. (2003). *Política y poética del sujeto poscolonial*. El Colegio de México.
De Oto, A. (2011). *Tiempos de homenajes/tiempos descoloniales: Frantz Fanon*. Ediciones del Signo.
Decraene, P. (1970). *El Panafricanismo*. EUDEBA – Editorial Universitaria de Buenos Aires.
Decree nº 528 (1890, June 28). Regularisa o serviço da introducção e localisação de immigrantes na Republica dos Estados Unidos do Brazil. Câmara de Deputados (Brazil). Portal da Câmara dos Deputados (camara.leg.br).
Decree nº 847 (1890, October 11). Promulga o Codigo Penal. Câmara de Deputados (Brazil). Portal da Câmara dos Deputados (camara.leg.br).
Decree nº 1,904 (1996, May 13). Institui o Programa Nacional de Direitos Humanos – PNDH. Presidência da República (Brazil). D1904 (planalto.gov.br).
Decree nº 3,952 (2001, September 4). Dispõe sobre o Conselho Nacional de Combate à Discriminação – CNCD. Presidência da República (Brazil). D3952 (planalto.gov.br).
Decree nº 4,228, (2002, May 13). Institui, no âmbito da Administração Pública Federal, o Programa Nacional de Ações Afirmativas e dá outras providências. Presidência da República (Brazil). D4228 (planalto.gov.br).
Decree nº 4,229. (2002, May 13). Dispõe sobre o Programa Nacional de Direitos Humanos – PNDH, instituído pelo Decreto no 1.904, de 13 de maio de 1996, e dá outras providências. Presidência da República (Brazil). D4229 (planalto.gov.br).
Decree nº 4,887. (2003, November 20). Regulamenta o procedimento para identificação, reconhecimento, delimitação, demarcação e titulação das terras ocupadas por remanescentes das comunidades dos quilombos de que trata o art. 68 do Ato das Disposições Constitucionais Transitórias. Presidência da República (Brazil). D4887 (planalto.gov.br).
Decree nº 95,855 (1988, March 21). Declara Monumento Nacional a Serra da Barriga, em União dos Palmares, Estado de Alagoas, e dá outras providências. Presidência da República (Brazil). http://www.planalto.gov.br/ccivil_03/decreto/1980–1989/d95855.htm
Decree nº 96.038. (1988, March 12). Declara de utilidade pública, para fins de desapropriação, a área de terra constituída pela Serra da Barriga, declarada Monumento Nacional, situada no Município de União dos Palmares, Estado de Alagoas. Presidência da República (Brazil). D96038 (planalto.gov.br).

Del Popolo, S. & Schkolnik, F. (2014). Pueblos indígenas y afrodescendientes en los censos de población y vivienda de América Latina: avances y desafíos en el derecho a la información. Notas de Población, 40(97), 205–247. DOI: 10.18356/04a95e4e-es

Diário do Nordeste. (2021, August 21). De janeiro a julho de 2020, Estado somou 31 denúncias do tipo; neste ano, número subiu para 55. https://diariodonordeste.verdesmares.com.br/metro/denuncias-de-racismo-crescem-77-no-ceara-em-2021-ocorrencias-podem-ser-registradas-pela-internet-1.3124263

Dias, A. A. M. (2007). Os anacronautas do teutonismo virtual: uma etnografia do neonazismo na internet. [Master Dissertation]. Unicamp.

Díaz, M. C. & Velázquez, M. E. (2017). Estudios afromexicanos: una revisión historiográfica y antropológica. Tabula Rasa, 27, 221–248.

Díaz, R. (1993). Hacia una investigación histórica de la población negra en el Nuevo Reino de Granada durante el período colonial. In Díaz, R. (Ed.), Contribución africana a la cultura de las Américas (pp. 15–22). Instituto Colombiano de Antropología-Biopacífico.

Díaz, R. (2011, October 18–21). La manumisión de los esclavos o la parodia de la libertad en el área urbano-regional de Santafé de Bogotá, 1700–1750. [Paper presentation] Simposio internacional "Pasado, presente y futuro de los afrodescendientes. Cartagena, Colombia.

Domingues, P. J. (2005). A insurgência de ébano: a história da Frente Negra Brasileira (1931–1937). [PHD Thesis]. FFLCH-USP.

Domingues. P. (2021). Agenciar raça, reinventar a nação: O movimento pelas reparações no Brasil. Análise Social, 53(227), 332–361. https://doi.org/10.31447/AS00032573.2018227.04

Dos Santos, S. A. (2021). Comissões de Heteroidentificação étnico-racial: lócus de constrangimento ou de controle social de uma política pública. O social em questão, 50, 11–62.

Du Bois, W. E. B. (1903). The Souls of Black Folks. Penguin Books.

Dube, S. (2001). *Sujeitos Subalternos*. El Colégio de México.

Dubois, L. (2005). Avengers of the New World: The Story of the Haitian Revolution. Harvard University Press.

Dutra, R. & Ribeiro, M. A. (2021). Existe Um Autoritarismo Brasileiro? *Revista Brasileira De Sociologia*, 9(22), 246–273

Economic Commission for Latin America and the Caribbean (ECLAC). (2018). Afrodescendent women in Latin America and the Caribbean Debts of equality. United Nations publication. https://repositorio.cepal.org/bitstream/handle/11362/44387/1/S1800725_en.pdf

Economic Commission for Latin America and the Caribbean (ECLAC)/Office of the United Nations High Commissioner for Human Rights (OHCHR). (2020). People of African descent in Latin America and the Caribbean: developing indicators to measure and counter inequalities. https://repositorio.cepal.org/bitstream/handle/11362/45202/1/S1900854_es.pdf

Escalante, A. (1964). El negro en Colombia. [Master Dissertation]. Universidad Nacional de Colombia.

Fanon, F. (1952). Peau noire, masques blancs. Les Éditions du Seuil.

Fanon, F. (1959). Fondement réciproque de la culture nationale et des luttes de libération. Présence Africaine.

Fanon, F. (1961). Les damnés de la terre. Éditions François Maspero.
Faustino, D. M. (2020). Revisitando a recepção de frantz fanon: o ativismo negro brasileiro e os diálogos transnacionais em torno da negritude. Lua Nova, 109. https://doi.org/10.1590/0102-303331/109
Feres Júnior, J., Campos, L. A., Daflon, V. T. & Venturini, A. C. (2018). Ação afirmativa: conceito, história e debates [online]. (Coleção Sociedade e política). EDUERJ. https://doi.org/10.7476/9786599036477
Fernandes, F. (1972). *O Negro no Mundo dos Brancos*. Difusão Europeia do Livro.
Fernández Retamar, R. (2011). Fanon y la América Latina. Revista Casa de las Américas, 31, 269–281.
Ferreira, G. L. (2017). A Lei de cotas no Serviço Público Federal: sub-representação legal nas ações afirmativas. Lumen Juris.
Ferreira, G. L. & Igreja, R. (2017). Narrativas como metodologia crítica para o estudo das relações raciais no Direito. Revista de Pesquisa e Educação Jurídica, 3, 62–79.
Ferreira, M. C. M. & Santos, M. H. G. (2000). Programa Brasil, Gênero e Raça: Superando a discriminação no trabalho. Boletim de Mercado de Trabalho – Conjuntura e Análise, 13. IPEA.
Ferreira, R. & Borba, A. (2006). O mapa das ações afirmativas no ensino superior. Laboratório de Políticas Públicas/UERJ, 2006. <http://www.lpp-buenosaires.net/olped/acoesafirmativas/documentos/4_Mapa_das_cotas.pdf >
Firmin, A. (1885). De l'égalité des races humaines. Lib. Cotillon.
Folha de São Paulo. (2007, June 8). UnB rejeita um gêmeo e aceita outro nas cotas. [Press release]. https://www1.folha.uol.com.br/fsp/cotidian/ff0806200718.htm
Folha de São Paulo. (2020, September 9). Tribunal do Paraná arquiva investigação contra juíza que citou raça em sentença. https://www1.folha.uol.com.br/cotidiano/2020/09/tribunal-do-pr-arquiva-investigacao-contra-juiza-que-citou-raca-em-sentenca.shtml
Fraser, N. (2004). Justice sociale, redistribution et reconnaissance. *Revue de Mauss: De la reconnaissance – Don, identité et estime de soi*, 23, 151–164.
Freire, G., Diaz- Bonilla, C., Schwartz Orellana, S., Soler Lopez, J. & Carbonari, F. (2018). Afrodescendants in Latin America: Toward a Framework of Inclusion. World Bank, Washington, DC. https://openknowledge.worldbank.org/handle/10986/30201
Freyre, G. (2001). Casa Grande & Senzala (45th. Ed.). Editora Record. (Original work published 1933).
Frühling, P., González, M. & Buvollen, H. S. (2007). Etnicidad y nación. El desarrollo de la autonomía de la Costa Atlántica de Nicaragua (1987–2007). F&G Editores.
Fry, P. (2002). Política, nacionalidade e o significado de raça no Brasil. In Bethel, L. (Ed.), *Brasil: fardo do passado, promessa do futuro* (pp. 153–202). Civilização Brasileira.
Fundação Cultural Palmares (2021, November 16). Superação do passado: Sem dívida histórica e olhando para o futuro. https://www.palmares.gov.br/?p=59573&fbclid=IwAR0URYj9Esa0y7YFlHOeOImKTILcVVEgEw_Mcdkne_mVDYiq5z7psAbRPfY
Garrido, M. C. M. (2018). Atuação militante de Lélia Gonzalez na discussão. Tempo e Argumento, 10(25), 435–463. Universidade do Estado de Santa Catarina, DOI: https://doi.org/10.5965/2175180310252018435
Gates J. (2011). Black in Latin America. New York University Press.
Geggus, D. & Fiering, N. (2009). The World of the Haitian Revolution. Indiana University Press.

Geggus, D. (2002). The Impact of the Haitian Revolution in the Atlantic World. The University of South Carolina Press.
Gilroy, P. (1987). There Ain't No Black in the Union Jack: The Cultural Politics of Race and Nation. Hutchinson.
Gilroy, P. (1993). The Black Atlantic. Modernity and Double Consciousness. Verso.
Gilroy, P. (2000). Between Camps: Nations, Culture and the Allure of Race. Allen Lane.
Gilroy, P. (2004). After Empire: Multiculture or Postcolonial Melancholia. Routledge.
Glissant, É. (1981). Le Discours antillais. Editions du Seuil.
Glissant, É. (1990). Poétique de la Relation. Gallimard.
Glissant, É. (2008). Creolization in the Making of the Americas. Caribbean Quatetley, 54(1–2), 81–89.
Gluckman, M. (1955). The judicial Process Among the Barotse of Northern Rhodesia. Manchester University Press.
Gobineau, C. (1915). An Essay on the Inequality of the Human Races. William Heinemann. (Original work published 1855).
Godoi, M. S. de, & Santos, M. A. (2021). Dez anos da lei federal das cotas universitárias: avaliação de seus efeitos e propostas para sua renovação e aperfeiçoamento. Revista de Informação Legislativa, 58(229), 11–35. https://www12.senado.leg.br/ril/edicoes/58/229/ril_v58_n229_p11
Gomes, F. S. (2005). Negros e política: (1888–1937). Zahar.
Gomes, F. S. (2015). Mocambos e quilombos. Claro Enigma.
Gomes, J. B. B. (2001). Ação Afirmativa & Princípio Constitucional da Igualdade – O Direito como Instrumento de Transformação Social. A experiência dos EUA. Renovar.
Gomes, J. D. (2013). Os Segredos de Virgínia: Estudos de Atitudes Raciais em São Paulo (1945–1955). [PHD Thesis]. University of São Paulo.
Gomes, N. L. (2017). O movimento negro educador. Saberes construídos na luta por emancipação. Vozes.
Gómez, L. (1970). Interrogantes sobre el progreso de Colombia. Populibro. (Original work published 1928).
Gonzalez, L. (1988). A categoria político-cultural de amefricanidade. In Tempo Brasileiro, 92/93, 69–82.
Gonzalez, L. & Hasenbalg, C. (1982). *Lugar do Negro.* Marco Zero.
Grin, M. (2001). Esse ainda obscuro objeto de desejo – Políticas de ação afirmativa e ajustes normativos: o seminário de Brasília. Novos Estudos CEBRAP, 59, 172–202.
Griner, A., Sampaio, L. M. B. & Sampaio, R. M. B. (2015). A política afirmativa "Argumento de Inclusão" como forma de acesso à universidade pública: o caso da Universidade Federal do Rio Grande do Norte. Revista de Administração Pública, 49(5), 1291–1317. https://doi.org/10.1590/0034-7612123593
Gros, C. (1997). Indigenismo y etnicidad: el desafio neo-liberal. In Uribe, M. V. & Restrepo, E. (Eds.), Antropologia en la modernidad (pp. 13–60). Instituto Colombiano de Antropología e Historia.
Gros, C. (2000). Políticas de la Etnicidad: identidad, Estado y Modernidad. Instituto Colombiano de Antropología e Historia.
Grosfoguel, R. (2006). La descolonización de la economía y los estudios postcoloniales: Transmodernidad, pensamiento fronterizo y colonialidad global. *Tabula Rasa,* 4, 17–48.

Grosfoguel, R. (2020). Para uma visão decolonial da crise civilizatória e dos paradigmas da esquerda ocidentalizada. In Bernadino-Costa, J., Maldonado-Torres, N. & Grosfoguel, R. (Eds.), *Decolonialidade e pensamento afrodiaspórico* (pp. 55–78). Autêntica.

Guimarães, A. S. (1999). Racismos e anti-racismos no Brasil. Editora 34.

Guimarães, A. S. (2002). Classes, raças e Democracia. Editora 34.

Guimarães, A. S. (2012). Preconceito racial: modos, temas e tempos (2nd ed.). Cortez.

Gutiérrez de Pineda, V. (1999). Miscegenación y cultura en la Colombia colonial, 1750–1810. Colciencias; Uniandes.

Gutiérrez, I. (1980). Historia del negro en Colombia. ¿Sumisión o rebeldía? Nueva América.

Gutiérrez, I. (1996). *Los Afroamericanos. Historia, cultura y proyectos*. Editorial El Buho.

Habeas Corpus HC nº 154,248 (2022, February 23). Habeas Corpus. Matéria Criminal. Injúria Racial (Art. 140, § 3, do Código Penal). Espécie do Gênero Racismo. Imprescritibilidade. Denegação de Ordem. Supremo Tribunal Federal (Brazil). https://stf.jusbrasil.com.br/jurisprudencia/1391052830/habeas-corpus-hc-154248-df-0067385-4620181000000/inteiro-teor-1391052932

Hale, C., Calla, P. & Mullings, L. (2017). Race Matters in Dangerous Times. A network of scholar-activists assesses changing racial formations across the Americas and mobilizes against renewed racist backlash. NACLA Report on the Americas, 49(1), 8–89.

Hale, C. (2020). Using and Refusing the Law: Indigenous Struggles and Legal; Strategies after Neoliberal Multiculturalism. American Anthropologist, 122(3), 618–631. DOI: 10.1111/aman.13416

Hall, S. (2000). Questão multicultural. In Sovik, L. (Ed.), Da diáspora: identidades e Mediações culturais (pp. 51–100). UFMG; Unesco.

Hanchard, M. (2001). Orfeu e o Poder – Movimento Negro no Rio e São Paulo. UERJ.

Hasenbalg, C. & Valle Silva, N. (1988). Estrutura Social, Moblidade e Raça. Vértice.

Hasenbalg, C. (1979). Discriminação e Desigualdades Raciais no Brasil. Graal.

Hasenbalg, C. (1988). Raça e Mobilidade Social. In Hasenbalg, C. & Silva, N. V. (Eds.), Estrutura Social, Mobilidade e Raça. Iuperj; Vértice.

Hasenbalg, C. (1996). Entre o mito e os fatos: racismo e relações raciais no Brasil. In Maio, M. C. & Santos, R. V. (Eds.), Raça, ciência e sociedade (pp. 235–249). Editora FIOCRUZ; CCBB. http://books.scielo.org/id/djnty/epub/maio-9788575415177.epub

Helg, A. (1998). Sentido e impacto de la participación negra en la guerra de independencia de Cuba. Revista De Indias, 58(212), 47–63.

Helg, A. (2016). Plus jamais esclaves! De l'insoumission à la révolte, le grand récit d'une émancipation (1492–1838). Editions La Découverte.

Henriques, R. (2001). Desigualdade racial no Brasil: Evolução das condições de vida na década de 90. Texto para discussão 807, IPEA.

Heringer, R. (2000). A agenda anti-racista das ONGs brasileiras nos anos 90. In Guimarães, A. S. A. & Huntley, L. (Eds.), Tirando a Máscara – Ensaios sobre o racismo no Brasil (pp. 343–358). Paz e Terra.

Herskovits, M. J. (1938). Les Noirs du Nouveau monde, sujet de recherche africaniste. Journal des Africanistes.

Herskovits, M. J. (1941). *The myth of the negro past*. Harper & Brothers Editors.

Herskovits, M. J. (1965). *Economic Anthropology: The Economic Life of Primitive Peoples*. Alfred A. Knopf.

Herskovits, M. J. (1952). *Acculturation: the study of culture contact*. Payot.

Hooker, J. (2005). Indigenous Inclusion/Black Exclusion: Race, Ethnicity and Multicultural Citizenship. *Latin America Journal of Latin American Studies*, *37*(2), 285–310. https://doi.org/10.1017/S0022216X05009016

Hooker, J. (2020). Introduction. In J. Hooker (Ed.), Black and indigenous resistance in the Americas: from multiculturalism to racist Backlash. Lexington Books.

Igreja, R. (2021). Populism, inequality, and the construction of the "other": an anthropological approach to the far right in Brazil. Vibrant: Virtual Brazilian Anthropology, 18, 1–22. https://doi.org/10.1590/1809-43412021v18a802

Igreja, R. & Tavolaro, T. (2015). Sciences sociales et discrimination positive au Brésil: défis et enjeux autour de la 'race' et du racism. Revue Socio, 4, 1–18.

Igreja, R. (2005). Estado, diferença cultural e políticas multiculturalistas: uma comparação entre Brasil e México. [PhD Thesis]. Universidade de Brasília.

Igreja, R. (2016). Combate al racismo y la discriminación racial en Brasil: legislación y acción institucional. Desacatos. Revista de Antropología Social, 51, 32–49.

Igreja, R. (2018). Catégories ethniques et raciales dans les recensements et politiques de discrimination positive au Brésil. In Wieviorka, M., Guerin-Pace, F., Igreja, R., Le-Bras, H. & Filippova, E. (Eds.), Catégories ethniques et raciales dans les recensements et politiques de discrimination positive au Brésil (pp. 111–145). Éditions de la Maison des sciences de l'homme (FMSH).

Igreja, R. & Ferreira, G. L. (2019). The Brazilian Law of Racial Quotas put to the test of labor justice: a legal case against Banco do Brasil. Latin American and Caribbean Ethnic Studies, 14(3), 294–317. https://doi.org/10.1080/17442222.2019.1667635

Igreja, R. & Negri, C. (2020). As ciências sociais brasileiras frente à ascensão da extrema-direita: uma reflexão urgente e necessária. Revista Plural, 2, 35–69.

Igreja, R. & Rodrigues Pinto, S. (2019). La Contribución de los Estudios Latinoamericanos para la Producción de un Conocimiento Global. In Igreja, R., Hoffmann, O. & Rodrigues Pinto, S. (Eds.), *Hacer ciencias sociales desde América latina: desafíos y experiencias de investigación* (pp. 15–26). FLACSO.

Iturralde, G. (2018). Reflexiones sobre la inclusión de variables afrodescendientes en instrumentos estadísticos. Entrevista a Odile Hoffmann. Diario de Campo Cuarta época, 2(5).

Izard, G. (2003). La construcción política de la identidad garifuna en el Belice contemporáneo. Revista de las Américas. Historia y presente, 1, 61–81.

Jaccoud, L. (2009). A construção de uma política de Promoção da Igualdade Racial: uma análise dos últimos 20 anos. IPEA.

Jaccourd, L. & Beghin, N. (2002). Desigualdades raciais no Brasil – um balanço da intervenção governamental. IPEA.

James, C. L. R. (2003). Los jacobinos negros. Toussaint L'Ouverture y la Revolución de Haití. Fondo de Cultura Económica.

Jaramillo Uribe, J. (1994). *Ensayos sobre historia social colombiana*. Universidad Nacional. (Original work published 1968).

Jesus, D., Conceição, F. & Marques, M. M. (Eds.). Racistas são os outros: contribuição ao debate lusotropicalista em África, Brasil e Portuga (pp. 18–34). Afirme-se.

Jesus, R. E. (2019). Reafirmando direitos: trajetórias de estudantes cotistas negros(as) no ensino superior brasileiro. Ações afirmativas no Ensino Superior.

Jesus, R. E. (2021). Quem quer (pode) ser negro no Brasil? Editora Autêntica.

Jiménez, M. (1920). Los problemas de la raza en Colombia. Biblioteca Cultura.
Kintê, S. (2013). Relato da reunião com a Presidenta Dilma Roussef. Centro de Cultura e Estudos Étnicos Anajô. https://anajoalagoas.com/2013/07/23/relato-da-reuniao-do-movimento-negro-com-a-presidenta-dilma-rousseff/
Knight, F.W. & Gates, Jr., H. L. (2016). *Dictionary of Caribbean and Afro-Latin American Biography*. Oxford University Press Current Online. https://www.oxfordreference.com/view/10.1093/acref/9780199935796.001.0001/acref-9780199935796
Kroubo Dagnini, J. (2008). Marcus Garvey: A Controversial Figure in the History of Pan-Africanism. The Journal of Pan African Studies, 2(3).
Kymlicka, W. (1996). *Ciudadania Multicultural*. Paidós.
Kymlicka, W. (2003). *La política vernácula – Nacionalismo, multiculturalismo y ciudadanía*. Paidós.
Lamounier, B. (1976). Educação. Cadernos do Cebrap, 15, 14–22.
Lao Montes, A. (2011). Fanon y el socialismo del siglo XXI: Los condenados de la tierra y la nueva política de des/colonialidad y liberación. In Los condenados de la tierra (pp. 7–46). Fondo Editorial Casa de las Américas.
Laó-Montes, A. (2008). Cartographies of Afro-Latina/o Politics: Political Contests and Historical Challenges. In Negritud: Revista de Estudios Afro-Latinoamericanos, 2(2), 237–262.
Laó-Montes, A. (2020). Contrapunteos diaspóricos: Cartografías políticas de Nuestra Afroamérica. Universidad Externado. https://publicaciones.uexternado.edu.co/gpd-contrapunteos-diasporicos-9789587902860.html
Law n° 70 (1993, August 27). Por la cual se desarrolla el artículo transitorio 55 de la Constitución Política. El Congreso de Colombia. https://www.minagricultura.gov.co/Normatividad/Leyes/Ley%2070%20de%201993.pdf
Law n° 1,390 (1951, July 3). Inclui entre as contravenções penais a prática de atos resultantes de preconceitos de raça ou de côr. Presidência da República (Brazil). Lei Afonso Arinos – Lei 1390/51 | Lei no 1.390, de 3 de julho de 1951, Presidência da República (jusbrasil.com.br).
Law n° 4,151 (2003, September 4). Institui nova disciplina sobre o sistema de cotas para ingresso nas universidades publicas estaduais e dá outras providências. Governo do Estado do Rio de Janeiro (Brazil). https://gov-rj.jusbrasil.com.br/legislacao/90604/lei-4151-03#:~:text=Para%20a%20Confenen%2C%20a%20Lei,tenham%20estudado%20em%20outros%20Estados
Law n° 6,620 (1978, December 17). Define os crimes contra Segurança Nacional, estabelece sistemática para o seu processo e julgamento e dá outras providências. Presidência da República (Brazil). http://www.planalto.gov.br/ccivil_03/leis/1970-1979/l6620.htm
Law n° 7,347. (1985, July 24). Disciplina a ação civil pública de responsabilidade por danos causados ao meio-ambiente, ao consumidor, a bens e direitos de valor artístico, estético, histórico, turístico e paisagístico (VETADO) e dá outras providências. Presidência da República (Brazil). http://www.planalto.gov.br/ccivil_03/leis/l7347orig.htm
Law n° 7.716. (1989, January 5). Define os crimes resultantes de preconceito de raça ou de cor. Presidência da República (Brazil). L7716 (planalto.gov.br).

Law n° 7,668. (1988, August 22nd). Autoriza o Poder Executivo a constituir a Fundação Cultural Palmares – FCP e dá outras providências. Presidência da República (Brazil). L7668 (planalto.gov.br).

Law n° 8,081. (1990, September 21). Estabelece os crimes e as penas aplicáveis aos atos discriminatórios ou de preconceito de raça, cor, religião, etnia ou procedência nacional, praticados pelos meios de comunicação ou por publicação de qualquer natureza. Presidência da República (Brazil). L8081 (planalto.gov.br).

Law n° 8,112 (1990, December 11). Regime Jurídico dos Servidores Públicos Civis. Câmara de Deputados (Brazil). Portal da Câmara dos Deputados (camara.leg.br).

Law n° 8,882. (1994, June 3). Acrescenta parágrafo ao art. 20 da Lei nº 7.716, de 5 de janeiro de 1989, que "define os crimes resultantes de preconceitos de raça ou de cor. Presidência da República (Brazil). http://www.planalto.gov.br/ccivil_03/leis/l8882.htm

Law n° 9,459. (1997, May 13). Altera os arts. 1º e 20 da Lei nº 7.716, de 5 de janeiro de 1989, que define os crimes resultantes de preconceito de raça ou de cor, e acrescenta parágrafo ao art. 140 do Decreto-lei nº 2.848, de 7 de dezembro de 1940.Presidência da República (Brazil). L9459 (planalto.gov.br).

Law n° 10,558 (2002, November 13). Cria o Programa Diversidade na Universidade, e dá outras providências. Presidência da República (Brazil). L10558 (planalto.gov.br).

Law n° 10,639. (2003, January 9). Altera a Lei no 9.394, de 20 de dezembro de 1996, que estabelece as diretrizes e bases da educação nacional, para incluir no currículo oficial da Rede de Ensino a obrigatoriedade da temática "História e Cultura Afro-Brasileira", e dá outras providências. Presidência da República (Brazil). L10639 (planalto.gov.br).

Law n° 12,288 (2010, July 20). Institui o Estatuto da Igualdade Racial; altera as Leis nos 7.716, de 5 de janeiro de 1989, 9.029, de 13 de abril de 1995, 7.347, de 24 de julho de 1985, e 10.778, de 24 de novembro de 2003. Presidência da República (Brazil). L12288 (planalto.gov.br).

Law n° 12,519. (2011, November 19). Institui o Dia Nacional de Zumbi e da Consciência Negra. Presidência da República (Brazil). L12519 (planalto.gov.br).

Law n° 12,711. (2012, August 29). Dispõe sobre o ingresso nas universidades federais e nas instituições federais de ensino técnico de nível médio e dá outras providências. Presidência da República (Brazil). planalto.gov.br/ccivil_03/_ato2011–2014/2012/lei/l12711.htm

Law n° 12,990. (2014, June 9). Reserva aos negros 20% (vinte por cento) das vagas oferecidas nos concursos públicos para provimento de cargos efetivos e empregos públicos no âmbito da administração pública federal, das autarquias, das fundações públicas, das empresas públicas e das sociedades de economia mista controladas pela União. Presidência da República (Brazil). L12990 (planalto.gov.br).

Law Project 6,738. (2013, November 7). Reserva aos negros vinte por cento das vagas oferecidas nos concursos públicos para provimento de cargos efetivos e empregos públicos no âmbito da administração pública federal, das autarquias, das fundações públicas, das empresas públicas e das sociedades de economia mista controladas pela União. Câmara de Deputados (Brazil). Portal da Câmara dos Deputados (camara.leg.br).

Lemos, R. O. (2016). Os feminismos negros: a reação aos sistemas de opressões. Revista Espaço Acadêmico, 16(185), 12–25. https://periodicos.uem.br/ojs/index.php/EspacoAcademico/article/view/33592

Léon-Gontran, D. (1988). *Primer Congreso de la Cultura Negra de las Américas, Cali, Colombia*. [actas] Unesco; Fundación Colombiana de Investigaciones Folclóricas; ECOE.

Lewis, R. (1994). Garvey's perspective on Jamaica. In Lewis, R. & Bryan, P. (Eds.), Garvey his work and Impact (pp. 229–239). (2nd ed). Africa World Press Inc.

Lima, M. (2010). Desigualdades raciais e políticas públicas: ações afirmativas no governo Lula. Novos Estudos CEBRAP, 87, 77–95. https://doi.org/10.1590/S0101-33002010000200005

Lima, M. (2014). A Obra de Carlos Hasenbalg e seu Legado à Agenda de Estudos sobre Desigualdades Raciais no Brasil. Dados, 57(4). https://doi.org/10.1590/00115258201428

Lins Ribeiro, G. (2018). Giro global a la derecha y la relevancia de la Antropología. Encartes Antropológicos, 1(1), 1–4.

López De Mesa, L. (1970). De cómo se ha formado la Nación colombiana. Ed. Bedout, (Original work published 1934).

López, R. (2011). Tensiones y continuidades en la historicidad de la negritud: Aimé Césaire ante Frantz Fanon. In Oliva, E., Stecher, L. & Zapata, C. (Eds.), Aimé Césaire desde América Latina. Diálogos con el poeta de la negritud. Centro de Estudios Culturales Latinoamericanos; Facultad de Filosofía y Humanidades, Universidad de Chile.

Loveman, M. (2014). National Colors: Racial Classification and the State in Latin America. Oxford University Press.

Machado, M., Eurístenes, P. & Feres Júnior, J. (2017). Políticas de ação afirmativa nas universidades estaduais. Iesp/Uerj.

Machado, M. (2009). A legislação anti-racismo no Brasil e sua aplicação: um caso de insensibilidade do Judiciário? Revista Brasileira de Ciências Criminais, 76, 79–105.

Maio, M. C. & Santos, R. V. (2005). Política de Cotas Raciais, os 'olhos Da Sociedade' e Os Usos Da Antropologia: O Caso Do Vestibular Da Universidade de Brasília (UnB). Horizontes Antropológicos, 11(23), 181–214. doi:10.1590/S0104-71832005000100011

Maldonado-Torres, N. (2005). El Fanon de Alejandro De Oto en el contexto latinoamericano. Caribbean Studies, 33(2), 233–238.

Maldonado-Torres, N. (2007). Sobre la colonialidad del ser: contribuciones al desarrollo de un concepto. In S. Castro-Gómez & R. Grosfoguel. El giro decolonial. reflexiones para una diversidad epistémica más allá del capitalismo global (pp. 127–168). Editorial: Universidad Central; Pontificia Universidad Javeriana; Siglo del Hombre Editores.

Mbembe, A. (2017). Crítica da razão Negra. Antígona.

McLemee, Scott. (1996). Introduction. In McLemee, S. (Ed.), C.L.R. James on the Negro Question (pp. 11–37). University Press of Mississippi.

Migalhas (2021, July 15). Bolsonaro pode ser investigado por fala racista: "criação de barata". https://www.migalhas.com.br/quentes/348589/bolsonaro-pode-ser-investigado-por-fala-racista–criacao-de-barata

Millán, G. L. (2017). Visibilización en los censos. Afrodescendientes en la Encuesta Intercensal 2015 en México. Legajos Boletín del archivo general de la Nación, 12. https://aries.aibr.org/storage/pdfs/1225/2017.AR0016590.pdf

Ministério da Mulher, da Família e dos Direitos Humanos (2022, January 20). Liberdade religiosa e de crença são temas de evento on-line, nesta sexta-feira. https://www.gov.br/mdh/pt-br/assuntos/noticias/2022/janeiro/liberdade-religiosa-e-de-crenca-sao-temas-de-evento-on-line-nesta-sexta-feira-21

Mintz, S. W. & Price, R. (1992). *The birth of African American culture: An anthropological perspective.* Beacon Press.
Moura, C. (1977). *O negro, de bom escravo a mau cidadão?* Editora Publisher.
Moura, C. (1990). As injustiças de Clio. Oficina de Livros.
Moura, C. (2001). A quilombagem como expressão de protesto radical. In Moura, C. (Ed.), *Os quilombos na dinâmica social do Brasil* (pp. 103–118). UFAL.
Müller, J. W. (2016). What is populism? University of Pennsylvania.
Munanga, K. (2001). Origem e histórico dos quilombos em África. In C. Moura (Ed.), *Os Quilombos na Dinâmica Social do Brasil* (pp. 21–34). UFAL.
Munanga, K. (2004). Uma abordagem conceitual das noções de raça, racismo, identidade e etnia. Programa de educação sobre o negro na sociedade brasileira. EdUFF.
Munanga, K. & Gomes, N. L. (2016). O negro no Brasil de Hoje. Global Editora.
Nabuco, J. (2011). O abolicionismo. Centro Edelstein de Pesquisas Sociais. <http://books.scielo.org>.
Nagel, T. (2003). John Rawls and Affirmative Action. The Journal of Blacks in Higher Education, 39(Spring, 2003), 82–84. The JBHE Foundation, Inc. http://www.jstor.org/stable/3134387
Nascimento, A. (1966). Lettre ouverte au Premier festival mondial des arts nègres. Présence Africaine 58, 215–234.
Nascimento, A. (1980). O Quilombismo. Documentos de uma militância panafricanista. Vozes.
Nascimento, A. (2002). Universidade e Cidadania: o movimento dos cursos Pré-vestibulares Populares. Revista Lugar Comum, 17. E papers Ed.
Nascimento, A. (2004). Teatro Experimental do Negro: trajetória e reflexões. Estudos Avançados, 50, 209–224. USP.
Nascimento, A. & Nascimento, E. L. (2000). Reflexões sobre o movimento negro no Brasil, 1938–1997. In Guimarães, A. S. & Huntley, L. (Eds.), Tirando a máscara- ensaios sobre o racismo no Brasil (pp. 203–236). Paz e Terra.
Nascimento, A., Ramos, A. G., Ribeiro, J. & Fischlowitz, E. (1950). Relações de Raça no Brasil. Edições Quilombo.
Nascimento, B. (1977). O Quilombo e a historiografia. In Quinzena do Negro (mimeo). Arquivo Nacional. Fundo Maria Beatriz Nascimento, Caixa 29.
Nascimento, B. (1985). O conceito de quilombo e a resistência cultural negra. Afrodiáspora, 6–7, 41–49.
Negri, C., Igreja, R. & Pinto, S. R. (2019). It happened in Brazil too: the radical right's capture of networks of hope. Cahiers des Amériques Latines, 92, 17–38.
Ngou–mve, N. (2008). *Mesianismo, cofradías y resistencia en el África Bantú y América Meridional* (pp. 10–18). Centro de Estudios Afro-iberoamericanos.
Nisbett, N. (2008). Universal Emancipation: The Haitian Revolution and the Radical Enlightenment. University of Virginia Press.
Nobles, M. (2000). *Shades of Citizenship: Race and the Census in Modern Politics*. Stanford University Press.
Nogueira, O. (1985). *Tanto preto quanto branco: estudos de relações raciais*. T. A. Queiroz.
Nogueira, O. (1998). *Preconceito de Marca – As relações Raciais em Itapetininga*. Edusp.
O'Dwyer, E. C. (2002). Os quilombos e a prática profissional dos antropólogos. In O'Dwyer, E. C. (Ed.), Quilombos: identidade étnica e territorialidade (pp. 13–42). FGV.

Notícias UOL (2021, November 20). Número de registros de racismo dobrou no Rio em 2021, mostra estudo. https://noticias.uol.com.br/cotidiano/ultimas-noticias/2021/11/20/numero-de-registros-de-racismo-dobrou-no-rio-em-2021-mostra-estudo.htm

OAS (2016). Plan of Action for the Decade for People of African Descent in the Americas (2016–2025) (adopted at the second plenary session, held on June 14, 2016) AG/RES.2891 (XLVI-O/16). https://www.oas.org/en/sare/documents/PA_Afrodesc_ENG.pdf

Obregón, L. (2002). Críticas tempranas a la esclavización de africanos. In Mosquera, C., Pardo, M. & Hoffmann, O. (Eds.), *Afrodescendientes en las Américas. Trayectorias sociales e identitarias a 150 años de la abolición de la esclavitud en Colombia* (pp. 2–45). Ed. UN; ICANH; IRD; ILSA.

O Globo (2007, May 30). Para UnB, um gêmeo é negro e o outro, não. [Presse release] https://extra.globo.com/noticias/brasil/para-unb-um-gemeo-negro-o-outro-nao-668078.html

O Globo (2018, October 24). Bolsonaro diz que política de cotas é 'equivocada' e que política de combate ao preconceito é 'coitadismo'. https://g1.globo.com/politica/eleicoes/2018/noticia/2018/10/24/bolsonaro-diz-ser-contra-cotas-e-que-politica-de-combate-ao-preconceito-e-coitadismo.ghtml

OHCHR – Escritório do Alto Comissariado das Nações Unidas para os Direitos Humanos. (2021). Combate ao racismo e à discriminação: 20 anos da Declaração e Programa de Ação de Durban. https://www.ohchr.org/SP/Issues/Racism/Pages/20th-anniversary-DDPA.aspx

Oliva, E. (2017). Intelectuales afrodescendientes: apuntes para una genealogía en América Latina. Tabula Rasa, 27, 45–65.

Ortiz, F. (1940). Contrapunteo cubano del tabaco y del azúcar. Editorial José Montero.

Osorio, R. G. (2003). O sistema classificatório de "Cor e Raça" do IBGE. Texto para discussão, 996. IPEA.

Osório, R. G. (2006). Desigualdades Raciais e de Gênero No Serviço Público Civil. Secretaria Internacional Do Trabalho, OIT.

Paixão, M. (2014). *A lenda da modernidade encantada: por uma crítica ao pensamento social brasileiro sobre as relações raciais e o projeto de estado-nação.* CRV.

Paixão, M. & Carvano, L. M. (2008). Censo e demografia: a variável cor ou raça no interior dos sistemas censitários brasileiros. In Pinho, O. & Sansone, (Eds.), *Raça: novas perspectivas antropológicas.* (2nd ed. pp. 25–61). EDUFBA. <http://books.scielo.org>.

Parekh, B. (2000). *Rethinking multiculturalism: cultural diversity and political theory.* Palgrave.

Paschel, T. (2016). Becoming Black Political Subjects: Movements and Ethno-Racial Rights in Colombia and Brazil. Princeton University Press.

Paschel, T. (2018). Repensando la movilización de los afrodescendientes en América Latina. In De la Fuente, A. & Reid, G. (Eds.), Estudios afrolatinoamericanos: una introducción. CLACSO; Massachussetts: Afro Latin American Researcher Institute; Harvard University.

Pereira, A. A. (2013). O mundo negro": relações raciais e a constituição do movimento negro contemporâneo no Brasil. Pallas; FAPERJ.

Periódicos UEPG (2020, December 18). Número de denúncias de racismo e injúria racial tem aumento de 440% no Paraná em 2020.https://periodico.sites.uepg.br/index.php/direitos-humanos/2010-numero-de-denuncia-de-racismo-e-injuria-racial-tem-aumento-de-440-no-parana-em-2020

Petruccelli, J. L. (1996). Doutrinas francesas e o pensamento racial brasileiro, 1870–1930. Estudos Sociedade e Agricultura, 7, 134–149.

Picard, J., Diaz, M. R. & Nuñez, N. (2020). Vers une ethnologie nationale: folklore, science et politique dans l'œuvre de Jean Price-Mars et de Fernando Ortiz. In Agyriadis, K., Gobin, E., Laëthier, M., González, N. N. & Byron, J. P. (Eds.), Cuba-Haití: Engager l'anthropologie. Anthologie critique et histoire comparée (1884–1959). CIDIHCA.

Pierson, D. (1945). Brancos e pretos na Bahia. Estudo de Contacto Racial. Brasiliana. Biblioteca Pedagógica Brasileira; Campanha Editora Nacional.

Pieterse, J. N. (1992). White on Black: images of Africa and blacks in Western popular culture. Yale University Press.

Pires, T. R. O. (2013). Criminalização do racismo: entre política de reconhecimento e meio de legitimação do controle social dos não reconhecidos. [PHD Thesis]. Pontifícia Universidade Católica.

Piza, E. & Fúlvia, R. (1999). Cor nos censos brasileiros. Revista USP, 40, 122–137, December/February.

Price-Mars, J. (1928). Ainsi parla l'oncle: Essai d'ethnographie. Imprimerie de Compiègne.

Price, R. & Mintz, S. (1976). An Anthropological Approach to the Afro-American Past: Institute for the Study of Human Issues.

Quijano, A. (1999). ¡Qué tal raza!. Revista Venezolana de Economía y Ciencias Sociales, 6(1), 141–152.

Quijano, A. (2007). Colonialidad del poder y clasificación social. In Castro-Gómez, S. & Grosfoguel, R. (Eds.), El giro decolonial. reflexiones para una diversidad epistémica más allá del capitalismo global (pp. 93–126). Editorial: Universidad Central; IESCO; Pontificia Universidad Javeriana; Siglo del Hombre Editores.

Quijano, A. (2014). "Raza", "etnia" y "nación" en Mariátegui: cuestiones abiertas en Cuestiones y horizontes: de la dependencia histórico-estructural a la colonialidad/descolonialidad del poder. CLACSO.

Ramos, A. (1937). As Culturas Negras no Novo Mundo. Civilização Brasileira

Ramos, A.G. (1950). O negro no Brasil e um exame de consciência. In Nascimento, A., Guerreiro Ramos, A., Ribeiro, J. & Fischlowitz, E. Relações de Raça no Brasil (pp. 33–46). Edições Quilombo.

Ramos, A. G. (1979). O problema do negro na sociologia brasileira. In Schwartzman, S. (Ed.), O pensamento nacionalista e os Cadernos de Nosso Tempo (pp. 39–69). Ed. UNB.

Ramos, A.G. (1996). A redução sociológica. UFRJ.

Ratts, A. (2007). Eu sou Atlântica: Sobre a Trajetória de Vida de Beatriz Nascimento. Imprensa Oficial; Instituto Kuanza.

Ratts, A. & Rios. F. (2021). Lélia Gonzalez: retrato do Brasil Negro, Editora Selo Negro.

Rawls, J. (1971). A theory of justice. Harvard University Press.

Rego Oliva, L. M. C. (2020). Sistema de cotas na universidade pública brasileira: avaliação da experiência da UnB após a Lei 12.711/12. [Master Dissertation]. Universidade de Brasília (UnB).

Reis, D. B. (2007). Acesso e permanência de negros(as) no ensino superior: o caso da UFBA. In Lopes, M. A. & Braga, M. L. S. (Eds.), Acesso e permanência da população negra no ensino superior. Ministério da Educação, Secretaria de Educação Continuada, Alfabetização e Diversidade; Unesco.

Reis, J. J. & Gomes, F. (1996). Liberdade por um fio: a história dos quilombos no Brasil. Companhia Das Letras.

Reis, J. J. & Silva, E. (1999). *Negociação e Conflito – A resistência Negra no Brasil e Escravista*. Companhia das Letras.

Restrepo, E. & Rojas, A. (2008). Afrodescendientes en Colombia: Compilación bibliográfica. Universidad del Cauca, Popayan.

Restrepo, E. & Rojas, A. (2010). Inflexión decolonial. Universidad del Cauca; Instituto Pensar; Universidad Javeriana.

Ribeiro, M. (2014). Políticas de promoção da igualdade racial no Brasil (1986–2010). Garamond.

Ribeiro, M. A. (2020). Lilia Schwarcz e a persistência do nacionalismo metodológico nas interpretações do Brasil. Sociologias [online], 22(54), 358–373. <https://doi.org/10.1590/15174522-98440>.

Rios, F & Lima, M. (2020). Por um feminismo afro-latino-americano. Selo Zahar.

RMAAD – Red de Mujeres Afrolatinoamericanas, Afrocaribeñas y de la Diáspora. Plataforma política de las lideresas de América Latina y el Caribe ante el decenio. [Managua, June, 27th 2015]. https://www. jstor.org/stable/pdf/j.ctvn96gn4.20.pdf?refreqid=excelsior%3 A1163425e398b62417a4 3429fbd55e4f8.

Robinson, C. (2000). Black marxism: the making of the Black radical tradition. University of North Carolina Press.

Rodrigues, R. N. (2010). Os africanos no Brasil. Centro Edelstein de Pesquisas Sociais.

Roland, E. (2000). O movimento das mulheres negras brasileiras; desafios e perspectivas. In Guimarães, A. S. & Huntley, L. (Eds.), Tirando a máscara- ensaio sobre o racismo no Brasil (pp. 237–256). Paz e Terra

Romero, S. (1906). América Latina. Livraria Chardon.

Rydgren, J. (2007). The Sociology of the Radical Right. Annuual Review of Sociology, 33, 241–262.

Sabbagh, D. (2004). Affirmative Action Policies: An International Perspective, Human Development Report Office Occasional Paper Background paper for HDR 2004. United Nations Development Programme. http://hdr.undp.org/sites/default/files/hdr2004_daniel_sabbagh.pdf

San Juan Jr, E. (2002). *Racism and cultural studies – critiques of multiculturalist ideology and politics of difference.* Duke University Press.

Sansone, L. (2004). Negritude sem Etnicidade. Pallas; EDUFBA.

Santacruz Palacios, M., Antón, S., García Savino, S. B. & Viáfara López, C. A. (2019). Pueblos afrodescendientes en América Latina: realidades y desafíos. Editorial Lizardo Carvajal; Corporación Amigos de la Unesco

Santos de Paulo, C. A. (2002). Movimento Negro, Participação e institucionalidade: desafios para uma agenda pública. [Master Dissertation]. Universidade de Brasília.

Santos, B. S. (2003). Introdução: para ampliar o cânone do reconhecimento, da diferença e da igualdade. In Santos, B. *Reconhecer para libertar: os caminhos do cosmopolitismo multicultural* (pp. 25–68). Civilização Brasileira.

Santos, B. S. & Meneses, M. P. (2009). *Epistemologias do sul.* Almedina.

Santos, C. A. I. (2018). Marchar não é Caminhar Interfaces políticas e sociais das religiões de matrizes africanas no Rio de Janeiro contra os processos de Intolerância Religiosa (1950–2008). [PHD Thesis]. Universidade Federal do Rio de Janeiro.

Santos, G. A. (2015). Nem crime, nem castigo: o racismo na percepção do judiciário e das vítimas de atos de discriminação. Revista Do Instituto De Estudos Brasileiros, 62, 184–207.
Santos, H. (2000). Uma avaliação do combate às desigualdades raciais no Brasil. In Guimarães, A. S. A. & Huntley, L. (Eds.), Tirando a Máscara – Ensaios sobre o racismo no Brasil (pp. 53–76). Paz e Terra.
Santos, J. T. (2012). Ações afirmativas e educação superior no Brasil: um balanço crítico da produção. Revista Brasileira de Estudos Pedagógicos, 93(234), 401–422.
Santos, M. (1996). As cidadanias mutiladas. O Preconceito. IMESP, pp. 133–144. <http://www.miltonsantos.com.br/site/wp-content/uploads/2011/12/As-cidadanias-mutiladas_MiltonSantos1996–1997SITE.pdf>
Santos, M. (1997). O intelectual e a universidade estagnada. Revista ADUSP, 11, 16–20.
Santos, M. C. R. C. F. (2020). Lélia Gonzalez: a amefricanidade como contributo para a construção de uma nova epistemologia. Revista Espaço Acadêmico, 225.
Santos, N. N. S. (2015). A voz e a palavra do movimento negro na Assembleia Nacional Constituinte (1987/1988): um estudo das demandas por direito. [Master Dissertation]. Fundação Getúlio Vargas.
Santos, R. (2020). Maioria Minorizada – Um dispositivo analítico de racialidade (Coleção Pensamento Negro Contemporâneo). Editora Telha.
Santos, R. (2021). Branquitude e televisão: a nova África(?) na tv pública (Coleção Pensamento Negro Contemporâneo). (2nd ed.). Editora Telha.
Santos, S. B. D. (2010). As ONGs de mulheres negras no Brasil. Sociedade E Cultura, 12(2), 275–288. https://doi.org/10.5216/sec.v12i2.9102
Schwarcz, L. K. M. (2001). Racismo no Brasil. Publifolha.
Schwarcz, L. K. M. (2002). Questão racial e etnicidade. In Miceli, S. (Ed.), O que ler na Ciência Social brasileira (1970–1995) (pp. 267–326). Editora Sumarés; CAPES; ANPOCS.
Schwarcz, L. K. M. (2019). Sobre o autoritarismo brasileiro. Companhia das Letras.
Segato, R. (1998). Alteridades históricas/identidades políticas: una crítica a las certezas del pluralismo global (Série Antropológica 234). Universidade de Brasília.
Sene, A. (1978). Discours. In Négritude et Amérique latine: Colloque de Dakar, 7–12 janvier 1974. Nouvelles Editions Africaines.
Senghor, L. S. (1977). Le Brésil dans l'Amérique latine. In En Liberté 3: Négritude et Civilisation de l'Universel (pp. 27–30). Le Seuil.
Senghor, L. S. (1974, January 7). Allocution du Président de la République du Sénégal M. Lépold Sédar Senghor. In Négritude et Amérique Latine, Colloque de Dakar (pp. 17–22). Nouvelles Editions Africaines.
Sieder, R. (2002). Multiculturalism in Latin America – indigenous rights, diversity and democracy. In Sieder, R. (Ed.), Multiculturalism in latin America – indigenous rights, diversity and democracy (pp. 1–24). Palgrave.
Silva, J. (2005). Feministas negras entre 1945 e 1964: o protagonismo do Rio de Janeiro, São Paulo e Santa Catarina [Article]. XXV Congresso de Sociologia (ALAS) – Grupo: Gênero, Desigualdades e Cidadania], Porto Alegre. http://www.wwc2017.eventos.dype.com.br/fg7/artigos/J/Joselina_da_Silva_40.pdf
Silva, N. V. (1978). Black-white income differentials in Brazil. [PHD Thesis]. University of Michigan.

Silva, N. V. (1999). Uma nota sobre raça social no Brasil. In Silva, N. do V., Hasenbalg, C. & M. Lima (Eds.), Cor e estratificação Social (pp. 127–125). Contra- Capa livraria LTDA.

Silva, P. B. G. (2009). A palavra é... africanidades. Revista Presença Pedagógica, 15, 42–47.

Silva, T. D. (2020). Ação Afirmativa e População Negra na Educação Superior: acesso e perfil discente. Texto para discussão TD 2569. IPEA.

Silva, T. D., Calmon, P. P. & Silva, S. A. M. (2021). Políticas públicas de igualdade racial: trajetórias e mudança institucional no governo federal de 2000 a 2014. Texto para discussão, 2662. Instituto de Pesquisa Econômica Aplicada.

Silva, T. D. & Silva, J. M. (2014). Reserva de vagas para negros em concursos públicos: uma análise a partir do Projeto de Lei 6.738/2013. Nota Técnica NT. 17. IPEA.

Skidmore, T. E. (1989). Preto no Branco – Raça e nacionalidade no pensamento brasileiro. (2nd ed.). Paz e Terra.

Skrentny, J. D. (1996). The ironies of affirmative action: politics, culture, and justice in America. University of Chicago Press.

Sodré, M. (1999). Claros e escuros: identidade, povo e mídia no Brasil. Vozes.

Souza, J. (2021). Como o racismo criou o Brasil. Estação Brasil.

Souza, L., Ferreira, G. L. & Santos, M. C. R. C. F. (2021). Direito e meritocracia contra as cotas raciais: reajustes do dispositivo da branquitude. Revista Eletrônica Espaço Acadêmico (Online), 21, 35–45. file:///C:/Users/Rebecca%20Igreja/OneDrive/livro%20completo%20Ra%C3%A7a%20na%20Am%C3%A9rica%20Latina/bibliografia/Ferreira%20Direito_e_meritocracia_contra_as_cotas_r_branquitude.pdf

Souza Lima, A. C. (2022). Ações afirmativas no ensino superior e povos indígenas no Brasil: uma trajetória de trabalho. Horizontes Antropológicos, 50. http://journals.openedition.org/horizontes/1975

Swartz, M. (1968). Local Level Politics. Social and Cultural Perspectives. Aldine Ed.

Tardieu, J. P. (1997). *Los Negros y la Iglesia en el Perú: siglos XVI-XVII*. Ediciones Afroamérica.

Tavolaro, S. (2014). A Tese da Singularidade Brasileira Revisitada: Desafios Teóricos Contemporâneos. *Dados*, 57(3). https://doi.org/10.1590/00115258201420

Taylor, C. (1994). The politics of Recognition. In Gutmann, A. (Ed.), *Multiculturalism* (pp. 25–74). Princeton University Press.

Telles, E. (2003). Racismo à Brasileira. Dumará.

Telles, E. (2014). Pigmentocracies: Ethnicity, Race, and Color in Latin America. The University of North Carolina Press.

Theodoro, M. (2008). Exclusão ou inclusão precária? O negro na sociedade brasileira. Inclusão Social, 3(1), 79. http://revista.ibict.br/inclusao/article/view/1622

Theodoro, M. (2014). Relações raciais, racismo e políticas públicas no Brasil contemporâneo. Revista de Estudos e Pesquisas sobre as Américas, 8(1), 205–219. https://periodicos.unb.br/index.php/repam/article/view/18484

Theodoro, M. (Ed.), Jaccoud, L., Osório, R. & Soares, S. (2008). As políticas públicas e a desigualdade racial no Brasil: 120 anos após a abolição. Ipea.

UNDP – United Nations Development Programme (2004). Human Development Report 2004 Cultural Liberty in Today's Diverse World. http://hdr.undp.org/en/content/human-development-report-2004

UNDP – United Nations Development Programme (2019). Human Development Report 2019. Beyond income, beyond averages, beyond today: Inequalities in human development in

the 21st century. http://hdr.undp.org/en/content/human-development-report-2019" http://report2019.archive.s3-website-us-east-1.amazonaws.com
UNDP. United Nations Development Programme (2020). The Next Frontier: Human Development and the Anthropocene. UN Plaza, New York, NY. http://hdr.undp.org/en/2020-report
Vainer, C. B. (1990). Estado e raça no Brasil, notas exploratórias. Estudos Afro-Asiáticos, 18, 103–118.
Valderrama, C. (2013). Black Politics of Folklore: Expanding the Sites and Forms of Politics. [Master Dissertation]. University of Massachussetts.
Valderrama, C. (2021). La política cultural de la negritud en Latinoamérica: Debates del Primer Congreso de la Cultura Negra de las Américas, Cali, Colombia, 1977. The Journal of Latin American and Caribbean Anthropology, 26(1), 104–123.
Valdés García, F. (2017). Leer a Fanon, medio siglo después. CLACSO.
Valero, S. (2020). Los negros se toman la palabra. Primer Congreso de la Cultura Negra de las Américas: debates al interior de las comisiones y plenarias. Pontificia Universidad Javeriana/Universidad de Cartagena.
Valero, S. (2021). Cuarto Congreso de la Cultura Negra de las Américas (1989–1991). Condicionantes históricos y tensiones epistémicas de un congreso fallido. Historia Crítica, 81, 95–117.
Vasconcelos, J. (1979). *The Cosmic Race/La raza cósmica*. The John Hopkins University Press (Original work published 1925).
Velázquez, M.E. (2018). Mestizaje, racismo y afrodescendientes en México: un análisis histórico. Cultures-Kairós [online]; *Les numéros*. https://revues.mshparisnord.fr:443/cultureskairos/index.php?id=1600
Velázquez, M.E. (2011). Debates históricos contemporáneos: africanos y afrodescendientes en México y Centroamérica, México, Centro de Estudios Mexicanos y Centroamericanos. Instituto Nacional de Antropología e Historia; Institut de Recherche pour le Développement; Universidad Nacional Autónoma de México.
Velázquez, M.E. (2016). Balances y retos de los estudios antropológicos sobre poblaciones afrodescendientes en México. Anales de Antropología, 50(2), 177–187. UNAM. http://dx.doi.org/10.22201/iia.24486221e.2016.2
Velázquez, M.E. (2020). Racismo y afrodescendientes en México: cinco reflexiones para la "deconstrucción" de las nociones de raza y mestizaje. Boletín de Antropología. Universidad de Antioquia, 35(59), 17–34. http://dx.doi.org/10.17533/udea.boan.v35n59a03
Velázquez, M.E. & Hoffman, O. (2007). Investigaciones sobre africanos y afrodescendientes en México: acuerdos y consideraciones desde la historia y la antropología. Diario de Campo, 91, 63–68. INAH.
Velázquez, M.E. & Iturralde, G. (2019). Afrodescendientes en México: trayectoria, demandas y retos. Instituto Electoral Ciudad de México.
Velázquez, M.E. & Iturralde, G. (2020). Afromexicanas: trayectoria, derechos y participación política. (Colección Género y democracia). Instituto Electoral México.
Viana, O. (1938). Raça e assimilação. Editora Nacional. URI: http://bdor.sibi.ufrj.br/handle/doc/82
Vieira Júnior, R. J. A. (2006). *Responsabilidade objetiva do estado: segregação institucional do negro e adoção de ações afirmativas como reparação aos danos causados*. Juruá.
Wade, P. (1997). *Race and Ethnicity in Latin America*. Pluto Press.

Weber, M. (2004). *Economia e Sociedade: Fundamentos da Sociologia Compreensiva*. Editora Universidade de Brasília.
Werneck, J. (2005). De Ialodês e Feministas: Reflexões sobre a ação política das mulheres negras na América Latina e Caribe. Nouvelles Questions Feministes – Revue Internationale Francophone, 24(2).
Werneck, J. (2009). Nossos passos vêm de longe! Movimentos de mulheres negras e estratégias políticas contra o sexismo e o racismo. In Vents d'Est, vents d'Ouest: Mouvements de femmes et féminismes anticoloniaux. Graduate Institute Publications. https://books.openedition.org/iheid/6316. DOI:10.4000/books.iheid.6316
Werneck, J. (2013). Racismo Institucional, uma abordagem conceitual. Geledés – Instituto da Mulher Negra.
Whitten, N. E., & Torres, A. (1998). *Blackness in Latin America and the Caribbean*. Bloomington Indiana University Press.
Wieviorka, M. (2001). La différence. Balland.
Wieviorka, M. (2015). Multiculturalisme: le débat est-il clos? Hypothèses. https://wieviorka.hypotheses.org/351
Wieviorka, M. (2017). Introduction. In Wieviorka, M. (Ed.), Anti Racistes. Robert Laffont.
Williams, E. (1942). *The Negro in the Caribbean*. The Associates in Negro Folk Education.
Zea, L. (1975). La filosofía americana como filosofía sin más. (3rd ed.). Siglo XXI Editores.
Zuluaga, F. (1994). Conformación de las sociedades negras del Pacífico. In Llano, A. V. (Ed.), *Historia del Gran Cauca* (pp. 231–258). Universidad del Valle, Instituto de Estudios del Pacífico.

www.ingramcontent.com/pod-product-compliance
Lightning Source LLC
Chambersburg PA
CBHW050525170426
43201CB00013B/2081